I Am What I Am

Praise for John's first book, *Anything Goes*

'*Anything Goes* is a refreshingly honest, funny and engaging read that hooks readers from the opening chapter.'

Woman's Way

'John Barrowman, the immensely likeable actor behind Captain Jack, has written his autobiography … Charmingly lurid, the book has the right saucy, sassy, somewhat overexcited quality for an afternoon on the sofa with a box of violet creams.'

Daily Telegraph

'Multi-talented John Barrowman, the star of the *Doctor Who* spin-off *Torchwood*, tells of behind-the-scenes celeb high jinks, hilarious memories and the sometimes moving story of his two decades of work in the film, TV, music and theatre industry in this open and entertaining autobiography.'

The Herald

'Charting his rise to superstardom from humble beginnings in Scotland to life in LA, *Torchwood* star John Barrowman reveals how he has become one of the best-loved stars of the stage and screen. Four stars.'

OK!

'Gossipy, fun and endlessly entertaining, buy this out of curiosity, buy it for the insight into the worlds of stage and television, but most of all, buy it for his absolutely hilarious stories of a Glasgow childhood with a granny you'll just adore.'

Daily Record

'John Barrowman is on a bit of a roll at the moment. Everything he touches seems to turn to gold and his heartfelt autobiography is no exception … This is a charming read that really gives us insight into John Barrowman.'

Beige

I Am What I Am

JOHN BARROWMAN

with *Carole E. Barrowman*

Michael O'Mara Books Limited

First published in Great Britain in 2009 by
Michael O'Mara Books Limited
9 Lion Yard
Tremadoc Road
London SW4 7NQ

Revised and updated paperback edition first published in 2010

A CIP catalogue record for this book is available from the British Library.

Papers used by Michael O'Mara Books Limited are natural, recyclable products made
from wood grown in sustainable forests. The manufacturing processes conform to the
environmental regulations of the country of origin.

ISBN: 978-1-84317-493-6

1 3 5 7 9 10 8 6 4 2

www.mombooks.com

Designed and typeset by e-type

Plate section designed by Ana Bjezancevic

Printed and bound in Great Britain by CPI Cox & Wyman, Reading, RG1 8EX

Contents

Author's Acknowledgements

I've approached this book from a slightly different angle than the first one, *Anything Goes*. Rather than covering the panorama of my life, I've zoomed in on a few key events and experiences of the past few years, and sprinkled among them family stories that give you a chance to get a little closer to me. The brief vignettes scattered among the chapters are called 'Table Talks' – because when I was growing up, these more intimate, funny, quirky stories were the ones that made up the conversation at the Barrowman dinner table, as in, 'That's a story for table talk.' When you turn the page and enter my house in Sully, you'll see what I mean.

Wait! Not yet. This part's important too. I'll be quick.

Once again, Carole and I collaborated on this book and, once again, we have people to thank. We owe a great debt – to be repaid (we promise) in books, golf, shoes, purses and a slap-up meal or two – to Scott, Kevin, Clare ('Oh, my, there's a jewellery store'), Turner, and especially to our parents, John and Marion Barrowman (the Harveys and the Glenmorangies are on us, Mum and Dad). Our lives would be very boring and this book would be very short without each one of you. Both of us are grateful for your love, your support, and your sense of humour (even when it's mocking us).

To Gavin Barker (aka Patricia), my manager and our friend – you're the tops, and indispensable when it comes to remembering details and returning emails.

Hugs and kisses to the rest of Team Barrowman: Rhys Livesy, my personal assistant, and Michelle, Steven and Katie at Gavin Barker Associates.

We would like to sing the praises of everyone at Michael O'Mara Books, especially Alison Parker, Sarah Sandland, and our patient and stalwart editor, Kate Gribble – we owe you a karaoke night … or two, Kate.

Also thanks to Andrew, Dot, Andrew, Yvonne and Bridgett, and the Barrowmans in Scotland, for letting us share with the world how bloody barmy we all are.

Finally, and most importantly, this book is dedicated to all my fans.

With love,
John
2009

CHAPTER ONE

'PROMENADE'

'Outside of a dog, a book is a man's best friend.
Inside of a dog, it's too dark to read.'

Groucho Marx

Six of my favourite things in my house in Wales

1 A caricature depicting the *Torchwood* cast embracing Captain Jack and Captain John in an exuberant tangle of arms and legs (say no more).

2 The original sheet music for Cole Porter's 'I Get a Kick Out of You' (a gift from my Reno Sweeney, Sally Ann Triplett).

3 Model planes, ships and cars, and a telescope to view the stars (these are a few of Scott's favourite things, too).

4 Two goldfish that my niece, Clare, and I rescued from a friend's house and named after two of our 'pet' names for each other (Shaka and Nina).

5 My gran, Murn's, two 'Wally Dugs'.

6 A bust of Caesar and a statue of Buddha in the bathroom, plus an oversized, welded-steel statue of a male diver in a backward pike that dominates the interior courtyard.

Welcome, readers – to my home in Sully, Wales, and to my life in the spotlight. Watch out for my dogs tangling themselves at your feet: Harris, a boisterous black cocker spaniel; Charlie, a gorgeous red-haired Dogs Trust rescue spaniel; and the family's thug, Captain Jack, a rescued Jack Russell terrier from Cardiff Dogs Home. Try to avoid their frenzied doggy madness as you step into my front foyer, and consider yourselves very lucky – because, since there's so many of you, I haven't gently urged you into the foyer, switched off the lights, closed the outer door … and left you alone to discover that a full-size black Dalek looms in the corner.[1]

The Dalek is one of a kind, made especially for me by the *Doctor Who* tech guys; I requested that the *Torchwood* logo be tattooed beneath his menacing eye stalk. My *Torchwood* Dalek is one of two treasured pieces of memorabilia displayed in pride of place at the front of my home because of their importance to my success in the entertainment business.

The second piece is far less scary, but equally significant. Hanging on my interior front door – where a welcome wreath might normally be – is the SS *American* life preserver from Trevor Nunn's revival of *Anything Goes*, in which I played Billy Crocker. *Anything Goes*, as you may know, was the Cole Porter musical in which I made my West End debut with Elaine Paige in 1989.

Anyone can make a grand entrance promenading along this hallway towards the main part of the house; even the dogs love to skid up and down on the blond oak-wood floor. To your left is a guest bathroom that I call my 'superhero room'. It's decorated with comic-book art: a

---

[1] My sister, Carole, had to have a lie-down the first time she 'encountered' my Dalek – and she knew it was there.

poster-sized 'Spidey Saves the Day' comic cover, and on the wall opposite this is a poster from one of the first Superman movies. The film's tag line is 'Irresistible Force' – which is an appropriate mantra for a toilet, don't you think?

Most of the art and the photographs in this hallway – and elsewhere in the house – punctuate special moments in my life or Scott's. For example, next to the bathroom door, you'll notice the framed drawings and costume swatches for one of my *Dancing on Ice* costumes. The best art, though, is through the far windows in front of you.

The view of the sea and the distant English coast is stunning, isn't it? After a hectic week of meetings or rehearsals or recordings or whatever, I come down this hallway, see that expanse of water – the Bristol Channel, and beyond to the Celtic Sea – and the surrounding craggy cliffs, and my entire body kicks into relax mode.[2] One of the first things Scott and I do when we arrive home together is drop our bags at the bedroom door and step outside, where, for a few minutes, we simply stand and stare at the majesty of it all.

While sitting on my deck overlooking this spectacular view, I began exploring ideas for this second book. I re-read many of your comments about my first book, *Anything Goes*. I've received letters and emails from all over the world since *AG*'s publication, and after seriously mulling them over, a few things really struck me.

One of them was this. No matter what your family experiences, you found connections with the Barrowman clan. Sisters wrote to me about their brothers; brothers wrote to me that they, too, had a bossy big sis.[3] Mums shared the book with daughters, and then they passed it along to their sons. Gay sons gave the book to their parents, hoping for some understanding; and parents gave the book to their gay sons, saying they understood. A few of you told me you used the book as a way to mend bridges within your families, and a lot of you revealed that the book reminded you of your own family's silly antics. You

---

[2] Yes, I do have a 'relax' mode.
[3] Mum! Carole hit me.

sent me tales about your dogs, your children, your schools and your grans.[4] And all of them brought me great joy. Some of you shared stories of alienation and exile from your families, and I'm deeply touched that you found some comfort in the anecdotes from mine. It was a no-brainer, then, that this new book would include a few more Barrowman yarns.

Watch your step as you come down into my main living area, which runs the length of the house; its expansive windows frame the pool and the sea beyond.[5] This space is divided into three distinct living areas: two ranged with their own comfy reading chairs and oversized leather couches, while the third space, at the far end of the room, accommodates a massive wooden table that came from Thailand. The table is scarred with the knots, crevices and imprints of the two trees that produced it, as well as the countless cocktail parties, family dinners, lunches and buffets it's played host to, and the book piles, laundry piles and other everyday stuff and more stuff that ends up on all dining-room tables.

Dominating these main living areas – along with my 52-inch Sony flat-screen TV, which I have to admit is on most of the day – is big, bold, bursting-with-colour art by Steve Walker and bright pop images by Burton Morris. My dear friend in LA, Brett Vinovitch, introduced me to these artists.[6] Brett used to work for Andy Warhol and he knows his hues from his values better than most.

Currently above the fireplace is an oil painting by Paul Kenton, which captures in its broad strokes and blurs of colour the kinetic energy of New York's Times Square. On its left is a painting of a Tutsi woman warrior that Scott bought for me for my birthday while in South Africa, and on the right is an original artwork depicting some very fit baseball players by the Abercrombie & Fitch artist Mark Beard. Below the mantel sit my gran, Murn's, two Wally Dogs – or

---

4 Not meant to be in order of importance.

5 On a clear day, I can see the white-peaked tents of the Minehead Butlins. Wave!

6 Thanks, Vageena!

'Wally Dugs', as they're known in Glasgow. ('Wally' is slang for 'made with china'. Use in a sentence? You could drink from 'wally cups' if you lived in a 'wally close'.[7])

Another thing that struck me from your feedback was that lots of you wanted to know my perspective on aspects of love and life from under a celebrity spotlight. You don't necessarily want to know what I think about big global issues,[8] but you do want to know my opinions on what matters to me. That's why inside this book, among other things, you'll find my insights about being Captain Jack, about being a talent-show judge, about being a family man, a gay man, a brother, a son, and a lover.

And that's why I've invited you into my home: to give you an opportunity to spend time with me in a more intimate setting, listening to some Barrowman table talk and learning more about my personal escapades and professional experiences from the past couple of years. So, please, join me at my table. I've made dinner[9] and I have lots of terrific table talk to dish.

---

[7] An exterior hallway decked out with tile instead of only Glasgow marble (aka concrete).

[8] I can rant about those as much as the next guy, but I'll restrain myself.

[9] Salmon, corn on the cob and baked potatoes, all done on my *Battlestar Galactica*-sized BBQ grill.

CHAPTER TWO

'WE ARE WHAT WE ARE'

'From scenes like these, old Scotia's grandeur springs,
That makes her lov'd at home, rever'd abroad:
Princes and lords are but the breath of kings,
"An honest man's the noblest work of God."'

Robert Burns, 'The Cotter's Saturday Night'

'Skinny Malinky long legs, big banana feet,
Went tae the pictures, an' couldnae get a seat.
When the picture started, Skinny Malinky farted,
Skinny Malinky long legs, big banana feet.'

'Wee Jimmy'

Twelve things I've learned from my parents

1 Don't go to bed angry (but if you do, wake up first and make the coffee).

2 Don't let anyone make you feel bad about yourself (that's your mother's job).[1]

3 Take responsibility for your actions (especially if you've been caught red-handed).

4 To love another person is to see the face of God (or the Face of Boe, depending on your beliefs).[2]

5 You always have room for dessert (there's a special section in your stomach).

6 You always have time to read (there's a special section of your brain that melts if you don't).

7 Laugh every day (especially at yourself).

8 Speak up for yourself (especially if you have something to say).

9 Speak up for others (especially if they can't).

10 It doesn't take much to be kind (if it does, time for you to be off to that remote island).

11 Where e'er ye be let yer wind gang free (just ask David Tennant, who was once trapped in the TARDIS with me when I followed this advice).

12 Always have a party piece ('Skinny Malinky' doesn't count).

[1] I'm kidding, Mum!
[2] Okay, so that was Victor Hugo's lesson via *Les Mis*.

When we were growing up, my dad was perpetually late. Never for work or anything business-related, but if it involved a family outing, we'd all be sitting waiting in the car, crisp and clean and ready to go, and my dad would be nowhere to be found. My brother, Andrew, would already be unbuttoning his collar and untucking his shirt from his trousers; Carole would be ten pages into the emergency book she'd hidden under the seat; and like a pinball I'd be bouncing from the front to the back to the side of the car and again from the front to the back to the side – ping!

'Has anyone seen your dad?' my mum would inevitably ask.

'He's cleaning the garage,' one of us would inevitably say.

The genesis of the phrase is from early in our childhoods in Scotland. It was a Sunday morning, and my mum was expected to be singing with the choir at the Church of Christ in East Kilbride within the hour. Carole, Andrew and I were decked out in our 'itchy clothes' and had all clambered into the car, when my dad spotted something out of place in the garage, something he had to change, clean or repair at that precise moment.

We did not make it to the church on time.

Throughout my childhood, and even today, this was our response whenever we were waiting for my dad.

'Where's your father?'

'Cleaning the garage.'

My dad even has a recurring dream about his chronic lateness, which stems from a real-life incident that occurred in America. As you may know, in the mid seventies, my family, including my gran, Murn, emigrated to the US. One summer, we were all travelling back to Scotland for a visit. (For our first few years living in the States, we went back to Scotland fairly regularly, especially so my dad could see his brothers and his parents.) This particular trip home, the entire family was waiting in a hired limo, which was ready to take us to O'Hare Airport in Chicago for an evening flight to Prestwick. We were already cutting it a bit too fine in terms of getting there on time.

'Where's your dad?'

In unison: 'Cleaning the garage.'

Fifteen minutes later, my dad emerged from the house after having double-checked for the fourth and fifth time that every light was out, every plug unplugged, every switch in the off position. The house was sealed so tight we'd be lucky if there was oxygen left inside when we returned.

Of course, we were heading to one of the busiest airports in the world, so there was a lot of traffic. When we were about two miles from the terminal and no longer moving, my dad realized we might not make our flight. The driver pulled over and called the airline and got assurance that if we could get there in the next fifteen minutes, the plane would wait for us. Keep in mind this is the late seventies. Airlines actually had live people answer their phones back in the day and international flights often waited for their late passengers.

With eight minutes left in our fifteen, the limo squealed up to the kerb at the terminal. We all scrambled out. Carole and Andrew helped Murn into a wheelchair. I piled bags on her lap and my mum distributed the other cases among the rest of us.

My mum looked at my dad, and nodded ever so slightly. The look that passed between them in that instant was one that kids often see parents exchange in moments of crisis, when children know instinctively not to argue – just to do what they're told. My mum grabbed my hand. Carole and Andrew watched my dad's face for the sign. We were poised like runners from *Chariots of Fire*.

Then my dad yelled, 'Go!' And like bats out of hell we went.

Dad led the way, propelling Murn forward like a battering ram, followed by Carole and Andrew, with Mum and me bringing up the rear. The crowds parted before us as if my dad was Moses. Murn was shouting in broad Glaswegian, 'Oh dear God! Oh dear God! Oh dear God!' and my mum was yelling after my dad, 'John! John! For goodness' sake, slow down!'

With seconds to spare, my dad, who by this time was a few lengths ahead of the rest of us, spotted the flight attendant closing the gate. He made a deep lunge and let go of the wheelchair. Murn – still screaming, mind you – went rolling forward and just missed the ankles of the flight attendant.[3] The near miss bought the needed extra time for the rest of us to catch up. However, it was at that moment that my dad realized he'd left all our passports in his briefcase in the hired car.[4]

When my parents first met, my dad knocked my mum off her feet – literally. He stuck his size-eleven shoe out and tripped her as she walked past him on her way to the cloakroom at a dance at Wellshot Hall in Tollcross. She was with her girlfriends and my dad and his friends were trying to make slouching against a wall look cool. My dad admits the bit with the foot was not his best move, but it was one he was sure would get my mum's attention. And, of course, it did.

My mum picked herself up from the floor, brushed off the dress Murn had made from a picture they'd seen in a fashion magazine, and the words just tripped from her tongue: 'My God, what a smooth move that was. I want to have your children some day.' Well, maybe not exactly those words. According to my mum, she already thought my dad was a bit of a nutcase, so this latest move didn't really surprise her.

Humiliated and angry, my mum ignored my dad for the rest of the evening. In fact, when my mum tells the story, she reminds us of how she dismissed the entire event as just more 'carry-on' from those Barrowman boys, and she kept her dance card filled with dances from other young men.

My mum never lacked dance partners. Even today, aged seventy-

---

[3] No grans were ever in any real danger in this incident.
[4] Serves him right that the entire incident still gives him nightmares.

five, she still has some good moves – as she proved onstage during my recent concert tour.[5]

This talent is not the only reason I love to have my mum perform with me onstage, though. When she was first married, she had an opportunity to audition for a television show. She chose not to go because she had just found out she was pregnant with Carole, and she decided to follow that particular path instead. When she sings 'Amazing Grace', or our other family favourite, 'The Wedding', onstage with me, I like to think I'm giving her a taste from her road not taken.

Although my parents didn't officially meet until this auspicious moment, they grew up in fairly close proximity to each other. My mum spent most of her childhood in Shettleston, a village nestled near Tollcross, where my dad grew up. I remember a neighbour in Mount Vernon (where I spent my childhood) telling me that one of her earliest memories as a young girl in Tollcross was of my dad and his brothers getting chased out of the fruit shop for stealing apples. My father, of course, denies this, especially when his grandchildren are within earshot.

My mum finally agreed to go out with my dad after he delivered extra bags of coal to her house for a week; my Papa Butler 'felt sorry for the boy'. For the longest time after my mum and dad started dating, my mum's girlfriends thought she was actually going out with my Uncle Charlie, my dad's older brother, because Charlie did not wear glasses and when my dad was with my mum, he refused to wear his.[6]

Growing up during the Second World War, my mum lived in a much toffier neighbourhood than my dad's family. The Butler house had its own back garden, complete with an Anderson bomb shelter; a necessity during the war, given the proximity to the Clyde shipyards and docks. This shelter survived well into the seventies, when my gran still lived at that address. I can remember playing hide-and-seek in it with Carole and Andrew when we'd visit Murn. It made a great fort.

---

5 Check out YouTube for the proof.
6 Oh vanity, thy name is John.

Emily would open the door and, of course, she'd pretend that she couldn't see anything or anyone. Then she'd look down ... down ... down, and see, standing in front of her, my Uncle Charlie, who'd be dressed up as the Glasgow icon, the butt of a million Glaswegian jokes, Glasgow's genial Everyman: 'Wee Jimmy'.[17]

'Ach, it's Wee Jimmy,' she'd call back to the living room, 'and you'd better come and talk tae him because I don't want him in my hoose. He smells like he's been drinking straight since the bells.'

This was the cue for everyone to rush to the door. Of course, the real reason Wee Jimmy couldn't cross the threshold was that if my Uncle Charlie moved, us kids would see the bottom half of his legs sticking out from behind his oversized jacket – and, yes, in case you're curious, he actually had shoes strapped to his knees, too, as an added convincer. I loved Wee Jimmy!

After we'd all crowd round the door, he'd take a small tin filled with cigarette butts out of his jacket pocket, and offer one to each of us kids (who were just a bit creeped out by the sight of this strange wee man, but also completely enthralled by the little bit of danger and mischievousness he might represent). Wee Jimmy would then banter with one or two of the grown-ups, flirt with Emily, regale us with a few war stories and – always my favourite – tell a couple of naughty jokes.[18]

The visit would end with a round of 'Skinny Malinky', or some other Glasgow ditty, after which Uncle Alex would pass a pound note to one of the kids to give to Wee Jimmy. He'd take it, then he'd tip his 'bunnet' and wish us all a 'Happy New Year'.[19]

Let me pause here, and offer a brief defence on the intellectual prowess of my cousins, my siblings and me, for not spotting Wee Jimmy's true identity much earlier in our childhoods. We were not stupid children, and we have all, as it happens, grown up to do fine, important things with our lives. What we were, readers, were children

---

[17] If you've ever stood at a Glasgow bus stop on a Saturday night, you've met him.
[18] Usually about bums or farting.
[19] My Uncle Charlie died in 2001 and, sadly, no one's seen Wee Jimmy since.

raised in a family that loved to play jokes, dress up, perform skits, and generally have a good laugh with and at each other, and who among us would want to spoil one of our better family performances?

And, I have to say, I truly believe that this ability to suspend your disbelief and give your imagination free rein is a critical life skill. Look at it this way: we might not be in such a global economic mess if more people in the financial world had been imagining what might go wrong if we kept buying and selling those dicey mortgages …[20]

This is one of the reasons why I'm committed to supporting arts and music programmes in our schools – because if children are not lucky enough to have the kind of home life where their imaginations are nurtured, then our schools must fill the gaps. In the Barrowman family, the ability to suspend our disbelief was finely tuned, even as we grew old enough to know reality better. I'm especially happy to say that the tradition's been nurtured in the next generation of my immediate family, too.

Here's a case in point: in 2002, when I was performing in the Stephen Sondheim Celebration at the Kennedy Center in Washington, DC, I invited my whole family to fly out and see *Company*, featuring yours truly as Bobby, the part of a musical lifetime. During the run, I was living in a two-bedroom suite in an extended-stay hotel on the edge of Arlington and Georgetown. As this was summer in Washington, when I called to book two more suites in the complex for my visiting relatives, I was met with a distinct snorting on the other end of the line. The best they could manage, they said, was one extra room and two foldaway beds. There were seven adults, three children, a baby, and two dogs in the family group. Of course the dogs were going to get the foldaways.[21]

Because Yvonne was an infant, my brother Andrew, his wife Dot, and my nephew, young Andrew, got dibs on the room; my parents took the second bedroom in my suite; Carole and Kevin, the bed settee in my rooms; and Clare and Turner got the two foldaways. On the first

[20] I didn't say there wouldn't be any political rants at all.
[21] Kidding.

night, after we'd returned from the theatre, we were all relatively restrained – only one guest called the desk to complain about the baseball game in the hall.

On our second night together, we decided it was time for the party pieces. Unfortunately, there weren't many props we could use for dress-up. I think what we did next had as much to do with our enclosed space and that distinct lack of props as it did our having a new baby in the family. Because quicker than you can say 'breathe!' and 'push!', wee Andrew was folded up inside the portable bed.

The bed had a really supple mattress. It was a normal single-bed size when opened up, but when it was folded in half, there was a soft squishy space in between the two parts that made the whole thing look like a giant birthing canal on wheels.[22] I grabbed salad tongs to use as forceps, and along with Dr Clare and Dr Turner's help, we re-enacted Andrew's birth. The 'wean' popped right out.

Hurrah! It's a boy!

Well, that was all it took. Pretty soon, all the children in the family had to be reborn[23] – including me, naturally.

I have to admit, mine was not an easy birth – and there were complications. For a second, I thought I might have to be born breech as my nephews and niece tried to deliver me. My 'birth' resulted in the bed breaking and most everyone in the room wetting themselves.[24]

Usually, these family high jinks are of the moment: a flare of laughter and silliness that fades to a memory, but one of my dad's – um, let's call them 'tall tales' – came back to haunt him in a big way. This happened back in Scotland, during my early childhood. It's a story that still makes all of us laugh.

For as long as we were old enough to believe him, my dad claimed he was a spy during the Second World War[25] and he took a bullet in his big toe[26] while he was fleeing from the Nazis. Like the von Trapps,

[22] If you really squinted your eyes and used your imagination.
[23] It was a deeply spiritual evening.
[24] Happens all the time in Labour and Delivery, I'm told.
[25] My dad was only seven when war was declared.
[26] I know … that should have been a clue.

he managed to climb – or, in his case, hobble – across the border into Switzerland, where he was hidden from the SS by all the lovely women in a local brothel.

Of course, being kids – not to mention kids who fell for Wee Jimmy's 'disguise' year after year – all the convincing we needed was for my dad to remove his sock and show us the painful deformity[27] on his foot.

One evening, after dinner but before we'd started our homework, a neighbour from up the street (who had a son who played with my brother) came to our door, with Andrew in hand. He must have been about seven at the time.

'What's he done?' my mum asked, preparing for the worst.

'I had to bring him home, Marion. You're gonna want tae talk tae him. He's telling everyone at my knitting bee that his dad met his mum at a brothel in Switzerland where she worked during the war.'[28]

I'm pretty sure my dad had to sleep in the garage that night. Thank God he kept it so clean.

---

[27] His bunion.

[28] Andrew thought a brothel was a soup kitchen where tasty broths were served.

'You People Can't Go in There'

'I feel a tremor in the Force,' I said, slowly lifting my umbrella and facing the gathering Stormtroopers in the main street of Oxford. 'Help me, Obi-Wan. You're my only hope.'

'We're in so much trouble,' Carole said.

When my sister and I were on the signing tour for my autobiography, *Anything Goes*, in the spring of 2008, we arrived in Oxford with, unexpectedly, a little time to waste. This stop in our book tour was about midway through a tightly packed schedule, which meant that we'd been confined to a car, and a multitude of store rooms and offices at the rear of bookstores, for three or four days straight by the time we arrived in Oxford.

(The exception to the bookstore routine was a signing at the Costco in Bristol, where the book tables were set up directly in front of a freezer of food. At one point, I had to shift my seat so a customer could manoeuvre in behind me and get his three-year supply of fish sticks and tartar sauce.)

I'd been to Oxford once or twice, but not for any extended amount of time. One of our nieces, Martha, on Scott's side of the family, went to Oxford University, and we'd experienced just a brief visit with her. I asked our publicists, Sarah Sandland and Ana Sampson, if we could wander around Oxford for an hour or so. I promised that I wouldn't call attention to myself,[1] and that I wouldn't loiter anywhere near the long queue that was already forming around the store in preparation

---

[1] I lied, as you'll discover.

for the signing session. I grabbed an umbrella big enough to cover both of us[2] since rain was threatening, and we headed out into the historic streets.

We decided to walk into the older parts of the city, especially the courtyards and buildings of Oxford University, given Carole's profession.[3] Honestly, I didn't put up much of an argument, good brother that I am, because I was just happy to be outside in the fresh air for an hour or two. After shopping in a few used bookstores, and stopping under the Bridge of Sighs – where, to be different, I laughed loudly – we then meandered aimlessly for a while, until we found ourselves deep in the heart of the medieval part of the city. I couldn't help myself. I ducked into a private courtyard at Exeter College, where I dashed onto the pristine lawn, threw my arms into the air and burst into song.

'The hills are alive –'

Carole cut me off. 'Sssh! Listen. Can you hear that?'

It wasn't an order of nuns calling from over the hill. It was a college choir rehearsing Handel's *Messiah*. For a beat, I thought this was part of the Oxford tourist experience and that pretty soon I'd see a riot of robed graduates, preferably hot and male, swooping across the courtyard, or Jeremy Irons and Anthony Andrews climbing from a second-floor window carrying bottles of champagne.[4]

I snuck into the chapel with Carole close behind me, and we stood at the rear of the building and listened to the choir rehearse for a few minutes. They sounded amazing, but once one or two of them began to recognize who was watching from the back, I became a distraction, and so I left. Plus, I was bored. We'd been wandering for close to an hour now and the only things I'd bought were a couple of posters and a pack of Post-it Notes for Carole that said: 'I'm the Queen of Fucking Everything.'[5]

---

[2] An important detail for later.

[3] Snore.

[4] I loved this eighties version of *Brideshead Revisited*.

[5] She should use them when she's marking students' papers, don't you think?

Before heading back to the centre of town and returning to the bookstore, Carole insisted[6] that I take a picture of her in front of the historic Radcliffe Library. Of course, asking me to take a quick snapshot is like asking Cole Porter to hum only a few bars, or Madonna not to call attention to herself, or Jensen Button to drive under the speed limit.

I suggested three scholarly positions for the picture.[7] The first was a typical pose, as in Rodin's *The Thinker*; the second a more reverential one, as in gazing up at the library in awe; and the third a traditional Barrowman pose, as in dropping your trousers and mooning. Carole's no fun and she refused to flash her bum outside the Radcliffe Library, so I had to settle for a lame number-two pose.

Not surprisingly, the process of picture-taking took a while, and involved a lot of laughter and general silliness. I'd just snapped some shots when this sturdily built woman in tweeds, brogues and a bad perm marched up to us, a book bag over her shoulder and a bicycle by her side. She didn't even wait to chain up her bike. She started to berate us immediately.

'You people can't go in there. This is a private library. Move along.'

I handed Carole the camera. 'Excuse me?' I said calmly. 'What "people" would that be, exactly?'

I'm not sure what I expected her to say. You tourists? You famous people? You siblings? Oh, it was none of the above.

'You, you Americans,' she blustered, 'are everywhere and you don't seem to respect the privacy of our historic institutions.'

Well, that was all I needed.

'Listen to me, you auld woman,[8] if it wasn't for a few brave Americans, this place might be run by Nazis and you'd be reading a few lines scribbled on toilet paper instead of yer books.'

---

[6] Huge, drooling sigh.

[7] I was being helpful; it's not about being in control.

[8] Afterwards, I decided she was probably younger than Carole, who, I must add swiftly under pain of death, is absolutely nowhere near 'auld woman' status.

I was just warming up, but luckily Carole was watching the time and pulled me away. We had to get back to the bookstore.

The woman's mouth had dropped open and it stayed open. She stared at us for the longest time as we walked off across the courtyard and back out into the main streets.

'Why is that woman still watching us?'

'Maybe she recognized you?'

'I don't think so.'

Before Carole could come up with the answer, I knew why. Because I was hanging out with my sister, I had let the 'auld woman' have a tongue-lashing in my Scottish accent, and I had completely upset her perceptions. We looked like Americans to her, I guess, but we sounded like we were Scottish.[9]

When we finally made it back to the square of shops across from the bookstore, I realized I'd made a bit of a tactical blunder. By now, it was mid afternoon and the streets were filling up with schoolchildren. One, and then two, and then three and then more began to recognize me. When I counted a posse of seven of them following close at our heels, I stopped, turned and faced them, raising my umbrella out in front as if it were my lightsaber.[10]

'I feel a tremor in the Force.'

The boys behind us were as into the whole lightsaber routine as I was, and pretty soon the crowd had grown considerably and we were all brandishing pointy things at each other.

'Run!' I yelled to Carole, who by this time was laughing so hard she could barely keep up.

We sprinted across the street and into the bookstore, with the Stormtroopers fast on our tails. I rushed us upstairs, spotted the back of a big cardboard display, and darted in front of it to block the view from the stairs as our enemy closed in on us.

After we'd caught our breath and stopped laughing, I turned to see what we were hiding behind.

---

[9] There's something to the cliché 'don't judge a book by its cover' after all.

[10] Of course I did the sound effects.

'We are so busted,' I laughed.

It must have been instinctive, a different kind of force that drew me to this hiding place.

I had ducked under the protection of a giant cardboard display of the TARDIS.

CHAPTER THREE

'WHERE DO WE GO FROM HERE?'

*'Since we're telling stories, there's something
I haven't told you.'*

Captain Jack Harkness
'The Sound of Drums', *Doctor Who*

Twelve things I admire most about Captain Jack Harkness

1 His loyalty to his friends.

2 His friends.

3 His bravery.

4 His coat (I own an original bought from BBC wardrobe[1]).

5 His unwavering humanity, despite all he's witnessed.

6 His ability to find humour (and aliens) in almost every situation (me too – except for the aliens).

7 His bold and honest sexuality.

8 His appreciation of Ianto's knowledge of things to do with stopwatches.

9 His adoration of Ianto.

10 His love for the Doctor (duh! Me too).

11 His ability to make impossible decisions under terrible pressure.

12 His ability to breathe underwater (forget I ever mentioned this).

[1] Scott loves to play 'Doctor'.

During the filming of *Torchwood* 'Children of Earth', I experienced something I've been immune to for most of my career – paranoia. I felt this way because of a number of major and minor events surrounding that third season. First of all, early in the filming, the Hub quite literally came crashing down around me. The underground tunnels collapsed, the massive security door imploded, the autopsy room was buried under rubble, and the tower that reached up under the Millennium Centre sparked and shook and erupted into flares of flame and light.

The destruction of the Hub may have been called for in the script, but given my state of mind, I thought everything the *Torchwood* team – cast and crew – had worked to achieve since our first episodes had been obliterated with the trigger of some well-placed explosive squibs[2] and a burst of brilliant pyrotechnics.[3]

Add to the annihilation of the Hub the fact that the number of episodes was reduced from thirteen to five for series three; the loss of Jack's Vortex Manipulator, his Webley gun – oh, and the Range Rover; and the gradual shrinking of the *Torchwood* core cast from five to three to two; and what would you think if you were me? I believed I was witnessing the fall of the house that Jack built.

Torchwood series one first aired in October 2006 on BBC3. Burn Gorman, Eve Myles, Naoko Mori and I all had strong television credentials – Gareth David-Lloyd was our television virgin[4] – but for each of us the fact that we were about to become part of a sibling of

---

[2] Technical term for a small electronic explosive, not to be confused with a squid -- which is neither small nor explosive.

[3] Thanks, Danny!

[4] Bet you were hoping for something naughty?

Doctor Who made us feel a bit like we were back at the beginning of our careers. There was a kind of giddy excitement about this new show and about the adventure we were now embarking upon.

When I first walked into the conference room at the BBC studios in Treforest – where *Doctor Who* was, and *Torchwood* was soon to be, filmed – I was a bit gaga. Everyone was packed around the table: the director of the first three episodes, Brian Kelly; the head make-up artist, Marie Doris (The Doris); Ray Holman, the costume designer; the assistant directors (ADs); the forty-two producers;[5] and just about everyone from BBC Wales it was going to take to get this thrilling new show up and running.

Funny story[6] about our first director, Brian 'the smelly' Kelly (aka Boabie Stroaker[7]). At the end of a long day's shooting of one of the first ever episodes, he and I let the other actors go home; we decided we could finish off the scene with just him and me and a small crew. It was a scene inside the Range Rover. Sometimes, when there's a lot of dialogue in a driving sequence, the car is put on a trailer to create movement and the crew essentially work from the outside of the trailer – hanging on for their lives. For this final shot, Brian sat in the back of the Range Rover and he started to feed me the lines. My line in reply was, 'Simple clean-up operation.'

However, because Brian is Scottish, every time he fed me the cue – and he was rubbish at it, by the way – I kept saying my line in a corresponding Scottish accent. In the end, we'd have been much faster asking everyone to stay because things, I'm afraid, went downhill from there … with the crew clinging onto the trailer for dear life with every take.[8]

At the threshold of the conference room, I paused for a beat, taking in who was there, and then I stepped through the doorway. I was Captain Jack, this show's number one, and although I was far from

---

[5] Okay, so maybe only three or four. It just seemed like a lot.

[6] Which you can see played out on YouTube.

[7] Think about it in Scottish as you say it phonetically.

[8] Their 'clinging' was well within the health-and-safety definition of 'clinging'. Trust me.

being a father figure to anyone around the table, I knew playing the lead in a BBC show of this calibre came with certain responsibilities. In fact, throughout each series since then, I've continued to take my leadership role seriously. If another cast member or someone on the crew has had an issue that needed to be raised with the producers, and he or she was not comfortable mentioning it him or herself, I'd always take it on and do my best to represent the person and his or her concern to the appropriate producer.

On the morning of that first read-through, Gareth was filling his plate at the small buffet with fruit, cheese and pastries. Eve, as my new leading lady, was introducing herself to some of the guest actors for that episode. She was beaming and when she spotted me, she waved me to the seat closest to her, Burn and Naoko. The atmosphere in the room was lively and energized. Although we were untested as an ensemble, the scripts were strong and we were all good at our jobs. However, we were very aware of the fact that not only would we have to prove ourselves with an audience, but also we'd need to prove ourselves with the BBC if we wanted to return for a second season.

We took our seats. Scripts were distributed. Gareth was dragged away from the snacks. Until a few minutes before we began, the two seats at the front of the room remained empty. Over the course of the next two series, and the many, many read-throughs in which I've participated since then, the final pair to take their seats became known fondly as 'our *Torchwood* mum and dad': Julie Gardner, *Torchwood* Executive Producer and, at that time, Head of BBC Wales Drama, and Russell T. Davies, Executive Producer and *Torchwood*'s creator (God, actually). Once they were seated, we'd begin reading through the scripts.[9]

Read-throughs are critical for actors because episodes are filmed in twos or threes and they are shot out of sequence. The read-throughs familiarize each of us with the story arcs, so we know what came before and what comes after a particular moment of a specific scene.

There is much about those first few weeks on *Torchwood* that is a blur, but I do remember the few days I worked closely with Ray, *Torchwood*'s

---

[9] Russell usually read the stage directions, and he did so with great gusto.

costume designer, as he fitted me for Jack's iconic RAF coat, his braces and his CAT boots. Russell's clear vision of 'Torchwood Jack' influenced the decision that Jack would wear a belt and braces. This was a fashion trend in the thirties and forties, and it projected an image of Jack as a kind of Midwestern farm boy. During this costuming and design process, we were re-envisioning and repositioning Jack as Torchwood's leader, as opposed to Captain Jack, the rogue Time Agent and follower in Doctor Who.

Everything I did during series one was with the intention of helping the show to find its audience and to forge an identity that was separate from our established BBC sibling. To achieve the former, I went on any TV talk show or radio programme that asked me to. I did guest appearances on This Morning, BBC Breakfast, Loose Women, Angry Women, Women On the Verge of Nervous Breakdowns, and Women Who Knit. I even stopped random women in the street, just to plug the series. One of the most fun highlights for me once the first season was up and running was finding out that Torchwood regularly beat out the football match on the other channel.

Hand-me-downs happen in every family, and the younger sibling, Torchwood, was no exception. We inherited some of the crew and materials from Doctor Who during series one because this kind of 'double dipping'[10] was less expensive, more efficient, and it ensured that each drama would have the best in the business working on it. The process made a lot of sense.

What bugged me, however, was when I'd be filming a scene and I'd overhear a crew member say, 'I'm going back to the mother ship next week,' or 'I'm back on the Big Show next episode.' This happened a few times as we were finding our feet, and I felt the same way about it as I did when I inherited a sweater, shirt or even a uniform from Andrew.

When I was about seven or so, my dad thought he'd give me a chance to play football, to be part of a team, and to see if I had any of the talents with a ball that Andrew had.[11] My parents must have been hedging their bets that I didn't because instead of buying me a new

---

10 Behave. Nothing kinky about this – well, in this context at least.
11 I'm so not going there!

uniform, they gave me one of Andrew's old strips and a pair of football boots he'd outgrown. Off I went with some of my pals to play a game with the local Boys' Brigade team. Oh, joy.

When I came home later, I stood on the back porch of our house in Mount Vernon, caked in mud from head to toe, with grass stains tattooed on my knees and turf burns on my bum.

When my mum opened the door, I glared at her.

'Did you have a good game?'

'Don't you ever ask me to do that again. I don't like being dirty.'

Before the close of *Torchwood* series one, I asked Julie Gardner and the other producers to make sure that the crew who stayed with us for series two was there because of their commitment to *Torchwood*. I didn't want anyone on set who viewed *Torchwood* as 'sloppy seconds'.

The following year, when we began filming the second series, the message was received and *Torchwood* had its own group of regulars in the crew; plus new trailers from a Welsh company that were roomier and more immaculate inside than the hand-me-downs we'd been using for the first series. We also had a new catering company for our meals on set. In general, we were well looked after, and I felt we had weaned ourselves nicely from the mother ship.

Series two saw *Torchwood* move to BBC2, and at that point as an ensemble of actors and as a drama, I believed we had found our feet. We were no longer the infant sibling. We were all grown up and walking well on our own. Then the first inkling that things were changing hit us like a falling spotlight.

Naoko, Eve, Burn and I were filming a sequence in the Hub (Gareth wasn't on set at that particular time). The Hub was a richly detailed and brilliantly imagined set, but filming there was always a bit of a pain in the arse because of how elaborately constructed it was.

The main parts of the Hub were built on three distinct levels. The lower level, where characters entered through the round steel door, or came up from the tunnels (which were constructed on a separate set, directly behind the Hub); the second platform level, where the computers and screens, the various *Torchwood* gizmos and gadgets, and the worn comfy couch were situated; and then, behind this main platform, were the steep steps down to the autopsy room. Jack's office, of course, was at the far side of the main level. When the entire team was on set for a scene, plus the crew, the lights, the sound, and the camera equipment, there was barely any room to think, never mind move.

The four of us finished our scene and we were walking together out of the Hub. We stepped through the thick, black safety curtains that separate the *Torchwood* set from that of *Doctor Who* and passed in front of the TARDIS, but when we got to the warehouse door, Burn cut out in front and stopped us.

'We wanted you to hear it first from us,' he said. 'Naoko and I are dying at the end of the series. Our characters are dying and they're not coming back.'

Eve and I were stunned and really upset. We had not seen this coming at all. We all hugged each other and by the time we had separated, we were all crying. It helped a little that Binny and Coco[12] added that they were okay with their characters' deaths. Since the whole Owen-of-the-living-dead arc had happened with Burn, he didn't think his character could go any further, while Naoko agreed that she too was ready to move on and try some other avenues.

When Burn, Naoko, Eve, Gareth and I had all finished our work for the day, we gathered in my trailer to talk about this turn of events. We cracked open a bottle of champagne and we drank and laughed and cried and cracked open another bottle of champagne. The impromptu gathering wasn't so much a party as it was a wake for Owen and Tosh.

Not long after these developments, word came down from the Producers on the Mount that *Torchwood* was moving to BBC1 for series three. Hurrah! How cool was that? Eve, Gareth and I were ecstatic. Who wouldn't be? We each felt as if all our hard work was finally being recognized and rewarded. Then came the caveat, the 'but' – the 'we loved your audition, but you're just not right for the

---

[12] Everyone had a nickname – or two – on *Torchwood*.

part' moment. The producers informed us that the third series would be running on BBC1, but it would only be five episodes instead of thirteen.

Before I go any further, let me make it really clear that this cut from thirteen episodes to five was a decision made at the production level. The fact that it was one more thing changing at *Torchwood*, and that this worried me as I've already suggested, doesn't diminish the truth that the decrease in the number of episodes was necessary for sound creative and programming reasons. The reduction had nothing to do with my schedule, or Russell's, or Eve's, or Gareth's – or anyone else's, for that matter.

When a television show moves to BBC1, it's important to make a dramatic impact: after all, this is the flagship of the BBC and *Torchwood* needed to perform there with a big bang. In order to achieve this, the producers, including Russell, decided to create a television event over five consecutive nights that would be so exciting and so suspenseful that it would be a not-to-be-missed viewing event around the country. The BBC wanted the kind of mini-series dramatic event that would give people something to talk about at the water cooler in their offices the next morning.

When I asked Russell about the episode cut, he revealed that there was also a powerful artistic motivation behind the move. Russell admitted to me that from the moment Captain Jack had first emerged on the page, he had had his secrets. Russell had been keeping a few pivotal details from Jack's back story under wraps ever since the character's inception, including the stunning family revelations in 'Children of Earth', which I think make Jack's character more layered and more complicated, his psyche darker, and his anguish for and about humanity more transparent. Russell felt that these disclosures needed to be framed in an epic narrative like 'Children of Earth' – one that, even in its thrilling aspects and its brutal, heart-wrenching moments, was really a story about what one person is willing to sacrifice for their own or their family's survival.

I got all of that, but – still – I have to admit I had mixed feelings about the decision. That, coupled with the loss of Burn and Naoko from the *Torchwood* team, sent me home to Scott on many a night during filming to ask him if he thought I was being paranoid and silly by reading something into this series of events. His response was always supportive and comforting, and then he'd make me some toasted cheese and a vodka tonic and rub my feet and I'd forget about what was bothering me for a while.

The problem with '[b]eing slightly paranoid is like being slightly pregnant – it tends to get worse'.[13] The second area that contributed to my fretfulness had to do with some scheduling issues on *Torchwood*.

Scheduling has always been a source of a little conflict between the *Torchwood* producers and me. When I'm filming *Torchwood*, it's my main gig. No ifs, ands or buts with that statement. However, unlike a lot of other actors, I want to keep my work diversified, my jobs balanced, and my plate full. It's how I roll – a little music, some theatre, a children's show, a concert tour, judging. I'm very good at multi-tasking in my professional life[14] and I like to plan my schedule in such a way that I get maximum entertainment value out of my time.

Life is short and it's not a rehearsal. I want to make the most of my talents and the opportunities they are now affording me. That's one of the reasons why my manager, business partner and friend, Gavin Barker, and I formed Barrowman Barker Productions (BBP) in 2008. This production company will give me the chance to broaden my entertainment interests even more.

Even while I was filming *Torchwood* series one, I could never get a hard-and-fast weekly schedule from the producers on a regular basis. Sometimes the schedule would get delivered the night before a shoot. I remember during series two, an AD dashed to my Cardiff flat close to midnight with a schedule for the following day that stated I was not needed until later in the afternoon. What annoyed me about this short notice was that I had cancelled a guest appearance on another show in London in order to return to Cardiff that night because I'd thought I had an early pick-up the next morning.

---

[13] Says Molly Ivins, political columnist in the US.
[14] Scott appeared to be choking on my word choice so I've added 'professional'.

I want to work because I love to work. This means I need a precise schedule to follow every week. Gav maps it out down to the second, and I check it every night to see what I have to do and where I have to be the next day. I also have a terrific PA, Rhys Livesy, who helps with the day-to-day demands of my life. Because my schedule is so tightly managed, I don't always know where or what I'm doing until I look at Gav's schedule.[15] I'm utterly dependent on it. My motto is definitely 'day by day'. Family members know this and if they need to ask me something about my schedule or where I will be on a certain date, they go directly to Rhys or they check their own copies of my schedule that Gav forwards to close family. I'm the last person they ask.

When it came to scheduling the shoots for season three of *Torchwood*, because of some other work I'd agreed to do before the producers had issued their itinerary, when filming began, I didn't start with everyone else. This meant that I wasn't there when the tone was set, and this added some alienation to the discomfort I was already feeling about the series.

When I first read the scripts for the five episodes, I truly thought they were of feature-film calibre. I thought they'd thoroughly engage new fans and fully satisfy the hard-core ones, but – I know, here comes another one – given everything I've been mentioning, I still felt as if *Torchwood* was being asked to prove its worth all over again. My paranoia was like a splinter in my brain, persistent and annoying. Now I was wondering if this sibling was being kicked out of its parents' house. So Scott made me more toasted cheese and another vodka tonic.

It didn't help that as soon as I stepped on set, I got into a battle of wits and styles with the director of the five-episode arc, Euros Lyn. Euros had directed a couple of *Doctor Who* episodes previously, including 'The Girl in the Fireplace' and David Tennant's final regeneration episode. I respect and like Euros immensely, and we ended up with a strong working relationship, but initially we were like two rams locking horns. Euros's style was more passive-aggressive

---

[15] Carole is convinced that some day I'll be scheduling my shites.

in his approach to a scene, and – as you know – I'm not very passive at all. Tell me what you want to change in my performance, help me understand why you want that aspect to change, and I'll likely change it.

One of the first scenes I was in with Euros directing, we were in the warehouse set that becomes the makeshift Hub during Day Three of 'Children of Earth'. Cameras rolled, the scene played out, Euros would call 'cut' and then he'd come up to me and the conversation would go something like this.

'Good, John, I liked it, but I'd like to go again. This time, bring it back a bit.'

Deep breath.

There I was, standing in that desolate warehouse, the Hub destroyed, the cast soon to be decimated again, down to five episodes from thirteen, the need to prove ourselves once more – aargh!

'If I bring it back any further, I'll be back in my fucking trailer!'

I know Jack well and I thought I was being asked to play him differently, less in your face and more under the radar, less ironic and more laconic. Euros's direction, as far as I was concerned at that particular moment, was turning me into a mumbling, introspective actor. The whole point of acting is to live the emotion, to say your lines and to be that person. I know it's not necessary to project as much on television as I do when I'm on a stage – I'm not stupid – but I wondered: when was the decision made that Jack was supposed to sound like Christian Bale playing Batman on *Torchwood*? Because if Jack did start to sound like Christian Bale playing Batman on *Torchwood*, then John Barrowman would have to spend four or five days in a dubbing suite because the dialogue would be so bloody understated not even a Weevil could understand it.

Exhale.

The set was deathly quiet. I finished the scene. Then I went to my trailer to calm down. After a few more takes, I got on with my job and Euros got on with his, and, according to Julie Gardner, Russell, and lots of viewers here and across the Atlantic, each of us did amazing work on 'Children of Earth'.

*

In the final scene of Day Five of 'Children of Earth', Jack stands at an emotional precipice. At a terrible cost to himself and those he loves, he has saved the children of Earth. He looks up to the heavens. For forgiveness? For release? For escape? He touches his wrist, activates his upgraded Vortex Manipulator, and in a beam of light … Jack's gone.

CHAPTER FOUR

'I CAN DO THAT'

'Be who you are and say what you feel, because those who mind don't matter and those who matter don't mind.'

Dr Seuss

Five things I've learned from being a talent-show judge

1 Be honest (preferably in a sound bite).

2 The public always chooses the right performer.

3 Don't contradict yourself (why not?).

4 The audience knows when you're talking shite (or shit).

5 Don't date a contestant (until he wins).

When Connie Fisher completed her first audition for the part of Maria in *How Do You Solve a Problem Like Maria?*, I leaned over to David Ian and Zoë Tyler, my fellow judges in the BBC's search to find the lead in the West End's revival production of *The Sound of Music*, and I whispered, 'That's Maria.'

David shushed me immediately. 'You can't say that at this point in the competition!'

Yes, I can. I wasn't suggesting to my fellow judges that Connie was going to win – because that decision would be out of my hands. I knew the public in the end would decide. I also knew, from my own years of theatre experience, that performers grow and change and adapt and rise to heights not always seen in an audition, but at that moment, given what I'd seen in the panel auditions, with very little additional work Connie could have stepped in to play Maria right then and there.

What did I see in her performance so early in the show's process? Connie had poise and confidence and she had talent. She could sing. She had a quality to her voice that impressed me from the beginning. To observe all of this from her first audition didn't mean I was biased and that no one else would have a chance to make a similar impression. Far from it. Many of the other performers for the successful talent-search programmes I've judged to date[1] have also made strong first impressions on me. A few of them faded as the performance challenges increased in difficulty and the show's pressure built, but a couple of them did go on to win their respective competitions. At a fairly early point in the audition process for *Any Dream Will Do* and *I'd Do Anything*, I made a similar comment to the

[1] *How Do You Solve a Problem Like Maria?*, *Any Dream Will Do* and *I'd Do Anything*, if you need to know.

51

other judges about Lee Mead as a potential Joseph and Jodie Prenger as a possible Nancy.

In these initial auditions, I noted my impressions and then I'd file them away in my head and in my notebook.[2] I can and I do step away from those primary observations, and here's why: Connie, Lee or Jodie, or any one of the other performers we auditioned in the early days of those shows, might have been terrific in that particular audition or during a specific performance on a given night, but when a performer is doing a show eight times a week for a year or more, there has to be consistency, energy, style and personality in his or her work at *all* times. Those qualities don't always emerge until well into the run of the competition.

This is also why it's not a good idea to have favourites too early. This applies to all of us – viewers and judges alike. I might have a notion of who may be emerging as the strongest in the programme, and I might begin to see the attributes blossom that will make, say, Connie or Lee or Jodie the best performer to carry the production, but, in the end, it's the audience that ultimately decides – and viewers can quickly turn against a performer if it appears that a judge is putting forward a favourite.

How do I know this? Because if I wasn't a judge on shows like this, I'd be sitting at home like everyone else, with my bowl of nibbles and my drink, and I'd be yelling through the TV at Barry Humphries or the Lord[3] that they 'must be mad' or 'tone deaf' or 'too bitchy' or 'so right!' or 'so wrong!' and then, when the phone lines opened, I'd say to myself 'those judges are being jerks to so-and-so', and I'd vote for him or her in spite of what the judges said.[4]

Even I had to audition to get a place on these talent shows. For my audition to be a judge on *How Do You Solve a Problem Like Maria?*, I was on a practice panel with Elaine Paige. The producers were also looking at Elaine for one of the judging spots. During this initial

---

2 It's easier to find stuff in my notebook.
3 Andrew Lloyd Webber, to be precise.
4 But I'd never yell at John Barryman. I love him!

audition process, I was under the impression that I was the only male lead from theatre and television being auditioned for the job. This did not turn out to be true, and the realization was a bit of a surprise.

Elaine and I have a long history together in the theatre and we're friends. We were both comfortable with each other in this audition and we had a good rapport. We were asked to sit at a table in a room at the BBC studios in London with a television in front of us, and the producers showed us a series of audition tapes they had from other shows. As Elaine and I assessed and debated the performances' strengths and weaknesses, the producers recorded our comments. They listened to everything I said and then they assessed my performance as a potential judge.

During a break from my audition, I headed up to the bar at the top of the BBC studio building, where guests gather after a show's taping to have a relaxing drink.[5] It's a comfortable and spacious area with lots of tables and a terrific outside balcony, which is used in the summer months for end-of-series parties.

For example, after the final episode of *Any Dream Will Do*, the producers threw an American-style BBQ[6] up there for cast, crew and guests. I filled my plate with sausages, chips and some other 'healthy' morsels, and then commandeered a table with Jonathan Ross and his family, who had been guests for the final episode.

We were a large group. Along with the Ross family were Scott, Carole, Gav and his husband, Stu. Jonathan and I were in fine form, so trying to get us all settled round an outside table on a crowded balcony was like herding cats. Just as we all finally managed to find places, David Tennant and his girlfriend at the time, Sophia Myles, joined us – and the musical chairs began all over again. We did, though, find a moment to squeeze in a toast to Lee and his future success.

---

[5] It's the BBC. No one gets rowdy and everyone drinks bitter lemon and Schweppes tonic water.

[6] In the interests of complete disclosure, although the food was tasty, it would never have passed the standards of a real American BBQ.

So, after I'd finished my first session for my *Maria* audition, I took the elevator up to the bar. I thought I'd see if anyone I knew was there, and have a chat before my next set of tapes. I scanned the room and didn't see anyone at first, but just as I turned to leave, I spotted Michael Ball sitting on one of the couches. When I saw Michael across the room, I wondered if he was also auditioning for the same judging position as me (I found out later that he had been considered for the job). Michael and I have a similar level of experience and history in the theatre world: the BBC was serious about wanting to cast a judge who could bring significant theatrical expertise to the panel.

Obviously, I got the judging gig. My first panel, on *How Do You Solve a Problem Like Maria?*, included producer David Ian – whose company was co-producing the West End production of *The Sound of Music* in which the winning Maria would perform – and vocal coach Zoë Tyler.

David and I got along really well. He is one of those producers who's been in the business himself.[7] He therefore knows actors well, and he knows the audition process intimately. He also appreciates what it takes to sustain your voice and your energy for eight shows a week. Plus, David was a lot like me in his views about the responsibilities of being a judge.

In all of the talent-search shows I've done, I've believed strongly that I had a duty not only to the contestants, but also to my peers working in the theatre and to my fellow musical performers. I didn't want to put a contestant into a leading role and then have that person not be able to hold up under the pressure. I also didn't want people I've worked with going to see *The Sound of Music* or *Joseph and the Amazing Technicolor Dreamcoat* and saying, 'What the fuck was Barrowman thinking?'

Perhaps most importantly, I also participated in these talent shows because I want to help launch careers. I'm not sitting on that lovely

---

[7] He performed in a number of West End musicals, including *Joseph and the Amazing Technicolor Dreamcoat*.

chair in my fabulous Neil Marengo suits just to find a performer for a single role. For example, from the beginning of *Any Dream Will Do*, I knew that Daniel Boys was something special and had a strong, confident voice, but I could sense that Danny wasn't going to be Joseph. For one thing, he was too mature for the role.

Whenever I talked with all the boys at Joseph camp, or during rehearsals, I'd tell them that they needed to see this show as a platform to showcase their talent. Danny and a few others listened and they took this advice to heart.

As a result, Danny has done really well since he was voted off. He recently released a CD and he's performed in a number of shows, including *Avenue Q* in the West End. Danny also toured with me on my 'An Evening with John Barrowman' tour in the spring of 2009, and our duet of the romantic ballad 'I Know Him So Well', from the musical *Chess*, has received all kinds of accolades. More on that in a later chapter.

Another Joseph contestant who has found success following the TV show is Ben Ellis. Ben didn't have the strongest voice in the competition, but he demonstrated week after week that he was an entertainer. He reminded Denise[8] and me of a young Robbie Williams – and, let's face it, he was very pleasing on the eye. Ben, like Daniel, has done well in his career since the show, playing the male lead in *Hairspray* and doing numerous presenting jobs on TV.

Helping to launch the careers of such talented individuals has been a real point of pleasure and pride for me – and for many of the other judges.

So, partly as a consequence of our shared values, David Ian and I had a lot of fun together on that first panel. I learned a lot from him – but he also learned a lot from me during our time together. I once explained to David and his wife what tea-bagging was.[9] I'm sure he was forever grateful, and thinks of me every time his wife dunks a Tetley.

---

[8] Van Outen, who joined me on the panel for *Any Dream Will Do* and *I'd Do Anything*.

[9] I can only explain this to those of you over eighteen.

I'd never met Zoë Tyler before, but I liked her immediately. She was outspoken, and wasn't afraid to challenge the producers if something came up about which she felt strongly. She was ballsy. I like that quality in a woman.[10] Zoë was also the vocal coach for the Marias (and later the Josephs, too) and her style of teaching and developing them was fairly similar to mine. She always offered criticism fairly and honestly, and when she issued a challenge to a performer, she tried to help them see ways to meet it. I've always felt that, in any situation where you're trying to teach someone, it isn't helpful simply to describe and label what you see them doing wrong, without offering any suggestions as to how they can improve.

On *Any Dream Will Do*, the panel shuffled, and entertainer Denise Van Outen and producer Bill Kenwright joined Zoë and me. Bill and I had a professional relationship, but we never saw eye to eye about much during the show. As Bill was one of the economic backers and producers of this revival of *Joseph and the Amazing Technicolor Dreamcoat*, I felt he had a considerable financial motive in finding a marketable Joseph for the production. Unlike David Ian or Andrew Lloyd Webber, Bill was a businessman first and foremost, and for him, almost any Joseph would do, as long as he looked the part and could sing the songs.

From the beginning, Bill had his eye on two particular Josephs, Lewis Bradley and Craig Chalmers. Craig was voted out in week seven, but Lewis survived till the final. Unfortunately, having heard his vocal qualities and his full range, I knew Lewis couldn't hit the final note in the *Joseph* song 'Close Every Door'. The audience loved Lewis throughout most of the series, but I never believed he'd have the stamina or the spunk[11] to carry a West End show.

During my time on the talent shows, I particularly loved working behind the scenes at the Joseph and Nancy camps. I enjoyed the teaching part of the job and the chance it afforded me to share some of the nitty-gritty aspects of the business with the performers. I have

10 I like it in a man, too.
11 I mean this in the US sense of the word, of course.

to say, though, that the boys in the Joseph camp cried way more than the girls in Nancy School. The boys were always weeping!

Sometimes, the lessons learned on talent shows occur in unexpected ways. It's not just the performers or even the production staff who gain knowledge – the judges can learn a thing or two, too. I certainly did. Mel Balac, one of the producers, who worked with the judges during all three series and went on to co-produce with Gavin and me on *Tonight's the Night*, taught me about the importance of producing myself.[12] In the television biz, this means knowing when to speak up and when to shut up,[13] knowing when to butt in, and knowing what to say in a brief number of words without going over the top and losing the audience.

When I first worked with Mel, a pretty, petite, dark-haired woman with lots of savvy and chutzpah,[14] all she ever wore on her feet were trainers or flats. Throughout the rehearsals, I kept telling her she had to wear heels on the nights of the actual shows. In my eyes, there's nothing worse than a woman in a flattering pair of jeans, a lovely top and then a pair of flat, scuffed-up ballet slippers or manky tennis shoes. Talk about what not to wear.[15] Anyway, I gave her enough grief about her shoes that she broke down and bought a lovely pair of Marc Jacobs.[16]

On one of the first nights on the show, when Mel was wearing her fabulous shoes, Denise was making a point to one of the contestants after her performance when, suddenly, the path down which she was heading with her comment veered off in another direction. Denise was getting so far from the point she was originally trying to make that she had wandered next door to *Blue Peter*. In my head, I was thinking, 'Okay. Stop now, Denise. Anytime.'

Then I looked over to my right. Mel was jumping up and down off

12 No, I was not born that way!
13 My family still wants to know how to get me to do this.
14 Term I learned from another Mel, Mel Brooks, when I worked with him on *The Producers*.
15 Fashion tips are free with the purchase of this book.
16 Hot! Hot! Hot!

camera, waving one of her Marc Jacobs high in the air and then slashing it across her throat. Not because what Denise was saying lacked validity, it had plenty, but time is precious on live TV and Denise's wanderings would mean that someone else would have to say next to nothing to make up the time. Denise caught the waving shoe out of the corner of her eye and, with grace and poise, she brought her journey to an end.

One of the biggest challenges of being a talent-show judge is to avoid the temptation of saying something just for the sake of a sound bite. Of course I want to be pithy and say things that have punch to them – I'm an entertainer, for goodness' sake – but I always attempt to frame my critical bites with evidence from the performance. This is live television, after all, and this makes the entire series a very public casting call for these performers.

I'm very loyal to the folks I've judged, if they've wanted to keep in contact. In my family, we call this being on the long road with someone; staying in touch with them for their entire journey, even if it's only an occasional email that marks the connection. Along with Jodie, Daniel and Ben, the Joseph contestant Keith Jack has kept in touch. After the shows have ended, I've helped a number of the performers to get agents. The ones I thought were *really* good, I recommended Gavin represent, because not only do I think they'll have long careers, but I also want to work with them on my albums, my concerts and my future TV shows.

A good deal of this business depends on networking and forging relationships. Learning how to do this is an important skill. After all, you may not be right for the part of the gay lead in a US sitcom, but a friend of a casting director, who once worked with you on that other show two years ago, thinks you would be perfect for the role of a rakish sci-fi hero.

One of my favourite staying-in-touch stories from working as a judge is also a lovely romantic one. Denise and Lee Mead began dating after *Any Dream* was over and Lee had won. In the late spring of 2009, they were married. Immediately after the ceremony, Denise sent me a text from a tropical island to announce that they had tied the knot. I was thrilled for them.

Back in the spring of 2008, after my concert at the Hammersmith Apollo – which was staged, in part, to promote my album *Another Side* – Lee and Denise came backstage, having watched my performance. For fun, I gave them both concert T-shirts with my face on them.

One night a few weeks later, when Den and I were judging on *I'd Do Anything*, Den came into my dressing room before the show. She was giggling even before she'd sat down. She told me she'd put on the JB concert T-shirt before going to bed. In a moment of, um, passion, Lee had looked up and seen my face smiling down on him.

'Fantastic, fantastic, fantastic!' exclaimed Denise.

'Get it off! Off! Off!' cried Lee.

'We Have a Hostage Situation – Send in the Clowns'

I could hear my mum and sister laughing when I put my ear to the bathroom door. Refrain from going 'Ewww!' You know as well as I do that it's a fact of life that women travel like wildebeests and go to the bathroom in herds, especially when they're in restaurants and clubs, but when they're at home they rarely pee in pairs. I had to check. It was getting close to midnight on a Saturday night and my mum, my dad, Carole, Scott and I were getting ready for bed. The main bathroom in my house in Sully was certainly big enough to accommodate two people brushing their teeth, but for my plan to work I really needed to be sure that Carole and Mum had gone in there together.

They had. Check.

I reached above the bathroom door and found the spare bathroom key. Don't ask me why there's an extra key. I think it may have something to do with making sure children don't get themselves locked inside, but I did not build this house. Scott and I only bought it in the autumn of 2008, and although we love it, we do have plans to renovate in the future and add features that will make it even more our own. Until then, many of the quirks of the house remain. Like the fact that the bathroom can be locked from the inside and from the outside.

I locked the door. Check.

My dad and Scott were my fellow conspirators in this midnight game to terrify my sister and my mother. Insert Dick Dastardly laughter here. While I locked the bathroom door, my allies moved silently into position. Scott headed to the sliding doors at the rear of the house with the broom, a flashlight and my black hooded North Face ski jacket. My dad was a decoy in this plan, so he ducked into the bedroom that has become my parents' room whenever they visit, and he quickly got his pyjamas on. He found his book and sat on top of the bed, looking as if he'd been reading for hours.

Positions. Check.

The five of us had just watched the movie *Paul Blart: Mall Cop*, a silly, laugh-out-loud comedy in which Kevin James plays a slightly hopeless mall cop who tries to foil a gang of crooks from robbing the mall. Watching the film had made us all a bit squirrelly. Not that my family needed an excuse.[1] Add to this collective state of mind that we are a very competitive family, we love to play games, and no one likes to lose. The words 'surrender' or 'I give up' rarely feature in my family's vocabulary.

Our house in Sully is laid out a bit like an 'I', with two courtyards on either side of the main artery of the house, the entrance and a few other rooms along the top, and the widest living space running across the bottom, facing the lawn, the pool and the sea. The three bedrooms are on the side of the house with the smaller, more closed-in courtyard, and the bigger of the two courtyards has become the dogs' area, because it's the safe space that Jack, Charlie and Harris have access to via their doggy door in the laundry room when no one is home.

I've always loved it when my family can come and visit me, and now that I have a house and so much space to share, over the past year it's been a busy abode. During the spring and summer of 2009, for about three-plus months, my parents lived with me. The main reason for their extended visit was so they could be part of my concert tour that spring, but they also decided that because they're both in their later seventies, the trip across the Atlantic was only going to get more difficult in the coming years. They might as well travel while they still can. I seconded that.

Scott and I have always enjoyed my family's visits and we never feel as if we have company when any of them are staying with us. In fact, sometimes we can forget we have company – or, should I say, for a few hours the company can occasionally think that we've forgotten about them.

---

[1] It's probably a good thing we hadn't watched *Scarface* or *The Shining*.

A recent case in point: when Carole visits, she usually stays in the guest room directly next to our master suite. One night, she was startled awake by some very aggressive moaning, loud sighing and what sounded to her like chests being beaten and wild animals being skinned alive in our room. I was making the noises: I admit it. Of course, you can imagine what Carole was thinking …

She proceeded to scramble for her Bose headphones and switched on the noise reduction. She claimed it didn't help. She cranked up the tunes on her iPod. The clamour persisted for about twenty-five minutes. Early the next morning, when our paths crossed in the hallway, she gave me this weird, eye-crinkling look.

I didn't think anything of it. I was completely unaware of her annoyance.

'I had *the* worst heartburn I have ever had last night,' I told her over my shoulder, continuing on my way to the kitchen. 'I seriously thought I was having a heart attack. I thought I was dying. Scott thought I was dying. At one point, I even had Scott punch my chest 'cause I thought my heart was stopping.'

'Oh, thank God,' she said, 'I am so glad to hear you say that. I thought you'd forgotten I was next door and that racket was you two having rowdy sex.'

'What do you mean, "thank God"?!' I exclaimed. 'You're okay with the idea that I might have been dying – just as long as I wasn't having loud sex?'

'Well … yeah,' she said.

Luckily, that experience hasn't put her off staying with us in Wales – nor the rest of my family. And it's easy to see why. Along with more space in our Sully house than our London maisonette, there's easy access to golf courses and shops, so my mum and dad, especially, have been visiting more often and staying longer. They are capable of entertaining themselves when I'm off working in London, and as long as my mum has her glass of sherry at 5 p.m. and my dad has his single malt, they are quite content to sit by the sea and enjoy my hospitality.[2]

---

[2] Turnabout's fair play, I figure.

They still have a good sense of humour, they still know how to have fun, and each of them takes on a couple of chores around the house when they're here. As long as my dad was around, garbage never lingered and the dogs' poo never sat for too long in the courtyard, which was a very good thing given my plan that Saturday night.

No shite in the courtyard. Check.

As soon as my mum and Carole tried in vain to get out of the bathroom, I knew and they knew that a game was in play.

'The buggers have locked us in here,' said my mum.

'They'll be hiding somewhere,' answered Carole. 'I'm not going out there. We need a plan.'

But I knew they would come out – because not to come out would be to admit defeat. That never happened in our games.

Quickly, I unlocked their door, dropped the key, dashed out through the patio doors and took my position with Scott in the smaller courtyard outside my parents' bedroom, where I put together my home-made Scarecrow Man with the broom and my North Face jacket.

Meanwhile, inside the house, I could hear my sister and my mum come out of the bathroom and quickly dart into my parents' bedroom, where they were surprised to see my dad.

Remember, I was hiding in the courtyard directly outside my mum and dad's bedroom.

'Where is he?' asked my mum.

'He's not in here,' answered my dad, who is the master of deception and the king of hide-and-seek in our family, and lies through his teeth in these situations. Last Christmas – yes, last Christmas, when he was seventy-six – he fell behind the washer and the dryer during a game. Also, when I was home on a break from filming *Titans* for CBS, and I was visiting Clare and Turner in Milwaukee, I was playing hide-and-seek outside with them and their friends. My dad encouraged me to climb onto their low-hanging garage roof and stay flat and still. The kids, he said, would never find me. He was right. The kids eventually gave up and went inside to bed – and my dad had to come out and help get me down.

Needless to say, my sister and my mum were sceptical of my dad.

'Get up, so we can check,' Carole insisted. 'You're in on this with them.'

They then made my dad stand in front of them while they whipped open the closet doors, pulled back the duvet and checked underneath the bed for me. Once they'd decided I was not in the room, they figured there was a good chance I'd be in the other bedroom. The two of them then proceeded to march my dad into the next room, where they forced him to carry out a similar search.

I was, of course, watching all of this from outside in the dark courtyard, waiting for as long as it would take until my mum and Carole would give up and get into their beds. My dad was our inside man to ensure that Scarecrow Man could exact his wrath as soon as they went to bed.[3]

But things did not go according to my best-laid plans. First of all, I forgot that the jacket I'd grabbed had a fluorescent tag on the zipper, and, second of all, I completely underestimated my opponents.

Suddenly, I glanced into one bedroom and then the other – and discovered they were both empty. No dad, no mum and no sister. Shit. I sent Scott around to the back of the house while I ran to the front. He met up with me back in the courtyard.

'All the doors are locked.'

Through the bedroom window, I could see the three of them in the hallway, laughing – including my dad, the traitor. Later, my mum told me she'd spotted the glowing tag on my jacket through the window.

Oh, well played. Well, played. But not well enough. I darted to the other side of the house and cut off the power. First the pool lights went out, then the outside lights, and then all the electricity inside the house. Everything went dark.

'You bastard!' Carole yelled.

The only way inside, as far as I could figure at that point in the siege, was to crawl across the dogs' courtyard in the hope that my mum and Carole had forgotten to lock the sliding door that opens onto the main hallway that runs the length of the 'I'. I took off my white T-shirt

---

[3] Insert another evil laugh here.

so I wouldn't have any reflection from the moon. I stretched out flat on the ground and inched my way across the courtyard like I was in a James Bond movie, or maybe a taller Tom Cruise in *Mission: Impossible*, or maybe just John Barrowman, entertainer and nutcase.[4]

I could see my mum and Carole standing in the dark hall – giggling, yet scared enough that they were still holding my dad in front of them as if he were a shield.

I almost made it to the sliding door. I was so close, but Carole spotted me and immediately leapt across the hall and locked the sliding door. I heard my mum laughing and saying, 'This is like that Bruce Willis movie where the family is taken hostage.'

'By a couple of clowns,' my dad chuckled.

Ten minutes later, I found my way into the house – how, I will never reveal, because this game may not be over. I dropped down onto the bathroom floor, and crawled towards Carole and my mum, who had climbed into the whirlpool bathtub to limit their exposure on three sides, in a vain attempt to stop me from sneaking up behind them. When I did finally leap out at them, even though they had to know I'd been coming – stealth is not my middle name[5] – they still screamed like maniacs and pounced on me.

When we finally turned the power back on, and settled into our respective bedrooms,[6] I had gravel burn on my chest from crawling across the courtyard, dirt and grime on my shorts and my knees, and scratches on my hands from climbing through a window, but I won – and that's all that counts.

Scare the hell out of sister and mum. Check.

---

[4] Thank goodness my dad had done his poo chore for the day.
[5] Scot is.
[6] For a quiet night.

CHAPTER FIVE

'I KNOW HIM SO WELL'

'If I had a hammer ...'

Lee Hays and Pete Seeger, 'If I Had a Hammer'

Seven things I've learned from Scott

1 How to cook fish sticks (in the event I'm a survivor of the apocalypse and that's all there is to eat).

2 How to rewire a phone (especially one chewed through by a certain dog when a certain partner was not paying attention to that certain dog's actions).

3 That saying too much is usually better than saying too little.

4 That you could have a very serious ailment and not even know you have a very serious ailment and your highly trained doctor may not even know you have a very serious ailment, but whining and worrying about this very serious (and non-existent) ailment can make you feel much better.

5 That a new furnace can be a beautiful thing (it's not a classic Mercedes, but I do like to be warm in winter).

6 That two men are always better than one (I mean as partners … um, as a couple … oh, never mind, just read on).

7 That I couldn't live without him.

In the mid thirties, the Welsh poet, Dylan Thomas, hung out in what is now our guest bedroom in London. At that time, Thomas was in his twenties and in the infancy of his career. If you know anything of his reputation, you'll know it's likely Thomas spent more time in the nearby pubs than he spent penning poems in our front room, but inebriated or not, Scott and I have been told that Thomas's blithe spirit on occasion returns to the house.

Generally, my family is quite accommodating to spirits, ghosties, ghoulies and any beings hanging out from the other side. My gran, Murn, would regularly have a 'wee blether' with her husband, Andy, after he died. In fact, one night, when I was having a wee coorie[1] with her on the couch, she suddenly whipped her head to the side and told my papa not to interrupt the 'wean'; she'd be with him in a minute. So the fact that Dylan Thomas's spirit has a kip in our front room has never really bothered me.

My mettle was tested, though, one night not too long ago, when I heard this strange, supernatural noise in our bedroom. At first, it didn't really register that it was not a normal sound, but after ten minutes or so, the darkness got the better of my imagination and I roused myself from my sleep to listen more carefully.

The dogs were clearly not bothered by it: all three remained prone at the foot of the bed. I noted that somewhere under the fourteen pillows and the large mound of duvet, Scott slept. The noise seemed to emanate from behind the wall and it had a vaguely animalistic tone to it – as if a cat was in the wall, clawing to get out. You may smile at the reach of my comparison, but I want you to know, readers, that a cat stuck in the wall is a distinct possibility in the Barrowman–Gill home.

[1] A Scottish cuddle, not to be confused with a 'Glasgow kiss'. Ouch.

It's no secret that I love animals and as anyone close to me will tell you, I'm a sucker for a stray. One morning, I was running late for my return trip to Cardiff to begin filming the third series of *Torchwood*. It wasn't entirely my fault that I was late.[2] In our flat in London, until only recently, Scott and I have been living with what can only be described as a 'porcelain disaster'. When we first bought the flat together, we (and when I say 'we', I mean Scott) immediately wielded his sledgehammer – no, this is not a metaphor – and took out a number of walls. Some I wanted brought down, others not so much. I have to tell you that over the years, this is the first thing Scott usually does when we move into a new home. He demolishes something.

Shortly before Scott and I met, I bought my first flat, in Bow, east London. One night, when our relationship was in its infancy, I returned from matinee and evening performances of *Sunset Boulevard* to find Scott had knocked down a wall dividing the living room from the entryway – and he almost took out our fledgling relationship in the process. I liked that wall. I had no intention of renovating. Plus, here was a grand building that used to be the Bryant and May match factory, a building whose walls had withstood more than a century of strife – witnessed the London Matchgirls Strike of 1888, and likely even come close to burning down once or twice – until Scott Gill came along with his bloody great hammer.

By the time I really noticed the sledgehammering pattern, Scott had knocked down as many walls as we had cars or dogs or nieces and nephews, and I already loved him madly, so it was too late to do anything about this strange, destructive side to his nature. The problem is not so much that he knocks the wall down; it's more that he does not always repair the hole in a reasonable time frame.

The worst example of this tendency was the bathroom in our flat in London. We moved in. Sledgehammer out. Walls came down in biblical proportion. In Scott's defence, none of them were ever weight-bearing and most of them were redesigned eventually and their holes

---

[2] And no, before you ask, I wasn't cleaning the garage.

filled[3] – except for our en-suite bathroom. It remained stripped to its timbers, bare to its bones, as unfettered as the day Scott went charging in there. In order for us to use the shower, we had to drape the walls with blue construction tarpaulins. Over the years,[4] when the blue tarp got torn, or the strange creatures growing on it started to apply for NICE or FDA approval, Scott would enclose the entire space with new blue tarpaulin walls.

The bathroom became a battle between his stubbornness and my, okay, stubbornness – a game of chicken between two grown men. Who would break first and demand tile? Who would give in and apply the grout?

I realize you may be thinking that this blue-tarped bathroom was actually a symbol of something deeper than this, perhaps something still under construction in our relationship, maybe even something that has to do with marking territory when everything else is shared. I would agree; however, every time I'd try to put my finger on what it was and then in a quiet yell try to convince Scott that this could not continue, I failed miserably.

Over the years, friends and family have posited their own views of the tarp and what it might represent: Scott's need to keep the bathroom unfinished as a way of holding on to some part of himself, and the house he can control; my need to have the bathroom finished and not to be showering in a fucking building site.[5]

So, one of the reasons I was running so late that morning was because the blue tarp was torn, and I had to wash one-handed while holding up the tarp with my other hand. Scott had already left to take care of a problem at a construction site.[6] I was midway through my ablutions when I heard a stray cat mewling outside the bedroom window.

---

[3] For those who don't know, Scott is a fully qualified, creative and very experienced architect – and not just an extreme DIY enthusiast (though there's a bit of that in him, too).

[4] And I do mean *years*.

[5] In 2009, the blue tarp bathroom, like the Berlin Wall, finally came down.

[6] Probably a bathroom needing a tarp changed.

I recognized the cat's crying because Scott and I sleep with our window open and I can sometimes hear this cat mewing[7] during the night. The bedrooms in our London flat are on the ground floor, so I grabbed a towel, went upstairs to the kitchen, filled a dish with milk, came back down, put it out on the ledge, and then I carried on with my morning routine. An hour later, the cat was perched on the sill, looking longingly inside. It had also started to rain.

I couldn't leave the poor thing outside in the cold, could I?

I went out into the garden, tempted him with some chicken, and brought him inside. Our dogs at that time, Lewis, Tiger and Penny, were naturally not happy. The cat's impression of the dogs was equally disdainful, and by now, Sean, my driver, keys in hand, was pacing in the hallway, reminding me how late we were going to be.

What to do? What to do?

I found an old blanket, spread it on the bed, opened the window a bit more for fresh air, and locked the cat in our bedroom. I figured he'd be safe from the dogs until Scott came home. What I didn't know was that Scott would not return for the entire day.

Scott knew something was wrong as soon as he opened the front door. His first clue? The three dogs were apoplectic – especially Tiger, who was virtually folded in a knot against the bedroom door, thumping his behind against it. The second clue was the stench. Think about it. You're a scared cat and you've been locked in a strange room for well over six hours with three very angry dogs barking and tearing at the door trying to get at you. You'd wet yourself too. More than once, I bet.

To this day, the memory of the moment when he unlocked the bedroom door and confronted the chaos in the room can start Scott shaking all over again. Thank God I'd hidden his sledgehammer.

But that wasn't the worst part of the situation.

The worst part was that in my rush to leave the house, I'd forgotten to tell Scott anything about a rescued cat locked inside our bedroom.

---

[7] My mum calls this 'yammin'. I have no clue as to the origins of this Scottish term.

At some point in the day, the cat had actually squeezed itself out through the open window and fled for its life. When Scott unlocked the bedroom door, he and the dogs burst into a completely empty but totally destroyed bedroom, with initially no clue as to what had caused it.

Not only were the duvet and the pillows soaked in cat pee, but also the cat had clearly been so terrified that he'd torn at sections of the sheet and pissed through to the mattress. Books and clocks had been knocked off our bedside tables and the family pictures we have on our bedroom's mantel were smashed on the floor. There were even scratch marks gouged into the plaster above the bed.[8] It was as if the cat had circled the room at 90 miles an hour, banking the walls at every turn, while spraying shit out of its arse like exhaust fumes.

There are obviously a few lessons to be drawn from this story, not the least of which is that I am not Noah and our house is not the Ark, and animals should only be brought home under mutual agreement. The other, and more important, one is that in Scott and my relationship, sometimes our freedom and independence can get in the way of clear communication between us. Scott and I are used to a freedom of movement and a level of personal and financial independence that can sometimes result in minor amnesia about our responsibilities to each other as a couple.

We live in a world where there is a kind of accepted narrative for how non-gay couples should live and behave. Although that narrative may be full of stereotypes and clichés – notions like the wife is in charge of the house and children; the husband, the finances and the lawn – there's a narrative nonetheless, and it's one full of anecdotes and advice for guidance and support for straight couples. Women may be from Venus and men from Mars, but at least the heterosexual couple's solar system has books and articles and talk shows and lots and lots of country songs to describe it.

They also have mums, and aunties, and grans, who have no qualms about taking a married son or daughter aside and giving them a verbal

---

[8] They were not human.

slap upside the head, telling them to shape up. For the families of many gay couples, they may be too busy coming to terms with the issue of their child being homosexual to be offering advice about whether or not their son (or his partner) is pulling his weight in the relationship. Plus, since many parents of gay men are themselves not gay, there's a real fear of the unknown that makes these kinds of conversations even more difficult.

In my family, we've been lucky that from the beginning of my relationship with Scott, we have been as visible in our family's life as any of my siblings and their partners. This has meant, for example, that for most of Clare and Turner's lives, they have grown up knowing Uncle John and Uncle Scott as a couple and they see few fundamental differences between us in that role and their parents. They've seen us argue and squabble, yell and scream, laugh and kiss and make up. They can tell you which one of us has more patience than the other.[9] They can tell you which one of us is aggressive-aggressive and which one of us is passive-aggressive. They can tell you which one of us talks in specifics and is very pragmatic, and which one is more vague and much less decisive. They know which one remembers every birthday and anniversary because of a nudge from the other one. They know which one is more likely to take them to the museum and which one to the mall. They know which one loves to cook and which one is always willing to clean up after. They know which one is rarely late and which one needs backup alarms. They know which one takes ten minutes in the shower and which one takes an hour. They know which one can scarf down five bags of Frazzles until he's frazzled,[10] and, most importantly, they know how much we love each one of them, and how much we love each other.

Carole and Kevin, Andrew and Dot, Scott and I, and my mum and dad are all as different as couples in any family can be, and we're also exactly the same. In each coupling, we're continually working out the balance and the choices that make the relationship work.

[9] You decide which one is which.
[10] Both of us!

Only a few chapters in the public narrative for gay men and women have been written, and I've made a conscious decision as a gay man that I want to be part of shaping it. Given my visibility in the media and in the arts, I believe I have a responsibility to help other gay men see what's possible in their own lives or even what's possible for the lives of their brothers and sons. Our rules of engagement may not always be as clear as we'd like them to be, but whose really are when you get past the surface stereotypes and false perceptions of what it means to be in a relationship – gay or not?

That said, though, there is one big difference between Scott and me and, say, Carole and Kevin. Scott and I are a couple made up of two males of the species. This means that not only do we love differently, but also there's a different emotional balance in our relationship. For the most part, on any given day, Scott and I are on the same wavelength. Our hormone levels tend to run on a similar monthly path. With two men in a hurry in a relationship, it's not surprising that one might find a demented cat has trashed the bedroom.

In the middle of the night, the odd noises continued, and, for a second, I thought the aforementioned stray cat may have crawled back in through the open window and got caught under our bed,[11] or, in my half-asleep head, that Dylan Thomas's ghost was refusing to go quietly into the good night.

I turned onto my side, trying hard to ignore the hacking sound that was now accompanying the moaning and the weird tapping, which, in fact, was suddenly much louder.

'John, wake up!'

'What?'

Scott was standing naked in front of me – and not buried deep in the duvet as I'd first thought.

'I think I have Lyme disease,' he said.

Oh, dear God, it wasn't a cat or a poet, there was actually a monster

[11] Scott has another name for the cat (and for me) when he recalls this story, so we shall speak no more of it.

in the room: the *Gillus hypochondriacus*. This creature is a beast – albeit a strikingly handsome one and in the middle of the night usually a naked one – but a monster nonetheless. The *Gillus hypochondriacus* suffers from multiple ailments, physical and psychological: all the result of way too much self-taught medical knowledge. Yet this beast insists on self-medicating and generally avoiding anything with the label 'organic', 'for your health' or even 'may be just a little bit good for you if you'll go ahead and try it'.

Not me. I'll happily take a pill if the pain demands it and I'm thoroughly convinced of the benefits of massive doses of vitamin B, C and broccoli.

'Say again?' I faced him, realizing that not to could result in prolonging my torment.

'I think I have Lyme disease.'

'Are you fucking kidding me?'

'Definitely Lyme disease.'

'You had one vodka tonic last night and it was with a lemon.'

'I ache all over.'

'Take two Nurofen and talk to me in the morning.'

I burrowed deeper under the duvet.

The moaning continued.

'Please, stop that noise. Trust me. You can only get Lyme disease from an infected tic bite and only deer carry infected tics. Where the hell did you encounter a deer in the middle of Chelsea?'

'Maybe it's lead poisoning? Or lupus?'

Ah ha! A pattern was emerging. I sat up and turned on the light on my nightstand. Lyme disease, lead poisoning, and lupus. Scott had been wandering around the online medical encyclopaedia in the 'L's. The weird clicking sound I'd been hearing was the computer keys, with his moaning coming through the wall from his office.

Scott was like the main character in Jerome K. Jerome's *Three Men in a Boat*,[12] who walks into the British Library to check on some mild

---

[12] You may have seen the Tim Curry/Michael Palin version on TV or read the book?

symptoms he's experiencing. He makes the mistake of flipping forward in the medical dictionary, and discovers that his symptoms are multiplying with each page he turns. He walked into the library 'a happy healthy man' and, hours later, he walks outside a 'decrepit wreck'. The only thing he doesn't have is 'housemaid's knee'.[13] I was pretty sure Scott didn't have that either. The last time he was on his hands and knees ... well, none of your business.

I grabbed my extra pillows, stacked them behind my head, and punched them a few times while glaring at Scott.

'What exactly is wrong with you? And don't describe what you've just read on WebMD.'

'I feel like I've been beaten with a cricket bat. Even my hair hurts.'

'Seriously?'

He nodded.

I placed the back of my hand against his forehead to see if he had a fever. I couldn't tell, so I kissed the top of his head instead. It's not a foolproof method, but it has the credibility of generations of mothers and grandmothers behind it.

'Maybe it's something you ate? Did you throw out the sausages that've been in the fridge since Easter?'

It was August. Scott holds the culinary misconception that if food has been refrigerated, even for long stretches of time (like years), it's fine to eat the said food as long as you cook it on a really, really hot flame ... and add fish sticks.

'It wasn't the sausages. It's not that kind of pain. It's more inside my muscles.'

I leaned over and kissed his head again.

'Ow.'

By this time, our three dogs, currently Charlie, Harris and Jack, were thinking it was morning and they were scratching and whining to go outside.

---

[13] Let me clarify for readers under, say, sixty-five. Back in the day, this is what women used to get when they waxed their floors – and you thought a Brazilian hurt.

I reached for the phone. 'Do you want me to call someone?'

'Yes.'

A few minutes later, Carole answered her phone in Milwaukee.

'What are the symptoms for Lyme disease?'

As you know, Carole and I are close, but that wasn't the primary reason I called her first. She lives in Wisconsin, a state with high instances of Lyme disease. I knew she would know the symptoms. Without so much as a 'do you even know what time it is over here?' or 'my God, don't you have doctors in England?'[14] she told me: severe muscle aches, slight fever and, the most important one, a target rash somewhere on the body.

So, we looked for the target – very slowly and carefully. This distracted us for quite a while. Scott eventually forgot he was dying and fell asleep. Later, the next morning, I solved his medical mystery, and I have to tell you I'm including it here because the causes of Scott's ailment are related to another essential element about being in a committed gay relationship that may interest you.

Gay men love to flirt, and we love to do it in the company of our significant others. To us, a nod's as good as a wink and it's as natural as smiling. We pass a hot male on the street, we do a double take, and then after the hottie has passed, we whisper to our partner that he missed something special. He, then, will insist on turning round and trying to see what he did indeed miss, usually just at the moment the hottie is turning to see who's staring at him. At a party, if we see a hot male, we chat him up … together. We flirt with temptation because our intentions are generally pure. In fact, we have no intentions at all. We like to window-shop. While in a non-gay relationship, regular flirting with members of the opposite sex may result in sleeping on the couch – or worse – with Scott and me there's no jealousy, no awkwardness, and especially no harsh recriminations when we get home.

This is not to say that gay men are less inclined to succumb to casual sexual encounters than straight men because I think the opposite is probably true; however, I do think that in a committed gay

[14] Actually, after a fit of laughing, Carole said both.

relationship, flirting is a behaviour that is assumed to be healthy and even stimulating to the relationship.

The morning after the 'Lyme disease' night, while Scott was enjoying his Weetabix, I spotted a phone number and a name on a scrap of paper on his desk. I picked it up and went upstairs to the kitchen, stopping Scott on his way out.

'Hold on a minute!'

I passed him the slip of paper. He looked at it sheepishly.

'You're not suffering from any strange disease,' I laughed, 'you just couldn't let a couple of hot young soldiers get one up on you.'

Under the pressure of my hilarity, Scott then admitted his aches and pains were a result of shameless flirting. Two days before, he'd run into an acquaintance, a twenty-something soldier with whom he'd worked when he was volunteering in Cambodia for the UK charity Cam's Kids. Scott had been chatting with the ex-soldier when, out of the blue, he invited Scott to join him and some friends for a hike at a park the next day.

Scott naturally felt obliged to say 'yes'. He is, after all, a man, and like all males, gay or not, he is prone to macho posturing every now and then.

It turned out that the park was not so much a place of picnics, ponds, trees and swings as it was an outdoor military obstacle course, with zip lines and rock walls; and the hike was not so much a brisk walk as it was frantic scrambles up ropes and competitive sprints in and out of paths made of tyres.

Turned out, *Gillus hypochondriacus* was suffering from Middle-Aged Musclitus. I kissed him on the mouth and gave his bum a love tap as I left the kitchen, because I knew how he felt. On occasion, I suffer from a similar ailment.

`Kiss, Kiss, Bang, Bang!'

'Blat! Blat, blat, blat, blat! Blat!'

During the first two seasons of *Torchwood*, Burn Gorman and I had this game we'd play whenever we were rehearsing a scene involving guns or weapons, and, on occasion, we'd play it in the parking area between our trailers at the BBC studios in Treforest, Wales.

Before 'places, everyone' and 'action' are called, the actors and the crew do what's known as a 'crew' or a 'camera' rehearsal. This allows the director to be sure everyone knows where he or she is supposed to be during the scene,[1] so that the boom-mic operator isn't suddenly tripping over the camera-dolly operator because the sound guy didn't know the camera was heading his way. Obviously, this 'crew rehearsal' also gives those of us acting in the scene a chance to rehearse our lines one more time.

When we're filming *Torchwood*, as I leave the BBC lot at the day's end, one of the producers gives me what's called the script 'sides' for the following day. The 'sides' have the next day's schedule attached to the front, and they also list my individual scenes, with my lines separated out from the script as a whole.

The last thing I do before going to sleep[2] on the nights before filming is to learn my lines for the next day. In the morning, when I get to my trailer and before I'm called into make-up, I run through my lines again. This is one of the few times in my day when I'm on set that I really insist on not being disturbed.

Some directors, like Euros Lyn, who directed 'Children of Earth', will call for an 'artists' rehearsal' first, which allows those of us in the

---

[1] You'd be surprised how easy it is to get lost.

[2] If Scott's not around …

scene to run through the script without the clutter of cameras, cables and all the crew.[3]

Sets can be crowded at the best of times and when I'm in a big studio, I don't always notice how crowded. For example, when rehearsing or taping *Tonight's the Night*, sometimes close to sixty crew people could be working around me and in the close vicinity. Imagine similar numbers in a space like the set of the Hub, which was easily half the size of a BBC entertainment studio, and, as I've mentioned, far more complicated and layered in its design.

Whenever Burn and I were given our guns for a scene – in my case, Jack's Webley – and we'd run through the script for the artists' or the crew's rehearsal, Burn and I always did the guns' sound effects.

When weapons or explosives are used in a scene, the set-up is complex and time-consuming because of the obvious safety concerns, the noise levels, and the fact that gunfire and explosions are expensive to create. Burn and I were always happy to substitute our man-made sound effects during these rehearsals. We were like little boys with big toys. We'd charge into the scene, point our weapons and in unison yell, 'Blat! Blat, blat, blat, blat! Blat!'

As we were filming one particular scene, after Burn and I had done a number of rehearsals with our guns, the director was ready for the real action.

I ran into the scene, pointed my gun, and then I did all the gun's sound effects with great expression: 'Blat! Blat, blat, blat, blat! Blat!' At the same time, the real sound effects and squibs were fired.

'Cut! Erm, John, everything okay?'

'Fuck!' I realized what I'd done. I'd ruined the take with my sound-effect 'blats'. Can you imagine watching that scene? How stupid would Jack have looked catching up to an alien and making his own gun noises as he shoots him? I'm sure my sound effects made our end-of-season blooper reel.

Another shoot that may have made a few contributions to that reel was the filming of the episode 'Adam', which I've always thought was

[3] In truth, there are always cables everywhere.

one of the better written in the *Torchwood* canon. Catherine Tregenna penned the script.

Since so much of this episode was in flashbacks, with Adam in Jack's childhood memories, the cast and crew had to be mobile. I spent a significant part of my days on location in the sand dunes at Merthyr Mawr; I then came home and spent a significant part of my nights finding sand in every nook and cranny of my body.[4]

If you remember the episode, at one point Jack screams for his brother during a windstorm, which was created on the sand dune, with me standing in front of a huge green screen with an industrial-sized fan blowing sand directly at me. The intensity of the sand swirling around me would be added later with CGI, but I still had to have my eyes rinsed out after each take. I went through a couple of pairs of contact lenses that day.

My memories of the 'Adam' episode are of a number of things going wrong. The first scenes we shot were filmed in tunnels created on the set to look like the sewers of Cardiff. Captain Jack is searching for a Weevil when his father appears to him. The set was dark and dank and really did look like a sewer. The problem was that the prop crew had run too much scummy water on the ground – so two things happened. The first was that the water running into the tunnel was dripping onto a couple of the fake pipes, which were, in fact, made of styrofoam. Andy Goddard, who was directing this episode, along with Jeff Matthews, the sound recordist, could hear that they sounded like styrofoam when the drips hit them. The crew had to figure out a way to stop the dripping. The second thing that happened as a result of too much groundwater was that when I climbed down into the sewer, too much water splashed up on my trousers and on the cameras. Solution? Everyone on crew grabbed a bucket and hauled water out to the real sewers.

One of the things I learned quickly when working on a television drama is that you have to have a lot of professional patience.[5] After a

---

4 Really not as much fun as it sounds.
5 Notice I've said 'professional' 'cause I know myself too well.

scene is filmed from one angle, the director then asks for a 'turnaround', which means, funnily enough, that the cameras are all turned round and the scene is filmed from another angle; and, if necessary, another after that. In the sewer scene, the director needed a close-up of my face when Jack realizes the figure in the sewer is his father, so we had to do several turnarounds on this shoot.

After the crew had completed their impersonations of Mickey from *Fantasia*, the filming shifted to Captain Jack's office, where Jack has to interrogate Ianto, who, thanks to Adam, Jack thinks has committed murder. The challenge of this scene was that the green lights from the lie detector that Jack is using were creating a distracting glare on my cheek. The scene had to be reshot several times with the lie detector in a variety of different angles. Ordinarily, a scene like this should take an hour and a half at the most, but this took close to three.

Then, just when we thought it was safe to go back into the Hub, the light shorted out on the lie detector gizmo, suggesting that Ianto was only intermittently telling the truth. Solution? A young woman from the prop department had to crawl under Jack's desk, out of sight of the camera, and every time the light needed to flash, she controlled it manually from a crouched position between my legs.[6]

During the filming of 'Children of Earth', our bloopers or blunders were not as memorable. The shoot didn't lack significance, though. So on the day we were filming in the Hub for the last time, I made sure Jack did two things.

First, I stole[7] a souvenir from the props spread across Jack's desk. I took a pulp sci-fi paperback from the forties that sat on his desktop. Every time I'd been in Jack's office, waiting for a take, I'd picked it up and read a few words.

The second thing I did was to make sure that the passionate kiss between Jack and Ianto that takes place moments before Jack and the Hub are destroyed was a kiss to die for. It certainly was.

---

[6] A place where no woman has gone before.
[7] Children, cover your eyes.

CHAPTER SIX

'I'D DO ANYTHING'

'Respect my authori-TEY.'
Eric Cartman, *South Park*

Five more things I've learned from being a talent-show judge

1 Trust your judging panel has your back
(unless one of them doesn't).

2 Trust your opinions even when they're not popular
(with the other judges).

3 Beware of pissed-off parents of performers.

4 A sense of humour makes a good first impression
(especially on me).

5 Coordinate your outfit with the beautiful woman to your left
(not Barry Humphries).

may have already helped to pick the right Maria and the best Joseph, but when it came to choosing a Nancy,[1] when I joined the panel on BBC1's *I'd Do Anything*, the expertise I'd developed as a judge was really put to the test.

I found my feet as a judge in the early stages of the *Maria* show. During the panel auditions for *How Do You Solve a Problem Like Maria?*, David Ian wore the earpiece and I went to school on him.[2] I listened, I watched and I learned. If the producers saw something on their monitors from the other room that they wanted to see again or that they wanted highlighted in a particular way, they talked to David through this earpiece.

Meanwhile, I discovered that if I asked the performers questions and established a bit of a rapport with them as soon as they came in front of me, they relaxed a little and this helped them to get their breathing calmed before they actually performed. So, with all this knowledge at my fingertips by the time *I'd Do Anything* began, I was more than ready for the challenges ... or so I thought.

Zoë Tyler was not on the panel this time. The other judges were Denise Van Outen, the Lord and Barry Humphries. As I did in *Any Dream*, during the panel auditions, when the contestants are performing for only the judges and the producers, I wore the earpiece. I was the judge with the voices in my head.[3]

I'd never worked with Barry before, but we got along really well. I've always admired and enjoyed his work. There's a whole group of performers from those early days of British theatre and television that

---

[1] Puhleeze. In any other context, with my eyes closed.

[2] I said 'went to school on him'. Clean out your ears.

[3] Well, new ones anyway.

I think contributed to the definition of what it means to be an entertainer, one that in my own twenty-first-century-when-everything-changes way I'm trying to shape, too. Angus Lennie, Rikki Fulton, Bruce Forsyth, The Two Ronnies, Danny La Rue and, of course, Stanley Baxter were all in that same category.

Little-known fact about the Barrowmans.[4] My mum grew up across the street from Angus Lennie and she remembers that when he was a teenager, he'd leave his house every afternoon for his violin lessons and the other kids would taunt him, yelling, 'Go on yer own, Hal the Fiddler.'[5]

You may remember Lennie from *Crossroads*, or more recently *Monarch of the Glen*, but, as far as my dad's concerned, Lennie will always be Flying Officer Archie Ives, aka The Mole, in one of my dad's favourite movies of all time, *The Great Escape* with Steve McQueen. His other favourite is *Von Ryan's Express* with Frank Sinatra fighting Nazis. Why Sinatra, you may ask? Well, because he could. When my mum catches my dad sneaking another viewing of the film late at night on some obscure US cable channel, he'll tell her he's watching it because he 'keeps hoping this time he'll catch the bloody train'.[6]

Don't tell my mum, but I keep a DVD set of these two movies, plus *The Guns of Navarone* as a bonus, hidden among my collection at the house in Sully – in case my dad ever needs a hit while he's staying with me.

Unfortunately, despite Barry Humphries's talents and versatility, and his undoubted place in the entertainment hall of fame, some of the Nancy contestants thought he came across as a bit of a 'dirty old man' on camera. Here's why. Imagine one of the Nancys has just performed, then read this dialogue in a low-pitched, not-quite-Dame-Edna-ish voice:

'You don't look so much like a milkmaid –' (pause for slightly heavy breathing) '– but you look very much like the milker.'

---

4 There are still one or two.

5 Young people back in the day really knew how to hurt a kid, didn't they?

6 If you need this spoiler explained, put the film on your movie rental list and discover the pleasure for yourself.

How do you respond to that? 'Hmm, thanks, Barry. I'll take that on board. Let me just dart out and get a breast reduction.'

Here was another one: 'Please, Samantha, I want some more!' And then there was: 'You were gorgeous! You had a touch of the guttersnipe, and I mean that in the nicest possible way.'

Sometimes, his comments could be a bit irrelevant, with little constructive purpose, especially when he was commenting on Jodie Prenger.

During the auditions, when I first met Jodie, she said something sassy and she made me laugh. A sense of humour makes good television, so I knew she had to be involved in the programme. I also knew the audience would like her because she was very down to earth and honest in her presentation of herself. She came across as your sister, your co-worker, or the girl you'd want to talk to if your boyfriend dumped you.

I know a lot of people may not believe me on this, given some of my comments after a few of her performances, but in the beginning I also thought Jessie Buckley was very talented. I still think she is. From the initial auditions, I thought Jessie would have incredible growth during the series, and I thought the same thing about Ashley Russell. I believed that, given the chance, both women would develop into strong performers. Sarah Lark was equally formidable when she started because she was already working in the West End. Ironically, this may have worked against her because she may have appeared too polished for the role of Nancy.

All in all, the performers trying for the part were as talented a group as any of the artists I've had to work with on these shows. So it was a bit of a blow from left field, and certainly not one I saw coming, when the high drama of this series came my way from another member of the panel.

Sir Cameron Mackintosh was not officially a judge on this show, but as the main producer of *Oliver!*, he took a keen interest in the casting process and joined the judging panel once the competition came down to its final four contestants (Jodie, Jessie, Sam Barks and Rachel Tucker). Cameron was in the audience for all the panel auditions, the rehearsals post-Nancy camp, and for all the shows, but because of his decision to stay in the wings until the climax of the series, he didn't have much of a chance to build a public rapport with the contestants, or a relationship of any kind with the show's audience. In the end, I think this may have had an impact on the show's finale and Cameron's offstage confrontation with me.

Over the course of *I'd Do Anything*, as Jodie began to demonstrate to the panel that she was learning from all the feedback we were giving her, the viewers were beginning to recognize that Jodie might be the one to watch. This also meant that some people, Cameron in particular, were getting tougher with their critiques of her performances.

After every show, and this held true for *Maria* and *Any Dream* too, the contestants would come up to the BBC bar afterwards. If they asked me for advice or more feedback, I'd happily give it. Almost every week, Jodie would come over and chat with me. One night, after a tough show when things had not gone well for her, Jodie approached me in the bar to ask how she could help herself to improve. I told her to try to see herself at a distance, and as much as possible to view her performance without emotion.

This is a very hard thing to do, even for a seasoned performer, and I think it was advice that was applicable to us on the panel, too. When I give my feedback, I try to frame it in a way that makes it clear I'm not judging the performer as a person; I'm judging their work. I may be saying 'you're not right for this job',[7] but it's because of the performance, not the individual. Working in showbiz means facing and accepting rejection, and it's the toughest lesson to learn.

On Saturday nights before airtime, all the judges would gather for a confab before going on, and we'd prep ourselves for what might happen if each girl on the show failed or succeeded. We'd draft out a rough response that related to whatever points or challenges we might have given her earlier performances. I took very seriously the aspect of the show that expected development in the performers, and this meant I paid attention to whatever the other judges and I had said in the past.

[7] Heard that one, two or twenty times in my career ...

Since we didn't know what was going to happen, we had to be ready for both eventualities: the good and the bad. The show was live, and in live television there's no time after a performance for a judge to stare blankly into space because he or she was gobsmacked by the success or the failure of a contestant. A performer may have a great dress rehearsal, but things can change in a heartbeat when you're in front of a live studio and television audience, and it often did.

During those pre-show meetings, I began to get the impression that Cameron and Andrew were pushing a bit harder for Jessie Buckley. At this point in the series, about midway, I had not really made up my mind yet. It wasn't until the semi-finals, when I started to see enough growth in people, that I began to think seriously about which performer could carry a West End show.

The reasons, in the end, that I didn't support Jessie were that I didn't see enough maturation in her performances, and I thought she was too young to play Nancy. I also suspected that she might not be able to handle the leadership that a leading lady would be expected to demonstrate and, to be honest, I saw limited emotional depth in her repertoire.

For example, when Jessie was singing an emotive song, she'd raise her hand and touch her forehead to suggest she was feeling something. She would do this quite deliberately. Lots of performers have a trait or a small movement that becomes part of their onstage persona. For example, Carol Burnett always tugs her ear at the end of her performances, and in *Tonight's the Night*, when I stepped down from my 'illuminated ring',[8] I always did a spin at the front of the stage. Neither one of these rituals is an emotional move. Acting is about making the emotion seem real and if, to convey that feeling, an actor relies only on a superficial, choreographed move, it lessens the impact.

Having said all that, Jessie did have her good points. She was gorgeous, had charisma and she had a great voice. What Jessie, and a few other Nancy contestants, also needed, however, was a lesson in how to walk in high heels. At John Barrowman's Beauty, Charm and

---

[8] Really. That's what we called it. I had a pink ring, a green ring, a red ring …

Confidence School, this would be one of the first required courses. For this, I believe, is an important life lesson for women.[9]

I worry, I really do, that with so many younger women wearing flip-flops and flats these days – including my niece Clare, who has more pairs of flip-flops than anyone I know – walking correctly in heels will become a lost art. How tragic that would be! That's why, when Clare was old enough to wear high heels, I gave her lessons in how to walk in them. Heel first. Weight on hips. Back straight. Strut. She can walk in any inch heel now and never looks as if she's going to topple. Clare put her learning into action when she walked the red carpet with me at the New York premiere of *De-Lovely*, the Cole Porter biopic I filmed with Kevin Kline, and she strutted her heels with my co-star Ashley Judd like a pro. Jessie and a couple of the other Nancy contestants took advantage of my special skills in this area.[10]

As the series progressed, it became obvious to me that Cameron wanted Jessie to win. Of the four finalists, while he loved Sam, he felt she was too immature to take on the role. He said he would be happy with any of the other three women winning the part – Jodie, Jessie or Rachel – but it was apparent that Jessie was his first choice to be Nancy.

During the contest, Cameron did not want Ashley Russell to move forward. He really liked her offstage, but onstage he found that her performances grated on him, and that she was unable, somehow, to communicate her sparkling offstage personality through her songs. I liked Ashley too – both on- and offstage – but she lost my support as Nancy in the end because she just wasn't progressing as much as I would have liked, or even as much as some of the other performers.

But one of the funniest aspects of Cameron's dissatisfaction with Ashley was that Andrew's children had sussed this out. Any time they were within earshot of Cameron, Denise or I would yell, 'Who are you voting for?' and Andrew's kids would reply loudly, 'Ashley! We love her!'

---

[9] And a few men.
[10] Just call me Henry Higgins.

On the fourth show of the series, Ashley and Francesca Jackson were in the bottom two after the audience voting. Cameron must have been thinking this was it; now Ashley would surely be gone. He was wrong and, unfortunately, I bore the brunt of his wrath.

One of the things I admire about Andrew in this kind of context[11] is that sometimes if Denise or I were strong in our opinions and we had compelling evidence to support them, Andrew listened to us. A lot of times, especially when we were witnessing an amazing performance, we'd all confer across the panel with our eyes. On this particular night, Andrew watched, listened, and chose to save Ashley.

I came offstage and directly into a confrontation with Cameron. In general, I don't let people rim me out in anger, but if it's really warranted, I might bite my tongue. In this case, Cameron was furious that Ashley had been saved and he seemed to hold me partly responsible.

After the closing credits, Cameron stormed off the set. I thought we'd had a terrific show with lots of drama, and impressive vocal performances. We were making *I'd Do Anything* for the viewers – not Cameron – so they could pick a Nancy who they'd want to pay their hard-earned cash to see.

Speaking of which, even before the semi-final, the box-office advance for *Oliver!* was huge; two-thirds of the advance bookings came from people who did not even know who exactly was going to play Nancy – they may have booked hoping for Jessie, Jodie, Rachel or Sam – which just goes to demonstrate the calibre of the contestants. *Oliver!* also starred Rowan Atkinson as Fagin, who was clearly a massive draw. By the time the show opened, in January 2009, the stellar cast – Jodie as Nancy, Burn Gorman[12] as Bill Sikes, plus Rowan and many other fantastic performers – had attracted phenomenal box-office receipts in the region of £15 million.

On this evening, in week four, I congratulated Ashley, offered my heartfelt condolences to Francesca and stepped off set, where I

---

[11] I admire him in others, too, of course.
[12] Go, Binny Bots!

immediately ran into Cameron. He was furious. He'd thought that he and Andrew had agreed on the matter of Ashley, and he was astonished that this turnabout had occurred. When I defended Ashley, and Andrew for having saved her – after all, it was only the fourth week, and, had Ashley improved, she could even have won the competition – Cameron lashed out at me.

'I'm a bit worried about your judgement and taste now,' he yelled, 'because what you've just done has shown me that you don't have any taste. I'm the one producing this fucking show, not you!'

Of course, I continued to defend my opinion – and he continued to yell at me, in front of all the BBC runners, some of the staff and crew, and Denise. I think Andrew may have been in earshot, too.

I was stunned into silence.[13] After a few beats, I caught my breath and I thought, 'I don't need to take this from him.' Cameron is a friend, I respect him immensely, and we have a long history together.[14]

I leaned towards him and said, 'If you feel that strongly about these performers, then why aren't you on the panel? I'm up there to be a judge. I'm not a casting director.' I paused and then added, 'The viewers will cast this and there's a good chance they're not going to cast who you want.' I avoided him for the rest of the night.

Later, when the show was over and I thought about all that had happened, I think this incident may have been a defining moment for me in that series. The confrontation showed me that when Cameron felt strongly about a particular performer, he would communicate his views passionately. I realized that when the show reached the finals, I might have to balance Cameron's (and Andrew's) push for Jessie. From that moment, I decided I was going to stick up for the performers whom I thought could carry a West End show; performers I thought had the temperament and the talent to be in the West End.

A couple of days after this incident, Gavin received a call from Trevor Jackson, Cameron's casting director, asking if I was okay

---

13 I know. Hard to imagine.
14 Read *Anything Goes* if you want to know more.

because he'd heard about the blow-up. He wanted to know if I was angry with Cameron. I said I wasn't and I meant it. Yeah, Cameron was out of line and behaved badly, but I think he was caught up in the adrenalin of the moment – and the casting of the show – and, well, we've all been there.

There's a pace and a rhythm to these talent shows. At about show six, the crescendo begins, the momentum picks up and the pressure builds. Weaker performers slipped away, but Jodie was getting stronger, and, in her performance of 'Send in the Clowns' in week three, I thought I might well, at some point in the contest, see her pulling away from the competition. When the final arrived, as I'd expected, Jessie and Jodie were the two left in the contest for the very last sing-off.

Here was where I believe my experience allowed me to make a judgement call. I realized that after Jessie and Jodie performed in the finale, we would be expected to give our opinion and to offer our advice, but I knew from experience that I could trust the British viewing public to make the right choice and to pick a Nancy they'd fork out to see. In many ways, with these programmes, it almost doesn't matter what the West End show is, as the public are voting for the performer and they're going to sell out the production because of that performer.

Denise and I decided that we'd give our opinions strongly in the first show,[15] and then we would back off during the second one and let the viewers make their own decisions. In the second programme, we decided to give positive feedback to both Jessie and Jodie.

Honestly, this final contest was one of the best I've participated in since *Maria*. Both Jessie and Jodie sang really well. Their performances made for incredibly competitive and compelling TV.

When Graham Norton, the show's presenter, asked us for our comments after the contestants' final songs, both Denise and I praised them equally. Barry knocked Jodie and boosted Jessie. Cameron cut down Jodie and boosted Jessie. Andrew did the same. I looked at Den

[15] The final was in two parts.

and shrugged, because we knew that it was out of their hands and maybe, just maybe, they had hurt Jessie's cause.

After the phone lines closed and before the winner was announced, Graham asked us to make our choice.

'John, who is your Nancy?'

'Jodie.'

'Denise?'

'Jodie.'

Barry, the Lord and Cameron all picked Jessie.

'The winning Nancy is ...' – twenty-minute-long dramatic pause – '... Jodie!'

Denise and I jumped up so fast, I felt dizzy. We threw ourselves into each other's arms. I was in tears and was punching the air like a madman.

After the excitement calmed, and the show ended, I did what I'd done every week in every one of the shows on which I'd been judging: I went over to the family and the supporters of the performer who had lost and I told them that I thought their daughter or son was talented and would go far. I did this to every Maria and to every Joseph and to every Nancy who lost.

Only twice have my condolences gone badly. Once, I had a parent lash out at me. You know what? I'd likely behave in the same way if it were my son or daughter. It was always a hugely emotional moment for everyone involved.

What's really important for all of us to remember about these particular talent shows is that they put bums on theatre seats and 90 per cent of the finalists find work in musical theatre. Jessie was no exception. She was not Nancy, but she was good enough to perform in Stephen Sondheim's *A Little Night Music* in the West End, and she was wonderful.

'There's an Iguana in the Toilet and He's Grinning at Me'

Ever since one of the first family Christmas shows starring yours truly, Clare and Turner, when they played two of the von Trapp children and Turner belted out, 'So long, farewell, my feet are saying goodbye' instead of '*Auf wiedersehen*, goodbye,'[1] I've loved working with children. And I'm especially thrilled when children recognize me and ask me for my autograph – or, more accurately, when they ask to have a picture taken with Captain Jack.

One day, when I was in Costco, a young boy and his mother came up to me as I was finishing paying for my industrial cartload at the checkout. She said her son had been watching me going up and down the aisles, and finally he'd asked her why Captain Jack was shopping in Costco.

Why, indeed.

For younger children who are *Doctor Who* fans (and who are too young to watch *Torchwood*), when they see me in a store, on the street, or at the movies, it's Captain Jack they see, and not John Barrowman. I took the mum's lead and said to her son that Jack was undercover. I'd heard from the Doctor that there'd been a possible sighting of a Cyberman in Costco. I asked him if he'd noticed anything unusual while he was shopping with his mum. He shook his head in all seriousness and said no, he had not. I shook his hand and as he headed out of the store, he turned and said, 'Bye, Captain Jack, but I'll keep watching.'

---

[1] Made perfect sense to him … to me, too.

And he did. He watched all the way to his car, when he gave me a little wave as his mum fastened him into his booster seat. I gave him a quick salute. He was beaming as the car disappeared out of the parking lot.

Two summers ago, I opened a summer country fete in the south of England and agreed to set up a table and sign autographs, with donations for them going to a local charity. I didn't have a great deal of time open in my schedule, and, naturally, it was pouring rain and there were only so many pairs of welly boots to go around.[2] The line was very long, so I asked if everyone would be okay with allowing the children to come up and be first in line. No one argued at all and, in the end, I was able to sign an autograph for everyone who waited.

One of the last children to step up was a boy of about eight or nine. He handed me his Captain Jack action figure and asked if I'd sign it. He and I took a few minutes to decide where exactly was the best place to have the autograph[3] because this was clearly a well-played-with figure. While I was signing the toy, he leaned in really close to my ear and said, 'I don't care if Jack likes a man or likes a woman, he's still my favourite hero.' I was so chuffed. I gave him a really big hug.

During the summer of 2008, I filmed a number of segment links for my show on CBBC, *Animals at Work*. The show is made up of clips of animals doing really cool and amazing things, like an elephant in Thailand that cleans toilets.[4] The shoot for *Animals at Work* took place at a rural zoo that I'm convinced was run by Basil Fawlty. I arrived very early in the morning and after a quick wander round – noting the overgrown vegetation, the stinking cages, the swarms of flies everywhere, and the sign that read 'WARNING: Lions Roaming the Premises'[5] – I began to wonder exactly what I was doing there. I mean, I'm a proper celebrity. I get recognized in M&S.

---

[2] Carole and Scott had to arm-wrestle for the last pair.

[3] I signed across Jack's back.

[4] Try teaching that to your cat.

[5] Seriously. As if a warning sign was all you bloody needed to protect yourself from wandering lions.

The zoo's outbuildings consisted of a large bungalow, where Basil and Sybil Fawlty lived; a faux Swiss chalet that housed the zoo's office; and a floor of dormitories for children who were participating in the Fawltys' 'summer camp for kids whose parents don't have a clue'. Behind all of these buildings there was acreage dotted with cages overgrown with brush (thankfully, the animals inside looked healthy), gravel walking trails, and a large pond with wild peacocks, ducks, geese and a few llamas lurking nearby.

The producer for the segment met me at the parking lot and introduced me to some of the zoo's staff; many of them appeared to be young enough to be avid viewers of CBBC themselves. The guy who was the keeper and main animal wrangler had to have been all of twenty-two. After enquiring about his training, I learned it consisted of a certificate programme in animal training and having a 'great passion' for animals, which he clearly had. But so do I, and you don't want me taking care of your tigers. Trust me, you don't. He was a nice enough young man, but I have to admit he didn't inspire great confidence in me, especially when I learned that the director was planning to put me inside a cage with either a lion or a tiger cub for one of the segment links.

While the producer continued to review the day's shoot with me, a number of children – ranging in age from about seven up to early teens – straggled out of one of the buildings and headed to a Quonset hut for breakfast. I didn't want to ask what was on the menu in case I was sent out into the far fields and asked to hunt and skin it.

Before I headed to make-up, which had been set up in one of the Quonset hut classrooms, I asked to use the bathroom – and that's when I realized I'd need to keep my wits and my hand sanitizer about me during this shoot if I wanted to get back to civilization a) with all my body parts intact, and b) without some rare animal disease.

The toilet I was directed to use was in one of the main buildings, next to the zoo's administrative office. This consisted of three desks set in a row, each one stacked ridiculously high with paper and files. Behind one of the desks sat Sybil Fawlty, with her beehive hair[6] stacked

---

[6] I wouldn't have been surprised to find actual bees in it.

just as high, answering calls and giving orders to campers and staff who were wandering in and out.

I stepped into the toilet – and froze. The room looked as if it had last seen Dettol a few days before the First World War and it smelled as if the entire Foreign Legion had taken a piss in it. The toilet paper was non-existent; and if all that wasn't bad enough, someone had had the nerve to stick an incense stick in a glass jar on the cistern. As if lighting it would have done anything more than add to the odour that was so thick and putrid I could taste it. But, and bear with me here, none of those things was the worst part of this toilet. This was. Instead of where a bathtub or shower should have been, there was a huge, glass reptile cage with one of the biggest iguanas I've ever seen inside.[7] Two things struck me as being creepy and weird about having this reptile cage in the toilet at this zoo.[8]

First of all – and I know this is completely irrational – I didn't want to pee in front of this reptile. He looked big enough to be able to get up on his four stumpy legs and climb out of the cage. When I was in middle school, one of my science teachers kept a variety of reptiles in her classroom and one day, when we all sat down, she had one dangling from the tip of her finger. While she'd been feeding it, Dr Pepper (I think its name was[9]) had latched itself onto the end of her finger. She told the class not to pay any attention to Dr Pepper hanging there and eventually he'd get bored and drop off. She told the class that the more she tried to force Dr Pepper to release her finger, the tighter he pinched. I was never a very strong student in the sciences, but if I'd been taught more often by teachers who had reptiles hanging from their body parts, I may have been a better one. In the end, she had to leave the classroom before the bell rang because she noticed her finger was swelling and turning blue. I stepped into that bathroom and had a sudden flash of that teacher's finger when I started to unzip my fly. Can you blame me for not wanting to pee anymore?

[7] Trust me. I've seen a lot in my day.
[8] Yes, only two.
[9] I'm rubbish with details like this.

Secondly, when families paid their admission fee to the zoo, did they all have to crowd into this smelly space if they wanted to see the iguana?

Back outside, while I was looking for someone from the crew, wanting to ask if there was a toilet more acceptable for human use available – like in one of the other cages – I noticed a restaurant across the street. For the rest of that day and the morning of the next, any time I wanted to pee, I'd get in my car and drive across the freeway to the diner.[10]

I was given the script to review for a few minutes before beginning. Since I was mostly filming intro links, most of what had been written was puns and animal jokes. Given the state of the place, I wanted to write my own introduction.

'Good morning! John Barrowman here, working in a pigsty, picking up shit, and generally hanging out with animals.'[11]

When filming started later that morning, my first segment was with a friendly, well-behaved skunk (well-behaved mainly because the poor thing's stink had been removed). This was followed by a scene with a snake – a snake that I had to wear around my neck for part of the link.

I'm not really afraid of any animals; cautious and respectful of some of them, but not afraid. The snake weighed heavy on my shoulders and by the time the handler – remember the kid of about twelve? – had finished explaining to me what to do to stop it crushing my windpipe, I was breathing heavily and wondering why I'd never paid attention to the old cliché about working with children and animals.

Between every segment we filmed, I wanted to shower. The whole place was filthy and run-down. At one point, when I was dashing to my car to take a toilet break, I noticed that all the kids from the camp were actually cleaning the animal cages. To make matters worse, it had started to drizzle, and the caged monkeys hadn't stopped screaming since lunch[12] was served. I think the monkeys were planning a coup.

[10] Did I mention I was a proper celebrity?
[11] Sounds like a nightclub I went to once.
[12] Which I couldn't make myself eat.

By the end of the first day of filming, I'd lost my sense of humour along with my appetite, and I was thinking seriously about becoming a vegetarian.

I can count on one hand the number of times during my career in theatre and in television when I've lost my temper on set with producers or directors. The end of that first day of shooting *Animals at Work* was one of them. I pulled the location manager aside and told him I wanted a trailer with running water and a clean toilet. In other words, a place to go where I wasn't at risk from catching cholera or Ebola fever.

He said he'd see what he could do. He wasn't sure there was money in the budget, so if he could get Basil Fawlty's permission, would I be willing to use the main house as my dressing room if they couldn't get a trailer?

I've never been one who believes life is full of compromises. I don't think it is. I think life is full of choices.[13] I told the location manager that I'd try the main house, but if it didn't meet even minimum health standards – and when I said minimum, I meant not sharing the bathroom with a frickin' anaconda – I wanted a trailer.

The next day, I showed up at the main house. From the outside, the house looked as if you might find Heidi and her grandfather inside, but once I crossed the threshold, I decided that this house could easily have been the inspiration for H. G. Wells's *The Island of Dr Moreau*. The place smelled like wet fur and faeces. The living room – where my make-up artist had been set up – was decorated like a jungle palace, with marble columns competing with huge palm fronds and stuffed animal carcasses. To top it all off, there was a puddle of pee on the tiled floor right next to my make-up chair.

My trailer arrived at lunchtime.

The rest of the shoot was fairly uneventful – until the director asked me to wander among the llamas for the final segment link. The llamas were hanging out at the far end of the property as if they didn't want to have anything to do with the rest of the place.[14]

[13] And good chocolate, if you're lucky.
[14] Who could blame them?

As the shoot had gradually moved further into the zoo's acreage, instead of sitting under a tent in the cold drizzle between takes, I'd taken to driving my rented SUV as close to the location as possible. I sat inside the car as the director set up the shot, and I kept my eyes on those llamas.

Now, I don't know much about llamas, other than the whole 'head on the can of polish' thing and that they make a tasty sausage,[15] but I thought this particular group looked angry and just plain mean.

When the director called for me, I walked across the grass and made my way into the herd. I swear I could hear them hissing and taunting me.

'Can you get a little closer, John?'

I took two steps towards to the llama the director wanted in his shot. It turned and stared at me. I think I heard it chuckle malevolently.

'A little closer please, John.'

'This, Mr DeMille,' I said, 'is way close enough.'

[15] Aw, shit. That's an emu. See? I know nothing.

CHAPTER SEVEN

'MAKE THE DIRT STICK'

*'I want you all to know that I'm writing
this ... stark naked, with my knees behind my
ears, and I'm using only one hand.'*

A. A. Gill

A few good lessons learned from a really bad week

1 Sometimes going along for a ride can take you in the wrong direction (especially if it's in a wheelbarrow on the radio).

2 Apologize first, analyse later.

3 Just because I have confidence in me, doesn't mean my blues don't get black.

4 Being 'seen' on the radio is an oxymoron.

When I was growing up in America in the late seventies and eighties, I adored TV series like *The Donny and Marie Show*, *The Sonny and Cher Show* and *Barbara Mandrell and the Mandrell Sisters* because they had spectacle, surprises, banter and lots of music. Little-known fact: when I was performing at Opryland USA in Nashville in the eighties, my first TV gig was as a backing dancer and singer on Barbara Mandrell's *Opryland Special*, and, might I say, she was a treat to work behind.

About two years ago, when the BBC and I first began serious discussions regarding a possible series for a Saturday night, even before we imagined *Tonight's the Night*, I knew I wanted two things: firstly, that the programme hark back to those variety shows of my youth; and secondly, that the company set up by Gavin and me, Barrowman Barker Productions (BBP), be part of the production team.

Oh, I loved the style and tone and sheer razzle-dazzle of those entertainment programmes from the eighties, and lots of little details about them have stayed with me. I knew that I wanted every show to open with a big, glitzy, Busby Berkeley-style number; and towards the middle of the opening song, I wanted to cut in with that episode's menu. To me, this small moment was a quintessential element of a variety show.

I imagined the opening for *Tonight's the Night* to go something like this.

Big number. Big number. Dancers dancing. Music drops. 'Ladies and gentlemen, on tonight's show we have a Welsh woman who always wanted to perform as a Jersey Boy, four colleagues from Kent who can do amazing things with their flutes, plus … Chaka Khan!'[1]

---

[1] This became a ritual. During rehearsals for *TTN*, I'd always introduce Chaka Khan as a guest. She never was.

On *Tonight's the Night*, I wanted nostalgia, spectacle, audience surprises and compelling live drama. Unfortunately, the week before the show was officially commissioned by the BBC, my life was overwhelmed with more drama and controversy than even I could handle, and it sent me spiralling into a physical and emotional tailspin.

Big number. Big number. Dancers dancing. Music drops. 'Ladies and gentlemen, in this chapter we have the story behind the story of me flashing "my boys" on BBC Switch on Radio 1, plus ... Chaka Khan!'

When I think about the events surrounding the incident that was quickly labelled 'Ballgate', I go from good humour to anger in less than sixty seconds flat. I'm not angry at myself much anymore, and certainly not at the DJs, Nick Grimshaw and Annie Mac, their producer, or anyone at the BBC. Instead, what angers me most when I think about the episode is that much of the outcry in the days following the actual event was flamed by a couple of tabloid newspapers, and a handful of folks who had not witnessed the incident first hand.

How do I know this? Because the so-called 'flash' occurred on the radio – that's right, on the radio, a purely aural medium, and one, in this case, without a live studio audience and with its web cameras turned off. I'm not saying that my outrageousness didn't get out of control, it did, and I have taken full responsibility for any offence it caused those actually listening to the show, including making a public apology. But I've always felt that the incident got inflated into something bigger in the blogosphere than the actual act itself warranted. As a result, the flash of 'my boys' was heard, not seen – remember it happened on the radio – around the country.

Days later, the *Times* columnist A. A. Gill captured brilliantly what I believe was underpinning the consequences of the entire event. In a hysterically funny and politically pointed piece of satire, he wrote that '[t]he truth is nothing as salaciously vile as the imaginations of the prim'.

Here's what happened. Gav usually travels with me to my scheduled appearances, but he left me to my own devices on this day and took a much-deserved break from what had been a hectic weekend schedule.

Would I have gone as far as I did in my outrageousness if Gavin had stayed with me? Maybe. Maybe not. Anyway, Gavin went home, poured himself a glass of wine, put his feet up, and tuned his radio in to listen to the show from home, leaving me with Joe Bennett, my record-company publicity person, and Scott.

During this particular BBC radio show, it's not unusual for guests to play games and carry on with the DJs – and you know me, I rarely need an invitation to do either. On this Sunday evening, the antics got progressively more out of hand as the show went on. At one point, I put on a crash helmet and the DJs wheeled me around the studio in a barrow, playing a ridiculous 'grab and fill the bucket' game. The studio had been decorated with copies of my CDs hanging from all the surfaces and this was the booty I had to snatch.[2]

From the moment the show went on the air, the DJs joked about my habit of mooning people,[3] and asked if they should be worried about me taking 'my willy out'. After they'd egged me on throughout most of the programme, in the spirit of the show's shenanigans, I looked at the producer and pointed to the webcam. She nodded it was off, and it was, so I gave the DJs a quick flash of 'my boys'.

Anyone who has been on set, backstage, or spent any time with me at home knows that I like a good laugh, love to pull outrageous pranks and that, if the circumstances are appropriate, I can be adult in my antics. An edgy radio show on BBC Radio 1 seemed, at the time, to be an appropriate forum. In my head, I remember thinking, 'We're on the radio, the cameras are off, so if I do what they're encouraging me to do, only Scott and the DJs will see me.' Of course, Scott had seen my boys before.[4]

I called Gavin immediately afterwards to ask if he'd heard the broadcast, as I usually do after I've been on the radio or on TV and he's not been with me. His first words were, 'Did you really have to take your dick out?'

[2] In the interest of full disclosure, I grabbed all of them.
[3] Not just my habit – a family, and a Glasgow, tradition.
[4] More than once.

'I didn't! It was just my balls,' I said, and I added that I hadn't really taken them out completely.[5] The moment was but a brief flash in my palm.

If my antics had happened at any other time, I'm convinced everything would have been nothing by Monday morning, but, unfortunately, they occurred during what was a very sensitive period for the BBC. Some people – and when I say some people, I mean one newspaper and one public complaint during the show – interpreted my flash as one more black mark against the BBC and its talent, and the incident was quickly linked to the Jonathan Ross/Russell Brand prank calls made a few weeks earlier.

For me, one of the consequences of the Ross/Brand incident, and 'Ballgate', was that it brought to light what I've always thought is an anti-BBC bias in a couple of the British tabloids; newspapers whose pump is always primed to flood their pages with any behaviour they perceive to cross their thin blue line of propriety. They'll bend over backwards[6] to expose BBC personalities in a dim light. Regardless, I issued a heartfelt apology first thing on Monday.

After the stories ran in the *Evening Standard* and the *Daily Mail*, I realized that their response was out of proportion to what had actually occurred in the studio. Tellingly, both articles failed to explain until past their leads that no members of the public had 'seen' anything because, as the *Daily Mail* admitted further down the story, 'Barrowman's genitalia were not actually shown.'

In the *Daily Mail* piece, my autobiography, *Anything Goes*, was raided, with details taken completely out of context to add to the paper's litany of my 'lewd behaviours'. For example, in one of the paragraphs, the *Daily Mail* described me as 'a serial exhibitionist', citing random examples from *AG* of times when I've bared my bum.

I have to say, this newspaper's questionable journalistic practices were what angered me most about the incident's aftermath. I couldn't

[5] Which Scott attests to.
[6] Not easy to do when their morality is so rigid.

help wondering, even then, how much their continued attacks on the BBC and its personnel were, in part, because the *Daily Mail* is owned by the same company that has an interest in one of the BBC's competing television networks.

However, what was truly appalling about the *Mail*'s article was that in the same paragraph it detailed my supposed 'licentiousness', it also noted that I had 'married' my 'long-term partner' in a civil ceremony; suggesting by association with the other examples that my civil ceremony was another example of my 'lewd behaviour'.

And the *Daily Mail* called me outrageous!

Shame on the *Daily Mail* for equating being gay with being 'lewd', and shame on them for suggesting that a public expression of two people's love for each other – something non-gays have been doing forever – is equally licentious. This is Britain in the twenty-first century, and yet this kind of bigotry can still find space in a national newspaper.

As if this association wasn't awful enough, the newspaper's story closed with the line that I once 'kicked faeces into the audience'. Anyone who has read *Anything Goes* knows that this incident was neither premeditated, purposeful, or even my fault, and that the flying faeces happened while I was high-kicking during a dance routine onstage, after a rival performer spiked my water with a laxative.

This particular article really angered me, but I have to say that, for the most part, the response of the rest of the press was to see this for what it was.[7] Friends who monitored bloggers on even the *Daily Mail*'s website explained to me – when I could handle hearing the details the following week – that most folks generally felt it was a stupid antic that went too far and nothing more. The day the story hit the front page of the *Daily Mail,* a close friend from television emailed me, sending his support. He added: 'But a great pic of you, John.' It really was.

Even after I released my apology on the Monday, the reporting of the incident kept spreading like a bad cold. By Tuesday, I had

[7] Nothing worth writing about.

sunk into a deep funk that drove me into seclusion. By Wednesday, my body felt as if it had been pummelled and it simply shut down. I didn't read emails, avoided the press, and couldn't make myself answer my phone. Everything hurt. I don't have these dark periods very often, but when I do, Scott, Gavin and my family know to leave me alone as much as possible and to let me work my way out of them.

Poor Scott. He felt completely helpless. This incident was the first time that Scott had really seen me felled by something as public as this, something that he couldn't do anything about to help, and even his mothering and cooking, and hugging and silly jokes, and the smart retorts he imagined writing to the press couldn't break my ever-blackening mood.[8]

Gavin tried to throw all kinds of work distractions my way, but none of them made a difference. I was angry at myself for getting into this situation in the first place, that's a given, but – honestly – what I was most upset with was the blinkered, petty moralizing from folks who had neither seen nor heard the incident first hand, and who were simply responding to second-hand summaries, many of them inaccurate. Plus, can I just write this again – it happened on the radio! No one from the general public saw anything.

By Thursday, I'd crashed, physically and psychologically. I'd completely lost my voice and every part of my body ached. At the last minute, I was forced to cancel my BBC Radio 2 'Friday Night is Music Night' concert.

In the face of dead air on a Friday, Jodie Keane, who's produced many of my BBC Radio 2 concerts, Joe Bennett and Gav pulled in some favours on my behalf, and they found performers at the eleventh hour. I was in no condition to do anything at that point, and I certainly wasn't able to phone anyone up to ask them to help out. Jodie very calmly arranged for Sally Ann Triplett, who was my Reno in *Anything Goes* at the National, Matt Rawle, who was playing Zorro at the time in the West End, Shona Lindsay, who played opposite me

---

[8] Even his famous fish sticks didn't help.

QE2 Atlantic Voyage 1971.

Returning to Scotland on the *QE2* in 1971, after Barrowmans' Excellent Adventure in the States. From left to right: Dad, my brother Andrew, 'wee John', sister Carole, Mum.

In our 'itchy clothes' for a family wedding. I was the horseshoe bearer – hence the kilt.

Another family wedding, in 2009. Dad donned the kilt this time. My brother-in-law Kevin and Scott are the Barrowman bookends.

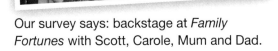

Our survey says: backstage at *Family Fortunes* with Scott, Carole, Mum and Dad.

The third generation of the Barrowman family: my beloved nieces and nephews. 'Uncle John' with …

… Clare.

… Turner.

Clare, Turner and my mum enjoying my bedtime stories.

... Andrew.

... Yvonne.

... Bridgett.

My dogs (from l to r) Captain Jack, Charlie and Harris.

Charlie and me practising for *Britain's Got Talent*.

Taking a dip in my pool with Captain Jack.

Finally, a vacation. We're in Barbados. Smile!

So here's to you,
'Mrs Barrowman' …

Scott introducing
Harris to his
brothers at our
home in Sully.

A few of my recent holiday snaps …

… en route to Glasgow.

… eating and drinking in Cape Town with Gavin (far left) and his husband Stu Macdonald (far right).

… voguing in Palm Springs with Brett (second left), Gavin and Javier.

… cruising in the Caribbean.

At BBC Radio 2 with David and Catherine.

Stealing a quiet moment in Jack's Torchwood office, during the filming of 'Children of Earth'.

On the *Torchwood* set with my make-up artist Claire Pritchard-Jones.

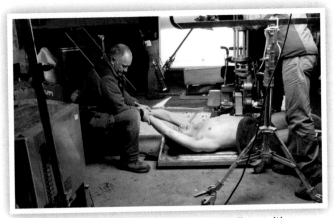

Getting prepped for Jack to be buried alive, with
Phil Shellard's help – and yes, I am naked.

Chatting with director Euros
Lyn between scenes.

On the set of 'Children of
Earth', enjoying a banana …
or two.

in *The Phantom of the Opera* years ago, and my concert duet partner, Danny Boys, to step up to the mic for me. They performed to my accompaniment as the programme's host (I sounded a lot like Shaggy from *Scooby-Doo*).

At the weekend, I had my voice back, but I still wasn't 100 per cent. I sang 'What About Us?' at the Royal Variety Performance – and I sounded like shit.

What did I learn from all this? Other than the obvious about not getting into that situation again, the entire week reminded me that, given my fame and status as an entertainer, certain members of the press, and even a few in the public, will always descend like a pack of wolves on any mistake I make, or flaw or weakness I appear to show. So be it. I will do my very best to limit any opportunities for feeding frenzies in the future. But I also decided that what I will *not* let a week like this do is make me into something I'm not: straight-laced, inhibited, unambitious and bland.

The consequences of events like these can make performers try to change; can even make them afraid to be themselves anymore. I felt this way for a while in the middle of that debilitating week. Fear can be a heavy anchor in your life if you hang on to it – and it can be heavier still if it's chained with regret. I'm sorry for what I did, but after I came to grips with myself at the end of that long week, I refused to be weighed down anymore by either one.

Admittedly, all of this was painful enough to live through, but the consequence that affected me most deeply was that the entire incident forced a delay in the announcement of *Tonight's the Night*'s commissioning. The day after 'Ballgate' broke in the tabloid press, Gav was called in to the BBC and ripped a new one, and, as my manager, he listened, he accepted the reprimand, and then he passed the message along to me, pretty much word for word. This made my depression even deeper – because a dream I'd had since childhood was suddenly threatened.

In the end, a comment from my dad helped me to put the whole episode into perspective, and began to bring me out from under my duvet. On the following Sunday night, when I called my parents to talk to them about what had happened, my dad allowed me to see some humour in the situation.

'Well, John,' he said, 'I guess you won't be hosting *Songs of Praise* anytime soon.'

`Blame It on the Flip-Flops ... and the Harveys'

'Lick him!'

    'Mum, please get the dogs away from me!'

    'Lick him!'

My mum blamed the flip-flops for my accident. I blamed years of practical jokes, silly games, prank falls and general Barrowman nonsense.

When Andrew, Carole and I were young, it was not unusual after dinner – when the three of us would be doing homework or playing in the living room – for my dad to stumble in from the kitchen, saying, 'Marion, I've cut myself. It's bad.'

We would all drop what we were doing and gather round him. He'd lift a blood-red hanky from his hand and expose his doubled-over thumb, which would be covered in ... tomato sauce. He'd vary the injury. Sometimes it would be his toe, sometimes his knee, but always the wound was presented to us with such award-winningly convincing pain that we never failed to get sucked into the drama. Even when we got old enough to know better, we'd see that bloody hanky and we'd have to peek.

And these fake accidents weren't staged only for my siblings and me. As I got older, if I was bringing friends home who hadn't met my dad before, it wasn't unusual for me to say upfront, 'Ignore my dad if he falls down. He thinks he's Dick Van Dyke.'

To this day, Dad plays similar pranks on his grandchildren – and anyone else who happens to be passing. He is always falling downstairs, tripping off kerbs and tumbling across furniture. One Christmas holiday in Florida, when Clare, Turner, Scott, Mum, Dad and I were doing some last-minute shopping, we went into a shoe store, where my dad proceeded to fake-fall. Because the people in the store were so genuinely upset – and security happened to be passing at the time and attended to him immediately – he had to spend the rest of the afternoon limping in and out of every shop we visited, because he was embarrassed they might catch him in his joke. Of course, the rest of us had no sympathy for him at all.

I have to own up to one or two fake falls myself over the years. And having forged a career on television and in theatre, I've had access to stunt professionals who have schooled me in some of their ways, which has made me even more skilled in walking into doors, or falling over real and invisible obstacles in the street.

At the Hub convention in 2008, however, my stunt moves didn't work out in quite the way I'd planned. Carole and I had retreated to our adjoining hotel rooms to chill before a signing session. I decided to stage a fake tumble across the room when she came to get me for the event.[1] When the adjoining door started to open, I launched into action ... only my foot caught on the edge of the coffee table's top; a slab of thick black marble that was perched precariously on a flimsy balsa-wood frame. As the door swung open, I went sprawling across the floor – and the table collapsed behind me.[2]

I also recently scared the hell out of a hotel maid in Glasgow, when I tumbled out of the elevator and barely missed her cart full of cleaning supplies. She was truly appalled when Scott, Carole and my brother-in-law, Kevin, walked out of the lift behind me, climbed over my prostrate form,[3] and kept heading to their rooms, without pausing for an instant to offer help.

So, you can see why my mum was not inclined to rush to my rescue when I fell over, poolside.

The last time I performed in the US was at the Stackner Theater in Milwaukee, Wisconsin, in 2002, when my cabaret sold out three

---

[1] Because she'd never expect such silliness from me.
[2] Carole took a picture – see the illustrated section.
[3] Scott may even have kicked me a little with his foot.

nights, and I played to lots of family, friends and fans from the area. When an opportunity came up to perform in the US again, this time in Chicago as part of the Torchsong convention, taking place from 5 to 7 June 2009, I was excited to include my cabaret in the event's programme as a special treat for my American fans.

The month of May 2009 had been a crazy, fabulous one for me. I'd performed at seventeen venues to seventeen sold-out audiences on my concert tour in the UK. As June began, I was settling into a couple of relaxing days at my house in Sully, before heading off to Chicago for the convention. My parents were staying with me, and Scott had taken a few days off. We were all lounging by the sea.

Directly after we moved into our house in Sully, Scott and I had a deck built at the end of the garden. (Scott had also, of course, found his trusty hammer within the first few days, and set about knocking down a few walls.[4]) The base of the deck is a couple of inches higher than the area around the pool, but the shoreline and the deck line combine to create the illusion when I'm lounging there that I'm floating out over the sea. When the weather is warm – which happens many more days than you might think on the southern coast of Wales – Scott and I regularly eat dinner out there, and cocktails when we have company[5] are de rigueur on the deck.

We were midway through the cocktail hour(s) on this particular night when I picked up my mum's glass to head inside for a refill of her Harveys Bristol Cream. In an instant, my plans for Torchsong and singing for my American fans went over the edge. I stepped off the deck and went over on my left ankle. I felt something inside snap, and I swear I heard a pop. I went down hard. The pain was instantaneous.

While I was writhing on the ground, my dogs thought I was playing games and they leapt and bounded all over me. My mum and dad thought I was playing games and they leapt and bounded all over me. Scott continued to watch the sunset.

'Get the dogs away from me,' I cried.

---

[4] At least this time, I told him which ones.
[5] And even when we don't.

My mum finally paid attention. She leaned over me and said, 'Stop goofing around, John. Just get up.'

'Get the dogs away from me.'

'Lick him! Lick him!' she chanted.

'Mother, I'm serious!'

It wasn't until she looked down and saw how much my ankle was already swelling – to at least twice its size in the few seconds I'd been writhing – that she and my dad believed that this was not a prank. I really was injured.

'It's those damn flip-flops,' my mum cried. 'I don't understand why you wear them. They're an accident waiting to happen.'

My dad and Scott helped me off the ground and out to the car. This move was made doubly difficult because Charlie, Jack and Harris thought the entire event was a game, and kept nipping and grabbing at my injured ankle.

In considerable pain, I made it to the emergency room, where I learned that I had pulled tendons and torn ligaments in my left ankle. Until the swelling went down, I was told there'd be no flying, and for four weeks I was permitted only limited movement on crutches, with my ankle encased in what I called a 'Beckham boot' cast.

When we got home from the ER, my mum felt so bad that she had not believed me right away that she immediately headed into the kitchen and made a pot of my favourite home-made chicken soup. After I'd eaten a couple of bowlfuls, she rubbed my feet until the pain medication kicked in and I fell asleep.[6]

A month later, a friend's young son was explaining to someone what had happened to me. He said, 'Poor John! He fell off his deck and tore all the testicles on his ankle.'

Now that would have really hurt.

[6] Feet rubbing is usually Scott's job.

CHAPTER EIGHT

'MR SATURDAY NIGHT'

'All my life I've had one dream: to achieve my many goals.'
Homer Simpson, *The Simpsons*

Five tips from *Tonight's the Night*

1 Gaffer tape holds up (and keeps down) anything.

2 Everyone loves you when you bring chocolate biscuits
(M&S Rounds especially).

3 Hold a little back during a rehearsal and the show will pop.

4 Don't edit me while I'm trying something new
(wait until the second time it doesn't work).

5 A successful variety show must have a personality
(and not only mine).

Saturday night was sweetie night in our house, especially when we still lived in Scotland and my gran, Murn, and her sister, my Auntie Jeannie, would come over to babysit. Carole, Andrew and I picked our favourites from their sweetie stash – making certain not to touch Murn's Fry's Chocolate Cream – and then we'd coorie on the couch and watch Cilla Black, Lulu, Lena Zavaroni,[1] *Opportunity Knocks* or anything with Bruce Forsyth. My childhood Saturday nights had magic and, can I say, a sweetness to them that continued when my family emigrated to the US.[2]

On special occasions, Murn brought a box of Cadbury's Milk Tray chocolates with her. We'd all tuck in excitedly, grabbing our favourites – the caramels and the creams – but we were notorious for nibbling the others first. We'd taste all of them, and then we'd return to the box the bitten sweeties we didn't like.[3] Did we ever think of reading the descriptions that came in the box? Puhleeze. For the most part, Barrowmans don't read directions of any kind. Putting together a table from IKEA? We use only our wits, a screwdriver, and a lot of swearing.

I'd pick a chocolate and if it was a flavour I didn't like – such as coffee – or something with a hard crunchy centre, I'd bite it to check it really was as yucky as I'd imagined, and then I'd put it back in the box, maybe turning it over so the nibbled bit couldn't be seen immediately. We all did this. I'm not sure what we were thinking – that maybe the next time someone opened the box, they'd say, 'Oh, thank God someone already bit into this sweet because now I can see that it's one I'd like to eat.'

[1] I used to pretend to be her in the playground at primary school.
[2] Relax. No 'life is a box of chocolates' here.
[3] Yeah, like you've never done it.

Instead, what would happen is that my mum would open the box to have a chocolate with her coffee the following afternoon or evening, and the box would look like it had been raided by a team of chocoholic mice. She'd eat one anyway, because no one wastes whisky or chocolate in our house. You can see now why 'life is a box of chocolates' is not a metaphor I like – because what on earth does it mean if our box of chocolates was always partially regurgitated and the centres were sucked out?

The BBC announced that it had commissioned the pilot of *Tonight's the Night* the week after the 'Ballgate' incident. I put 'my boys' behind me[4] and went to work on one of my lifelong career dreams: hosting my own Saturday-night variety show.

The BBC and I began talking two years prior to the actual commissioning announcement about the possibility of me having my own show on prime-time Saturday night. *The Kids Are All Right* had been a huge success, but the BBC wanted me to do something different: something bigger, with more variety.

A show with all those components was a very tantalizing prospect, and, best of all, it would give me the opportunity to be involved behind the scenes as well as in front of the camera. Gavin and I established Barrowman Barker Productions (BBP) in 2008 so that we'd have more creative input into whatever I do, and so that we could get involved in aspects of the entertainment business where I'm not necessarily a performer. Forming BBP made perfect sense at this point in my career because it united my performing side with my creative side.

During all my years in theatre, I was always bothered by the dichotomy that many producers perpetuated between their talent (that would be me and the other actors) and themselves, sometimes forgetting that without the performers, they could produce themselves right into the dole queue. *Tonight's the Night* was not only the unveiling of my Saturday-night entertainment show, it also marked my attempt to unify these two important sides of the entertainment business with Barrowman and Barker's debut as producers.

4 Careful.

Setting up BBP was in itself a new and exciting challenge. As well as attending hours of legal meetings, Gavin and I also created the company's logo. The image we decided on has a retro feel to it, with an element of the 'boy' in it – without being too gay. It's a man pushing a wheelbarrow with a dog sitting inside it.[5] We designed the logo in such a way that if we wanted to make beer mats or T-shirts for gifts,[6] the logo would work well.

A major benefit of this new development in my career, however, was that it added yet another string to my bow. I hate being pigeonholed – as an actor, singer, 'the talent', whatever. Sometimes producers, and even network heads, want to put me in a nice neat performing niche, but I refuse to go. This is one of the reasons I don't answer a question that's often put to me – 'Which do you prefer: singing or acting; theatre or telly?' – in the way the asker may want.

My response is always: 'I'm an entertainer. I love all of them.'

As a case in point, one of the most difficult decisions I've ever faced as an entertainer was having to make the choice between television and theatre when, a couple of months after Cameron's rant at me during *I'd Do Anything*, he offered me one of the biggest deals in the West End: the lead in *Barnum*. Oh, man, I really wanted to do it.

Barnum would have been a great musical to showcase my voice and my talents, what with its unique blend of music, comedy, drama and the razzle-dazzle of the circus. The Cy Coleman and Michael Stewart musical first opened on Broadway in 1980, and in the West End the next year. The plot follows the life of the innovative entrepreneur and outspoken entertainer P. T. Barnum, and his 'Greatest Show on Earth' as it travels from city to city.

Cameron had a lot of terrific ideas about making his revival more modern and accessible to today's theatre audiences. His production would be more in the style of Cirque du Soleil, with acrobats and high

[5] The dog was created from the likeness of a stray that Gav and Stu, his husband, befriended while on a holiday.
[6] Because this gay man gives so many 'beer mats' as gifts.

wires, rather than three rings with lions and tigers and bears.[7] What would have been really brilliant about playing Barnum was that I would have gone to circus school in Amsterdam, to learn the ins and outs of being a Big Top leader. Can you imagine me on a high wire? Doing a double backflip? In a ring with a whip?[8]

However, the more I thought about the details and the planning and the schedules of such a project, the more I realized that, at this point in my career, when there are so many new things I still want to do, I couldn't devote so much time to one single venture. If I were to return to theatre for a new show, I'd have to be with the production for a full year's run. That would be fair and reasonable. At that particular time, I couldn't and didn't want to commit to a full year of anything.

While I was negotiating with Cameron, I was also in meetings with the BBC, brainstorming the format for *Tonight's the Night*. As that dream was moving closer to reality, I finally had to admit that I'd have to give up *Barnum*.

I didn't relinquish it without a fight, though. At one point, I was so desperate to try to get my schedule to work that I even considered doing a variety show and a West End production at the same time.[9] But it would have been completely unreasonable of me to expect that Cameron would give me Saturday nights off from the theatre so that I could spend the time on television. There was no way I could do both.

To do or not to do *Barnum* was an emotionally difficult decision for me to make. My life as an entertainer began in the theatre, and being an entertainer has always been more than a career choice for me: my double helix is a treble clef in a belt with sparkles. In the end, I had to say 'no' to *Barnum*. But no matter how heavy this 'no' weighed on me, no matter how difficult and disappointing, it was also, in some quiet way, affirming that all the career decisions and choices I'd made

[7] Oh, my.
[8] You can.
[9] Insane … I know.

to date were paying off – because I was in a position, professionally, where I could say 'no' to a West End show, to say nothing of the thrill of being on the verge of launching my very own prime-time variety TV show.

If you're single and, say, between eighteen and twenty-five, it's unlikely that anything on the telly will keep you home on a Saturday night, but if you're my age,[10] you're married with children, or you're in my parents' generation, then sitting down to watch something light and entertaining on a Saturday night is exactly what you want from your licence fee.

In preparation for our initial meetings with BBC Entertainment, who are just the best at coming up with successful Saturday-night shows, Gav and I spent hours on the web and YouTube, researching the people and programmes we personally might want to watch on a Saturday night. I'd jot down ideas, fragments of ideas, and details of fragments of ideas – anything I liked and thought was worth considering. After six months or so, we realized that – given the success of the BBC's talent-search shows, and my own background as a performer – whatever the overall format turned out to be, a significant part of my Saturday-night show had to be performance-based.

My own performing dream came true in 1989, when I debuted in *Anything Goes* with Elaine Paige in the West End, and I believed this kind of programme was one way for me to give back a little. But you know what else? I think it's really nice to do good things for good people, and to see them have a chance to experience something that, for whatever reason, hasn't happened for them.

Good television is not only about what you see on the screen, it's also about what you don't see behind the scenes. The team working on *Tonight's the Night* was great and we all worked well together, collaborating with ease and with the purpose of a shared vision. Moira Ross,[11] the show's executive producer and our boss, was very experienced in the entertainment field, having produced *Dancing with*

---

[10] Um, forty-something and still very youthful …
[11] Mo – as we called her.

the Stars for American TV and *Last Choir Standing* for the BBC, among others. Mel Balac was the series producer and the one who talked into my ear during the Sunday-night recordings of the show,[12] and who'd done all three of the Andrew Lloyd Webber programmes with me.[13] Funnily enough, Mel also produced the Barrowman family[14] when we appeared on *All Star Family Fortunes.*

Finally, Martin Scott was the third executive producer on *Tonight's the Night.* He represented BBC In-House Entertainment and oversaw the entire production on behalf of the channel. I'd worked with him on all the BBC entertainment shows I'd ever done. Martin's a veteran of *Strictly Come Dancing* and the ALW talent searches, as well as lots of others.

Every series also needs runners and assistants. In fact, television shows couldn't operate without them. Runners are the young men and women, often interns or recent graduates directly out of university, who scuttle around a set taking care of the small details that hold all the big stuff together. Left your script in the dressing room, your phone in the car, your costume change in the rehearsal room, your sister in the wrong hallway miles from the studio? The runner solves these problems and makes everything okay.

My runner for the term of *TTN* was a terrific, hard-working young man named Alex Bender. I knew we'd work well together and the production was off to a great beginning when I saw the call sheet for show one. My runner's name was listed next to mine. The sheet read: 'John Barrowman – A. Bender.'

Even though I was a production virgin,[15] Gavin and I had lots of input into the production side of the show, and we worked very closely with Mo, Mel and Paul Domaine, the show's choreographer, to make the whole ensemble pop.

Paul was brilliant. He could take any show tune or pop song and choreograph it into something hip and flashy and breathtaking. With

[12] Mel, stop shouting at me!
[13] Remember Mel? I made her buy high heels.
[14] Well, a TV version: Mum, Dad, Scott, Carole and me.
[15] Long time since those words have been in a sentence together.

the talents of the show's eight dancers, the J8s, the dancing was always fresh, fluid and, well, pretty fabulous, I thought.

I was excited about the entire team. Plus, because I was one of the producers as well as the host, I was in a position to solve problems when they arose, in an efficient manner that didn't hurt our shared creative vision.

For example, the BBC producers, Gav and I wanted to do a big Bollywood number for one of the last shows of the series, to the track 'Rhythm of the Night'. The dancers and Paul were up for this kind of lavishly choreographed number. The problem was the budget. No money left. The budget couldn't cover our chocolate biscuits, never mind the eight additional dancers we required to make the number a true Bollywood piece with its array of colourful costumes and mix of dance styles.

As we sat around the production table, reviewing the past week's show and planning for the upcoming one (this meeting was a weekly one, and essential to the overall flow and ongoing success of each episode), Gavin and I decided that the Bollywood number *had* to happen. If the BBC didn't have the budget, then Barrowman Barker Productions would pay for the extra dancers. BBP coughed up the cash. In the end, the number was worth every extra penny. I think this kind of synergy made for better production values overall and was also great telly for our viewers.

When production started for the show, my schedule took on a pattern that was exhausting and invigorating – and as full of variety as *Tonight's the Night* itself. Since each show was taped in front of a live studio audience on a Sunday evening, the Saturday before was a full dress rehearsal for everyone. My work for each episode began early on the Monday at the Dance Attic on the Fulham Road, where I'd rehearse with Paul, 'Jennie Fabulous', his assistant, and all the J8s. They would dance through the opening and closing numbers with me, and I'd rehearse my moves in relation to theirs.

Sometimes, these rehearsals took longer than expected. One morning, I couldn't get my left hand to coordinate a parallel move with my right foot while moving forward in a chorus line using a complicated cross-step. At another session, the dancers were having a difficult time with a complex series of lifts and turns in their routine. I grabbed Jennie and moved to the front, next to the room's long wall of mirrors. I worked with her to simplify the lift routine – because if there's one thing a musical-theatre leading man knows how to do really well, it's how to lift his dance partner. I can't think of any musicals that don't expect a lift or two. One of the first dance lessons I had in college at the start of my theatre training was how to lift and turn my partner above my shoulders with ease.[16]

During these rehearsals early in the week, I would often try out one or two moves of my own to connect my routine with the choreography of the dancers around me. I always appreciated that Paul would let me work through my own innovations at least a couple of times before he would affirm them, critique them or, if necessary, ask me to cut them out.

On one of those busy mornings, rehearsals ran even later than usual – because a children's ballet troupe was rehearsing in the next room and the children spotted Captain Jack on the stairs. Their dance mistress popped in to ask me if I'd come and say a few words, because maybe then she could settle her dancers down.[17]

After rehearsing the choreography for a couple of hours on those Monday mornings, I'd sprint upstairs to another room, where Matt Brind, *TTN*'s musical director, and I would run through my songs and I'd learn any new arrangements he'd created. I'd repeat this same process the next day at the BBC studios, to make sure everything sounded good, and once again on Friday, the day before the show's dress rehearsal.

At some point during the morning, usually in time for a cup of tea and a biscuit, Gav would arrive to review my other work and to discuss commitments I'd already made or that had to be made. We'd dash upstairs to a smaller rehearsal room for privacy. As an example of the sort of things on our agenda, during a two-day period one week

16 And without dropping her, of course.
17 I did and they performed a short piece for me.

in April, I was offered a Broadway show, asked to make a number of guest appearances on UK television, finalized a few things for my concert tour, and arranged interviews and photo shoots for a handful of press requests.

When Gav and I had finished, I'd dart back down to the main rehearsal room and run through the opening and closing numbers with the dancers one more time. If my schedule permitted, I'd eat lunch with the J8s, Paul and Matt in the Dance Attic's cafe;[18] otherwise, I'd grab something to eat from M&S, while on my way back to the BBC studios to do a voiceover for one of the surprise hits I'd already filmed.

These surprise hits involved catching up with an unsuspecting person, who – unbeknown to them – had been nominated by a friend or family member to perform on *TTN*. The surprise hits caught on tape the moment when I pulled off a helmet, jumped from behind a screen or – in one young woman's hit – stopped shampooing her hair, and told them that they'd be entertaining millions on TV on Saturday night.

A typical mid-week afternoon also involved costume fitting for Sunday's taping of the show. The wardrobe room at the BBC was always lively, with banter flying like bullets and mostly men – and an occasional woman – working sewing machines at top speed. I spent a lot of time considering what I'd wear for the shows because, as you may have noticed when you watched, my suit colour always coordinated with the hue of the stage lights and the sparkle of the set. It's a variety show. Everything had to pop, including me!

Whenever possible, I travelled to the surprise hits at least a week ahead of the show in which we'd be broadcasting them. When this was not possible, I'd squeeze a trip to North Wales or Ipswich or Brighton into my Wednesday or Thursday of the same week. This meant that some contestants found out about their television debut on the Tuesday or Wednesday, and he or she had to be ready to perform on the following Sunday. In most cases, a family member

---

[18] It serves the best soups.

or a close friend had been in on the hit, so a lot of the arrangements that the person being surprised would have to make had already been handled.

Each hit required a separate crew with its own producer, Katy Mullan, and director, Marcus Liversedge, who would accompany me to the various locations we visited. This crew created all the videotape segments[19] for *Tonight's the Night*, including the wonderful opening sequence with the crazy dancing silhouette in the windows.[20]

When I first started working on the surprise hits, the VT crew didn't realize I was co-producing the show. I'd offer some input on a few of the shots, come up with ideas for how to shoot a hit, or suggest a camera angle or a different way for me to reveal myself to the guest, and they'd look at me as if I was just a meddling control freak,[21] even if my suggestion was good one. At one hit, I finally mentioned in passing that I was co-producing, and after that my suggestions were seen in a bit of a different light. We all truly worked well together to produce some great material.

After the first episode of *Tonight's the Night* aired, on Saturday 18 April 2009, a few on the crew, and the producers from the BBC, started calling me 'Mr Saturday Night'. I've been called a lot of things in my time, but this rates as one of the best.

Following that first broadcast, I read one or two reviews that came across my desk – this is not something I usually do. Honestly, in the words of my friend, Catherine Tate, I can't 'be bovvered'. A couple of critics described the show as, and I'm paraphrasing here, schmaltzy and cheesy. My response to those critics: 'Watch something else.'

I care what critics think – to a certain extent – but sometimes a few of them can be plain old bitchy because they forget (or have never known) what it felt like to sit on the couch on a Saturday night with their favourite family members and a bag of sweets and have a

---

[19] Or VTs, as they're known in the biz.
[20] It's all me behind the curtains.
[21] Am not! I don't meddle.

laugh, or a wee greet.[22] I don't do shows for the critics. I do shows for the men, women and families who're watching together and singing along.

One or two critics compared *Tonight's the Night* to *Britain's Got Talent*, but it was never our intention to be like or to compete with Simon Cowell's juggernaut. From the beginning, *Tonight's the Night* was different from Cowell's show because *TTN* was not making performers into stars. Instead, for one shining moment, Sam Horsfield of Ipswich, or someone like her, got the opportunity to perform on the BBC to millions of viewers and to have her dream fulfilled.

When I surprised Sam, who had given up her dream of performing professionally when her twins were diagnosed as autistic, she turned to her husband, who had nominated her, and with tears filling her eyes, she looked into his overflowing ones and whispered, 'Thank you.' I lost it too. If those moments don't move you, then your heart's made of Swiss cheese and your head's full of holes.

For Sam's hit, the crew and I arrived on a Wednesday afternoon at a local working men's club, where Sam would later meet with her amateur dramatics group. Sam thought she and her fellow am-dram members were auditioning final candidates for their local production of *The Producers*. What she didn't know was that I was one of the actors auditioning: a 'Norswedish' man named Bennie, who was the 'beegist Abba fan evaar!'

The crew and I commandeered two of the club's private function rooms, one for make-up and costume – as moustached Bennie had to look as if he'd drifted in from the seventies in two-foot-high, glittery, platform-heeled boots that would have broken most men[23] – and the other room for the monitors, equipment and VT crew. Inside the rehearsal hall, cameras were hidden, and Sam's friends prepped for the hit.

The rehearsal took twice as long as usual because I was having too much fun. I insisted on singing Bennie's audition number twice

---

[22] A 'greet' means 'a good cry'. As in, 'Ach, son, have a wee greet. You'll feel better.'

[23] And quite a few women.

through, while adding to the routine what I'd decided were Bennie's own, pretty slick moves. Bennie's deep, deep lunges and knee-high kicks had all the fluidity of a three-year-old trying to skip.

After Sam arrived and was seated with her friends and fellow judges, the hit began. We'd recruited two people to play actors interested in auditioning and they performed first. I could tell by Sam's responses to them that she had no clue she was being set up.

Then Bennie stepped out to centre stage. Man, I was so bad that I was really good. I'd hardly opened my mouth and I'd only completed one of my groovy moves, but I could already see Sam struggling desperately not to laugh. After all, this was some poor man trying his very best to get a part in her local production. Bless his heart. When I'd finished, the applause was polite. Then Sam did her best to let me know gently that 'she'd be in touch'. I interrupted her.

'Do you think you can do this any better?' I asked, in an accent that sounded a lot like the Swedish Chef from *The Muppet Show*.

She was a bit taken aback, even more so when Bennie stepped off the stage – not very gracefully, given his really tight trousers and his towering boots – and he … I walked right up to the audition table. She started to look back and forth among her colleagues for some assistance. None was forthcoming. At that moment, while she was blustering an answer to Bennie, I tore off the moustache, beard and wig,[24] and revealed myself.

Her facial expression was a mix of about twenty-two competing emotions that ended in sheer delight. 'Oh! Oh! I can't believe it's you … It's John Barrowman.'

But what Sam said next has remained one of the funnier lines of any of the hits I participated in. I asked her if she knew why I was at her am-dram auditions.

Without missing a beat, she replied, 'Because you've finally decided you can't live without me.'

These surprise hits were one of the best parts of the show to film – not only because of meeting and doing something special for people

---

[24] Ouch – they'd been taped on.

like Sam, but also because the hits gave me the opportunity to get out of the studio, to improvise, and to dress up. Most of all, though, I loved the drama and the emotion of the reveal.

There was no irony involved, no mocking, and no parody in *Tonight's the Night*. I wanted the show to be Sam's special night, or whoever else's dream we made come true. The rest of us were simply sharing the spotlight.

When Sam joined us in London to prepare to sing with the cast of *Mamma Mia!*, she met the cast at the Prince of Wales Theatre, she was given rehearsal time with them and with Paul, our choreographer, and she was given some of the best vocal training in the West End from Claire Moore, who was in *Miss Saigon* with me in the early nineties. I trust Claire's ear and her heart, and it was her job to work with all the performers and help them to sound the best that they possibly could.

My call time to the BBC studios on Saturday mornings was early, because the day before we taped in front of a live audience, we had what's called a 'camera rehearsal'. These camera rehearsals were more complicated than the ones I described in an earlier table talk, but they essentially served the same function: to make sure everyone knew their positions and had rehearsed the flow of the show.[25] On *TTN*, the camera rehearsal was a full dress rehearsal for all of us, as well as a chance for the director and his crew to figure out camera positions. Perhaps most importantly, for the performers whose wishes were being fulfilled, it was a chance for them to get comfortable on the set and to rehearse on the stage with lights, music … and me.

The camera rehearsal can take all day and well into the evening. The most difficult part of this day was keeping focused when there was so much chatter and commotion, and while the crew were constantly moving around. Given the chaos, I tried to keep the mood light and to have some fun.[26]

While I was rehearsing 'Boogie Wonderland' for one of the shows' opening numbers, I did my signature turn and then sang the first part

---

[25] Minus the gun sound effects, though.
[26] Imagine that!

of the song while doing my impression of Shakira – which wasn't half bad and cracked everyone up. When I shifted into Patti LuPone for the last half of the number, however, the laughter dropped to polite tittering because only Gav, Carole and Claire, our vocal coach, actually knew who I was mimicking. Oh, those television people.

Midway through taping the series of shows, Gav, Mel, Mo and I made a decision to cut a segment that the audience enjoyed and I really liked participating in, but which was taking up far too much of my time during the week. The segment was called 'Stage Fright', and it involved me competing against a celebrity in a performance smackdown during the live taping. One week, I learned how to fire-toss – and managed to singe most of the hair off my lower arm in practice. Another week, I trained to be a freestyle footballer. I was rubbish at dribbling the ball, but I did master a couple of tricks, including taking my shirt off while keeping a ball[27] balanced between my shoulder blades.

On Sunday, the studio audience is seated between 5.30 and 6 p.m. (which usually meant Scott dashed into his seat at 6.15 p.m.). This became one of my favourite moments on a Sunday: standing in the wings having my mic adjusted, my make-up touched up, and watching yesterday's craziness morph into … maybe not calm, but certainly a cool professionalism. The studio felt electric and alive with the energy from the band, the crew, the other performers and the audience, and when I stepped onstage, the energy ratcheted up two more notches.[28]

When I sensed the same passion and excitement I had for the show from the crew, the cast, and even the viewers I met in Costco when I was picking up dog food, it made me want to push myself even more – not just onstage, but also creatively. I loved co-producing television for the first time, and in the future I'd like to add to my résumé and produce a show in the West End. I love that Barrowman Barker Productions could have a hand in bringing TV recognition to all the terrific theatre performers who don't get much exposure. This was one of the reasons why so many of the dreams we fulfilled on *TTN* were

[27] A football! Honestly, people.
[28] I was the host – three notches.

related to musical theatre. The casts of *Mamma Mia!*, *Hairspray* and *High School Musical* were all part of *Tonight's the Night*.

Over the years, I've tried to learn something from every project I've ever been a part of. From this experience on *Tonight's the Night*, I've noted that when a show has a good team of producers and they are all in sync with the talent, they feed off each other's ideas and take the show to heights that may not have been planned for.

Murn and my Auntie Jeannie would have loved *Tonight's the Night*, and I thought of them often when I was watching the programme from my couch in Sully on Saturday nights.[29] The first time I saw the show's closing credits, and the Barrowman Barker logo came up right next to the big BBC one, I couldn't stop grinning. Seeing those images side by side made my night and fulfilled one of my longest-held career dreams.

---

[29] I worked hard to get where I am. Of course I watch my own shows.

CHAPTER NINE

'JOINTS AND JAM'

'Those who wish to sing, always find a song.'

A favourite sign I saw in a theatre dressing room years ago

Five highlights of my 'An Evening with John Barrowman' tour

1 The fans, the fans, the fans (you're all too good to be true).

2 Ripping my trousers in Glasgow (this may be a regular occurrence in the lives of some, but for me it was a first).

3 Performing at the Royal Albert Hall (Vegas, here I come!).

4 The standing ovations (never got old).

5 Having a catering service at my beck and call (for food, for food).

'm proud to confess that I've done something that I'm pretty sure the Rolling Stones, in all their years of touring, have not. Wait for it. To date, I've been on two concert tours: one in 2008 to promote my album *Another Side*; and another in the spring of 2009, for 'An Evening with John Barrowman' (also known as my *Music Music Music* tour). On each occasion – here it is – my parents were part of my entourage.[1]

My 'grey groupies' took their position in my tour so seriously that they went into training a month ahead of time to get ready for tour life. Their training regime consisted of sleeping at odd hours of the day and night for inconsistent lengths of time, eating catered dinners with big yummy desserts, dressing straight from a single suitcase and, finally, practising doing 'The Slosh' in their bedroom.[2] In truth, they really did get in shape for this tour, increasing their mileage on the treadmill at their home in Brookfield, Wisconsin, because they knew they'd need all the energy possible to keep up with their baby boy. When they stepped off the plane at Glasgow Airport to join me at the Glasgow Royal Concert Hall on 14 May 2009, they were ready for their marathon of music, music, music.[3]

For me, touring is one of the most satisfying things I do because when I'm singing in front of an audience, no matter how many, I feel more connected to my fans; and when I perform live, my audience never knows quite what to expect. I love being able to be spontaneous and to improvise. On my first tour in 2008, I scripted a lot of what I thought I might want to say between songs, but after the first night, when I realized I'd referred to the script only once, I binned it.

---

[1] Keith Richards, eat your heart out.
[2] Eeew! Don't go there. They're my parents!
[3] I'll stop that now, now, now.

For this most recent tour, I altered a few things from my *Another Side* concerts. My caterers on this tour had food as fabulous as their name – Eat Your Heart Out. I hired four of my J8 dancers from *Tonight's the Night* (known as the J4s for the tour) and they had a variety of costumes and a number of wardrobe changes. I added more flashy suits with buckles of bling for yours truly, plus a video screen, showing family pictures and photos exploring my life, to complement the music; I hoped the images gave fans more insight into 'JB'. I told stories that had either recently happened or that the majority of my fans would not have heard before, and most of my banter was pretty off the cuff. I sometimes had an idea about a bridge between my songs, or I used a repeated phrase at the end of my link to give my musical director, Matt, and the band their cue, but many times I didn't know exactly what I was going to say until I started to say it.[4] Oh, and I had Danny Boys with me every night.[5]

What remained the same? I hired the same musicians for the band who'd toured with me in 2008, and most of the same hard-working crew. Plus, I kept the same parents.

When Neil O'Brien, my tour agent, and Gavin and I were choosing the cities for the tour, I told them that I wanted to perform at bigger venues. Some day, I'd love to perform in Las Vegas, maybe even take my concert tour on the road in America, but promoters in the US are not interested in backing a tour until a performer can show that he or she can sell out in bigger venues. This tour was a step towards meeting that goal and, amazingly, I sold out every venue we booked. In fact, before I'd even reached my final performance at the Royal Albert Hall in London, I heard from their management that they wanted to make sure the Royal Albert Hall was on my itinerary for 2010.[6]

Every audience on this tour had a distinctive personality. I adjusted my banter and played and joked with them accordingly. For example,

---

[4] Like most days.
[5] Stop it. On stage.
[6] It is.

about ten minutes into the show in Glasgow, I realized I'd slipped into my Scottish accent and was blethering with the audience just as if I'd gotten off the corporation bus with them at George Square. Normally, this wouldn't have mattered, but the Glasgow concert was filmed for a DVD release – and so the accent might throw off viewers who don't know my family's history.

As it turned out, my accent was the least of my concerns in Glasgow. I was having some fun introducing the band and the dancers when, suddenly, I tore my trousers: the rip was big enough that my white briefs could be seen from the balcony.

Despite my comments in an earlier chapter about how well West End performers can lift their dance partners, I'd made a vain attempt to lift one of the J4s as she was leaving the stage. All I'd succeeded in doing was popping my trouser seam. Funnily enough, not everyone in the audience was aware of what I'd done, until I told them – in between bursts of hysterical laughter – because I initially kept my rear to the band. All was recorded for posterity on the DVD, of course.

After Rhys, my PA, made a mad dash to the tour bus and rummaged through my already packed suits, I took a quick break, dashed offstage and changed into an intact pair of trousers for the rest of the show. Bob's your uncle![7] Thank God for all those years of changing in the wings between scenes.

In Blackburn, the audience was ready to 'partay'. So much so that by the middle of the second act, they were dancing in the aisles and almost right onstage with me. Thank goodness the set was raised and I had some height on them. At one point, I cut out a couple of stories because I was worried about the folks in the front row ... and myself, to be honest. Even at the close of my encore, the Blackburn fans kept dancing and shouting for more.

At the Oxford concert, a hyperactive usher with a torch kept darting up and down the aisles, shining his light on anyone who was taking pictures on mobile phones. He was distracting everyone with his

---

[7] Bob Firth is my uncle, not yours. His wife, Ruby, from Sandyhills, has been my mum's friend since childhood.

diligence, including me. If there was one phone on, there were hundreds (even though the tour management had, as they so often do, asked that no pictures be taken). In fact, it was a bit like watching a wave wash across the hall when they all beamed on ... which reminds me of a relatively recent concert experience of my own.

I was attending a charity gig at Cardiff's Millennium Stadium. It was being held on behalf of one of the aid charities raising money after the terrible tsunami in 2004. David Tennant, Russell T. Davies, Julie Gardner, Phil Collinson (then a producer of *Doctor Who*), and I were seated together in a private box. We had filled our plates from the buffet and were jamming to Keane when, all of a sudden, Russell and I looked across the audience and saw that a Mexican wave had started across the stadium. Russell looked at me and we both cracked up. Doing the wave at a tsunami concert was so wrong.

At my concerts, which were slickly managed and precisely organized thanks to Paul Crockford (our tour producer) and Steve Rayment (tour manager), it turned out that there was a good side to the wave of mobiles in my audience. All those fans snapping pics and taking videos meant that my family in the States was able to track the tour via YouTube. When my mum and dad first joined me onstage in Glasgow, my mum to sing a duet of 'Amazing Grace' and both of them to dance with me, Carole and Clare texted 'bravo' to them within hours of their performances thanks to YouTube.

My parents had so much fun doing 'The Slosh', a line dance performed at Scottish weddings almost as much as the hokey-cokey or the Gay Gordons.[8] Although The Slosh can be set to any number of songs, our family's favourite is Tony Orlando and Dawn's 'Knock Three Times'. As the tour continued, I worked it out with the male dancers, James and Jamie, that they'd lift my mum at the end of the dance. Unfortunately, the female dancers, 'Jennie Fabulous' and Kate, had a bit more work to do to get my dad into the air; instead, they'd lift up only one of his legs. At every venue, during the interval, my parents had a line of requests for their autographs and photos.

---

[8] I'm serious. It's a traditional Scottish reel; I'm especially good at it.

I loved the fact that this concert tour was a family affair. What with having my parents physically with me, plus the company of the video of family photos, which showed snaps of the whole gang, I really felt as if the entire Barrowman clan was with me on this tour.

When I performed at the Cardiff Arena, it was like playing on my home turf. Cardiff was my largest audience of the tour because the venue was an indoor stadium. The numbers were easily in excess of 2,500; I was thrilled. After that concert, I threw a party for many of my neighbours and BBC Wales friends, including David Tennant, who I had made sure had seats in a private box for the gig. He'd have been mobbed otherwise.

From Cardiff, we headed to the Portsmouth Guildhall, where it was difficult to leave after the concert because the waiting crowds outside the stage door were massive. Regrettably, all I could do was thank them for their support, and then I had to get straight into the van.

If I were to sign autographs after each concert, I'd be standing outside for hours after being hot and sweaty and exhausted. No matter how much I'd love to spend time chatting with my fans, first and foremost I have to preserve my voice. This holds true when I'm in a West End show and for pantomime, too. The next day's audience, after all, deserves the same quality of voice and the same energy as the audience who are waiting outside after the show. To be fair to each audience, I no longer hang around for very long in the cool night air.

When I played Jack in *Jack and the Beanstalk* in Cardiff in 2006/07, for Qdos Entertainment and Paul Elliott Ltd., I got really ill from signing after the show; and the same thing happened when I was in *Aladdin* in Birmingham in 2007/08; and again the following year while I was performing *Robin Hood*.

Paul Elliott, by the way, is not only the Panto King,[9] but he also has a history as rich and as long in theatre as, well, Shakespeare. Paul has been involved in some of the most celebrated West End productions since his career as a producer began in the sixties, including *Private Lives* with Alan Rickman; the RSC production of *The Hollow Crown*

[9] That does not make me the Panto Queen.

with Dame Diana Rigg and Sir Derek Jacobi; and, more recently, *Thoroughly Modern Millie* starring Amanda Holden; *The Philadelphia Story* with Kevin Spacey; and *Macbeth* with Patrick Stewart. I love doing panto under Paul's auspices.[10] He understands a theatre audience better than anyone I know, he's funny, has lots of juicy theatre stories, a work ethic I admire, and he's become a dear friend and mentor as I branch out into the production side of this business. When Paul says he's going to do something, he does it. Oh yes, he does.[11]

Given what happened to my health during those panto seasons, I did experience a learning curve and I decided the best thing for me – and my voice – was to get into the van right away after a concert. During the tour, that wasn't always as easy as it sounds. You know me – I could never drive away from the stage door and not say anything to all the fans waiting, sometimes close to two hundred of them. That's not who I am. Instead, I tried to give my fans something special before I left, even if it was only standing up through the sunroof and waving, or walking over to where the fans were gathered and saying a quick hello.

Whenever I had a day off between concert venues, and if the journey was a reasonable one, my parents and I returned to my house in Sully, where I slept in my own bed, played with my dogs,[12] and cooked my own meals. Otherwise, the rhythm of the tour went like this.

My concert entourage travelled in two huge coach buses: one transported the crew and all the stage set-up, and the other carried all the musicians, dancers and their baggage. My parents, Rhys and I travelled in a kitted-out Mercedes Viano supplied by the Sinclair Group, Cardiff. My parents sat in the back on captain's chairs, with their feet up and their books and their sweeties on their laps. I took the middle chairs that became a bed if I needed to sleep while we travelled from venue to venue.

Immediately after a performance, my van and the band's bus would

---

[10] I'm donning my tights again with Paul and playing Robin Hood in Cardiff in 2009 – and more exciting surprises to come after that.

[11] Oh no, I'm so not starting that …

[12] And sometimes with Scott, too.

travel to the next concert location while the crew stayed behind and de-rigged the venue; then, instead of going to the hotel with the others in the entourage, the crew would travel directly to the next venue and immediately set up for the forthcoming show.

My parents and I often arrived at the hotel around 2 or 3 a.m. Rhys and Sean, my driver, would unload everything from the van. My mum and dad and I would sleep until midday, and then we'd go to the new venue for my soundcheck, rehearsal and a proper lunch. I always arranged for a late checkout from the hotels so that this schedule was possible and we didn't have to worry about housekeeping disturbing our beauty sleep.

After lunch, the crew would head to the hotel, where they'd sleep until the end of the show itself, and then they'd return to the venue when the concert was over, de-rig everything, and begin the process again. The only time the entire entourage came together for an extended time was when the folks from Eat Your Heart Out served lunch, or early dinner,[13] after the soundcheck rehearsal.

Don't let anyone tell you otherwise: food on the road was fabulous. Every night, we had a spread of dishes and desserts that was so luxurious that if I wasn't burning up so many calories each evening, I'd have been ripping my trousers at every venue – not just Glasgow.

The dancers and the band travelled in what I called the Super Bus. It was an amazing vehicle. I'd love to drive across this country or the US in one like it some day. The upstairs was kitted out as an entertainment room, with a big TV that was equipped with more video games than anyone had time to play. The bus had plenty of movies, and beds to cater to everyone's needs, in case anyone wanted a snooze while we journeyed to our hotel. The kitchen was downstairs and comfortably sat four, plus there were showers, toilets – naturally – and lots of comfy couches.

These buses were massive and expensive to run. I was originally planning to travel with my parents on a Super Bus, but because I wanted to have more dancers on the tour, the budget demanded I give up my bus.[14] It was a worthwhile sacrifice. I loved having the J4s –

---

[13] Or 'dunch', as Clare and Turner called it when they were kids.
[14] Next time.

Jamie, James, Kate and 'Jennie Fabulous' – with me. They made the show stronger, and since we had danced together on *Tonight's the Night*, we had a terrific working and playing relationship.

The second-to-last performance of any show or concert, whether it's in the West End, Broadway or on tour, is the performance where all the pranks and jokes are played, and this cast and crew made no exception. But instead of playing pranks with costumes, staging silliness with the sets, or even fooling with the music,[15] they wrote, acted, directed and produced their own tour film. 'Rhinestone Gayboy' debuted after our penultimate show and, believe me, no one – and I mean no one – other than those watching and participating at the time will ever see this video. Let me just say that it made me blush at times. Feel free to let your imagination run wild here ...

For me, the most difficult aspect of touring was finding some down time with Scott. While I was on this most recent tour, Scott was in charge of renovating our London flat. Bye, bye, blue tarp.[16] When it was possible, he travelled to a few of the venues and we'd grab a few hours together – with my parents as chaperones.

On the other hand, the brilliant part of touring was seeing my fans and letting them know how much I appreciated them. The whole tour was done for them. I chose songs that allowed them to get to know me even better. When I created the playlists for my concerts, I took the opportunity to include songs that I hadn't sung before; or that have a special meaning for me, but that I hadn't necessarily recorded yet. For example, on this recent tour I dedicated 'When You Tell Me That You Love Me', a Diana Ross song, to all my fans. I've always imagined my albums as love letters to my supporters; I see my concerts as my chance to 'read' to them in person.

When Sony BMG approached me a few years ago to record my album *Another Side*, I was ecstatic. Over the course of one month, I chose all the songs, and with the album's producer, Graham Stack, recorded the

[15] There was still some of that.
[16] That's why I'm out working so hard ... to pay for the remodelling.

album in London and Cardiff (while I was also filming the second series of *Torchwood* during the week, and being a talent-show judge on the BBC at the weekends).[17]

Another Side was my first real studio album. Since it was my first major release, I didn't have much scope for pushing or pulling away from what Sony or my producers wanted. I had to sit back a little[18] and go with their melody because I was a newbie and I wanted to learn.

Another Side sold well, going gold relatively fast. This album and *Music Music Music*, my second one, are full of songs with special meaning for me. And all my albums have thirteen tracks on them because my mum was born on Friday the 13th of July; in our family it's a really lucky number for us.

Here's a related piece of trivia that might net you the big money if you're ever on the game show *How Geeky Are You?* or the one I'd be a big winner on, *Are You Smarter Than a Person Who Doesn't Watch TV Endlessly?* In the scene in 'Children of Earth' where Gwen is being directed through lines of covered bodies to identify Jack and Ianto, the officer in charge says, 'Thirteen and fourteen.' I requested that Jack's body be number thirteen.

When it came to making *Another Side*, it was important to me that this first studio album reflected who I was as a person. Happily, there was, as I've said, great personal significance behind the selection of many of the tracks. For example, I recorded 'Time After Time' for a friend in LA who had HIV. His family was incredibly supportive of him, but his dad couldn't quite put his feelings into words, and so he quoted parts of this song to his son in a letter.

The Police's song 'Every Little Thing She Does Is Magic', meanwhile, was for Clare, whom I adore, but who did get a little less 'magical' between the ages of twelve and fourteen.[19] I sang 'Please Remember Me' for Sandie, Scott's sister, who died of brain cancer in 2005; and 'Heaven' was for Scott and me. 'Can't Take My Eyes Off You', which

---

[17] Nespresso, anyone?

[18] Oh, man, that was difficult to do.

[19] Ah, who among us didn't? She's twenty-two now, if you're keeping track.

appears on *Music Music Music*, was picked because … well, like Frankie Valli, the Pet Shop Boys and Andy Williams, who have all recorded it before me,[20] I just like the song.

One of the first things I learned about Scott after we met[21] was that he loves to sing along to an eclectic mix of music and to musical soundtracks while he works. He especially loves Dusty Springfield. Sometimes, when you've lived with someone for a long time, it's easy to take that person for granted and not always say aloud the things you should. Believe me. 'You Don't Have To Say You Love Me' was recorded for him, and captures a few of the things we don't always say to each other.

With 'I Know Him So Well', the tenth track on the second album, I had a bit of a fight on my hands with Sony BMG, who initially did not want to include the song the way I covered it. Originally from the musical *Chess*, it is a duet sung by two women – their characters a Russian chess champion's estranged wife and his mistress (Elaine Paige played the mistress in the West End production). In the song, the women share their feelings for their mutual lover.

I recorded the track as a duet between two men, singing with Danny Boys. In the end, Sony agreed to my version. I was really pleased I'd dug in my proverbial heels about keeping it as a male duet because I've always felt that the song crossed gender lines. When you're in love, gay or not, the feelings are the same, the doubts as debilitating, and the hurt as painful. I felt redeemed about the arrangement of this track, as it has established itself as one of the signature songs of the album. Tim Rice, the song's lyricist, loved the fact that the duet became a poignant 'gay anthem' – a point he made to me in a note he sent prior to a concert we both participated in at Truro Cathedral.

My favourite accolade about this song, though, came in an email from a young Australian man, who was coming to terms with being gay. He wrote that when he heard this version of the song, it made him realize that he wanted some day to know what that kind of love and passion between two men feels like.

---

[20] That has to be the only thing they have in common.
[21] Okay. Not one of the very first things.

When I hear from fans about how much a particular song has meant to them, I'm always moved and touched; and when I hear from the song's writer, like Tim Rice, or more recently Barry Manilow, I'm very chuffed indeed. I've been a fan of Barry Manilow's music for decades, and I've included his work in my concerts and cabaret for years. For *Music Music Music*, I recorded Barry's song 'I Made It Through the Rain'.

One morning, when I was a guest on *The Chris Moyles Show* on BBC Radio 1, Chris, in his usual, slightly mocking, tongue-placed-firmly-in-cheek mode, encouraged all his listeners to download this particular track from iTunes. Guess what? The result was that the song zoomed into the charts, which was amazing, given that the album had been released eight whole months before. The song actually got as high as number five on iTunes downloads, and then settled at number fourteen for a couple of weeks.[22]

If that wasn't incredible enough, a few days later I heard from the man who wrote the song himself. Barry was so thrilled with my cover of this song, and the fact that it had leapt into the charts again, that he called me while I was in the US filming my segment of 'Around the World in 80 Days' for Children in Need. He invited me to lunch with him in Palm Springs, but unfortunately I wasn't available.[23] Instead, we had a long chat – and he invited me to join him onstage, to duet on the number, when he performed at the Proms in the Park concert in London's Hyde Park.[24]

Creating albums isn't just about the individual songs, it's also about the CD's overall style and sound. With *Another Side*, I wanted glossy and showy, but with *Music Music Music*, I wanted a more down-to-earth and personal approach. I know a lot of people didn't like the cover of *Music Music Music* – which shows me in profile, in a relaxed, informal pose, looking down and laughing – Sony especially. They wanted a full picture of the front of my face, and possibly they were right on that.

22 Ah, the power of the web, the radio and fans.
23 I was so bummed that I couldn't go.
24 I'm so there – schedule permitting.

Whether the look ultimately succeeded or failed, though, at least I had some say in what the cover looked like: that creative input is really important to me. The picture on the inside sleeve, with the 'three Johns'[25] on the theatre seats, was also my idea and I was really pleased that the image worked out so well.

I recorded most of *Music Music Music* in London and LA. Occasionally, I'd lay down some tracks in a venue that happened to be next door to the studio where Britney Spears was recording her latest album, *Circus*. When she was there, the studio and the surrounding streets were a circus themselves, with all kinds of characters and photographers crowding the pavements. Sometimes, I'd arrive to record and the facility would be in lockdown, with as many security guards and paparazzi as there were fans.

When I'm singing in the studio, there's a 'click' track going on in my cans,[26] kind of like a metronome, helping me to keep time and hold my track line.[27] I'm not really sure why, but I found that *Music Music Music* was a bit more emotional to record. When I'm recording, I'm trying to get across the feelings at the core of a song, and when I was recording 'From a Distance' and 'Both Sides Now', for example, there were times when I just couldn't get through the songs without losing it. I've heard from other artists that this happens much more when you're in a studio recording than it may ever happen when you're singing the song live. I've wondered if it's because you're in such a confined space, often completely alone, and you're exposing yourself in a way that can be pretty raw. A few times, I'd have to stop, and then start the 'click' track all over again.

Music Music Music had a few hurdles to get over when it was released, and because of them the album did not sell as well as *Another Side*. One of the biggest was the recession, and Woolworth's going under. Woolworth's held a lot of CD stock in their warehouses that

---

[25] Sounds like a naff buddy movie – or the sign you'd be looking for after drinking *way* too much.

[26] The recording word for 'headphones'.

[27] Sometimes this track stays in my head and keeps me moving outside the recording studio.

didn't get distributed after they declared bankruptcy, and I wasn't the only performer caught in this economic situation.

The other hurdle I faced with this second Sony album was that Sony/Epic really wanted me to be a pop singer, and under no circumstances did I ever want to be one. I've always aspired to be a singer who puts out an album a year for a wide spectrum of listeners to enjoy. Don't get me wrong, I can sing pop songs with the best of them, but that's not the same as creating the persona along with the playlist.

Before recording *Music Music Music*, I'd been moved from Sony BMG to Sony Epic. Epic produces more of Sony's pop artists, whereas BMG covers a broader range of genres and artists. Epic decided to release *Music Music Music* on a day when there were about twenty-two other albums being released. Since I'm not primarily known as a recording artist – unless you were looking for my album specifically, you might not dig around for it – I think that decision also hurt my sales.

For my part, I was lobbying for a Mother's Day release, given the album's style, and because I thought my fans would appreciate the opportunity to receive or give the album as a gift for Mother's Day. In retrospect, I think *Music Music Music* lost its way.

That's not to say that there weren't a lot of things I loved about this album. The idea for the title and the style of *Music Music Music* originated from one of my signature responses to contestants when I'm a talent-show judge,[28] and the fact that I'm superstitious and do a lot of things in threes. The album also consisted of three distinct styles of music that I love: pop, country, and musical-theatre songs.

The single 'What About Us?', which Gary Barlow penned, was terrific. I was particularly proud of how well my idea for the video was received, exploring the parallels in a relationship between a male/male couple and a male/female couple. The song and the video received a lot of airplay.[29] On one memorable occasion, the video came on the big

---

[28] 'Fantastic, fantastic, fantastic!' T-shirts available.

[29] Thanks to all my mates at BBC Radio 2: Elaine Paige; her producer, Malcolm Prince; Steve Wright; and Jonathan Ross.

screen in a bar when I arrived at the Hub convention in 2008. Without any prompting,[30] I climbed up onto one of the tables and lip-synched to myself.

Another time, Clare and I snuck away from the Hippodrome in Birmingham, between my panto performances, to have a quiet meal at a local restaurant. We managed to remain relatively incognito through most of the meal – until the music channel broadcasting on the row of wall-mounted flat-screen TVs began showing 'What About Us?' I might as well have been dancing on those tables, too, we had so many people staring at us. So much for being sneaky.

I did find out something later, though, about the Barlow song that bothered me a little. 'What About Us?' came to me not quite in the manner I'd originally thought. I was told that Gary Barlow had penned the track exclusively for me, when the truth was that he and Sony had intended the song to be a release for another artist, who didn't want it. I love the song and I think I made it my own regardless of its provenance.[31]

Given all of this, my next album for Sony will be an album of songs from musicals. A good friend at Sony, Daniel Hinchliffe, who worked on both of the earlier albums and was once a dancer – or a hoofer,[32] as they are fondly called – in the West End, and who is now part of the Sony group responsible for Celine Dion and Barry Manilow, will be much more involved in the collaboration to make sure this next album is on track.

And, I hope, in time for Mother's Day.

---

[30] Please, it's me.
[31] You know what I say: 'If life gives you lemons, make a vodka tonic.'
[32] I said 'hoofer', not 'woofter' …

'Was That Captain Jack Racing a Rickshaw?'

'Stop the car!' I yelled.

Team Barrowman – my mum, dad, Carole, Scott, Clare and I – had just been escorted to our limo in the secure parking lot at the rear of the San Diego convention centre, where I'd spent the day at Comic-Con 2008, signing autographs and presenting on a lively panel with other *Torchwood* folks, including Naoko, Gareth, and the show's executive producer, Julie Gardner. We'd answered questions from a packed house, and, on the request of a fan, Naoko and I had sung, a cappella, an excerpt from 'The Last Night of the World' from *Miss Saigon* (which, as you may know, was the West End show on which Coco and I first met).

Comic-Con is the mother of all conventions for anything new, cool or will-soon-be-both in Popular Culture.[1] Movies, television shows, video games, and – of course – comics, graphic novels and anything related to sci-fi, superheroes or animation are previewed at Comic-Con. For me, the appeal is all of those things, but I also love looking at and meeting the fans who attend conventions like this one.

The massive convention centre is set up with rows and rows of kiosk-like areas, where collectible companies, television networks and movie studios pay celebrities to sit and sign; in some booths, it's even possible to watch artists creating their illustrations. As I sat behind my table at Mary Lee Holzheimer's booth, and signed autographs for hours on end, I loved to watch as the cavalcade of characters crossed my path. Someone[2] made the mistake of giving Gareth, who was signing at the

---

[1] Yes. With the capitals.
[2] I blame Clare.

same booth as me, a soft-tipped dart gun, and pretty soon he and I had a contest going to see how far we could fire the darts – and who we could hit as they passed in front of us.

'See that Stormtrooper over there?' Gareth would taunt. 'I can hit him in three darts.'

'I can hit him in two.'

And so it would go. One of the workers from the booth then dashed out into the crowd, quickly gathered up our missiles and rushed back with them. If people noticed who had nailed them, then we'd call them over and chat with them, but most of the time, they had no clue that they'd just been tagged.

After a couple of hours of this, I noticed that a distinct pattern had begun to emerge as to the nature of our respective targets. I was picking fans dressed as recognizable characters that I found to be intriguing or really impressively created, like a Lando Calrissian or a stunningly detailed Boba Fett, whereas Gareth was hitting on[3] scantily clad women in sexy leather costumes, like Batgirl or Elektra, or young women dressed in erotic chain mail – like an amazing Barbarella who strutted past.

The entire spectrum of sci-fi characters from TV, movies and games crossed my path in those couple of days. And I thought I was a geek. I couldn't have named half of them for you. I did, though, love the *Star Wars* characters I saw, including a few I'd completely forgotten about and a handful of droids I'd never even heard of. There were also lots of elaborately costumed superheroes, villains and aliens, some already real in the world of a particular television show or movie, and others imagined by the fan him or herself,[4] from planets even the Doctor has never visited.

Whenever I took a break from the booth, I needed an escort in order to make my way through the throngs to get to the bathroom. The same applied when I did a little retail therapy at the collector booths, where I bought a few figures for my ever-evolving collections:

---

[3] I mean that phrase in all that it implies.

[4] I have to say, the Comic-Con world is pretty balanced in its gender geekiness.

a 'Captain Jack Sparrow' doll that was brilliant in its execution, and a Superman figure that was equally remarkable. At the T-shirt stalls, I bought up all my favourite vintage Ts, from Spider-Man to Aquaman to the Green Hornet. On these buying trips, I had to have a posse with me because this crowd knew their Captain Jack from their Captain America.

I enjoyed and appreciated everything about Comic-Con, including the intensity and the imagination of the fans. So did Carole, who disappeared for a long time one afternoon. Just as I was thinking that I might need to send a security detail to find her – she was meant to be signing *Anything Goes* part of the time with me – she came dashing back to the booth, as excited as a twelve-year-old, clutching a bag full of Emily the Strange paraphernalia. Emily the Strange is a comic character I introduced her to many years ago, because Carole – middle name Emily – *is* Emily the Strange.[5] She had also waited in line to have her photo taken standing in front of a full-scale model of a 'stargate' from *Stargate Atlantis*. She's almost as geeky as I am.[6]

Scott, on the other hand … hmm, not loving the whole Comic-Con vibe nearly as much. After he and Clare walked the entire circuit of the main floor of the convention centre and made it back to the booth safely, they both looked more than a bit stunned. Scott had the look he sometimes has when I'm about five minutes into telling him something that involves a chore he really doesn't want to do. He looked as if his brain had completely shut down. I had to send him out into the streets of San Diego with a map of the museums and historic sites just so he could get back his equilibrium.

Clare, meanwhile, recovered more quickly, especially after she managed to work in a little shoe shopping. My parents – the troupers that they are[7] – sat behind me in the booth all day and took everything in their stride, loving the craziness and the exuberant theatre of it all. In fact, my dad even did a spot of modelling. Mary Lee was selling

---

[5] Except for the cats. Emily loves cats, Carole not so much.
[6] Almost. She does not own a lightsaber.
[7] Note not Storm …

T-shirts with my name and image on them, and my dad happily volunteered to wear samples of them. Of course, it helped everyone's energy level that Mary Lee had a steady stream of chocolate and sweets in supply for all of us, including Gareth.

After a long, exciting day, Team Barrowman finally piled into the large limo. I gave the driver our hotel information, but as we began to pull out into the road that ran behind the convention centre, I looked to my left and saw someone who, in a flash, flooded my head with television memories from my high-school years.

'Stop the car!' I yelled, leaping out of the door without closing it – and leaving everyone inside convinced that this time I'd *really* lost the few marbles I had left. I darted between the limousines loading and unloading other celebrities for events later in the evening, and I charged across the street towards the vision from my past.

'Where the hell are you going?' someone inside the car yelled.

'It's the Bionic Woman!'

To understand the full impact of this encounter, I have to explain here that once I'd been safely ensconced in my private car with Team Barrowman, my security guards had immediately moved over to the loading dock and gathered around the very person I was now charging excitedly towards. This meant that the security detail knew I was not a threat, but poor Lindsay Wagner had no clue.

She looked up and spotted this man charging through traffic, yelling, 'I'm a huge fan! Hello! Lindsay!' and, naturally, she turned to her security detail for some help – but they were all acting completely nonchalantly and ignoring this clearly demented man in a Captain America T-shirt who was about to pounce on her. By the time I got to Lindsay Wagner, the poor woman was attempting to move behind one of the security guys and she was looking more than a bit terrified.

Did I care? Are you kidding? Well, maybe a little. But come on, it was the Bionic Woman. Alongside *Space 1999* and *Thunderbirds, The Bionic Woman* was one of my three favourite sci-fi shows in my youth.

When I reached her, she was finally figuring out that while this fan might be a nutcase, he wasn't a threat. I introduced myself. I've no idea what I said to her after that; I'm sure I sounded completely incoherent. Then I strolled back across the street to the waiting limo.

'It was the Bionic Woman!' I exclaimed.

'That's a first,' Scott said.

'What do you mean?'

'I don't think you've ever cut through traffic that fast for a woman in all the years I've known you.'[8]

When I was at university, I lived in a condo that my parents owned in La Jolla, a city close to San Diego. In recent years, when I've returned to the area, the district known as the Gaslight has been completely reborn. It's now full of good restaurants, clubs, saloons, ice-cream parlours and lots of shops – yet in a style that's preserved the area's nineteenth-century traditions, including the gas lamps (thus its name). Getting around is done mostly on foot or by hiring a young man or woman in a bicycle rickshaw to use pedal power to get from A to B. Vehicle traffic is heavy, and pretty slow moving because of lots of one-way streets and pedestrian zones.

That evening, we went to dinner at a restaurant in the Gaslight District. It was one that a friend who was a regular at Comic-Con had recommended to me. After a wonderful meal and, admittedly, a couple or three bottles of wine,[9] I let my dad savour the last morsel of his cream-laden dessert, paid the bill and then stood up. As is usually the case at a Barrowman family dinner, there'd been lots of terrific table talk, so we'd been having a good laugh throughout most of the evening. I had the perfect way to close out our night, but I wasn't going to tell anyone until I had a head start.

We were nearing the front door of the restaurant when I suddenly grabbed my mum and dad and shoved them out the door in front of me. I whistled for a rickshaw, pushed them on and jumped up next to them, just as Carole, Clare and Scott were emerging from the restaurant.[10] They figured out quickly what I

---

8 It was the Bionic Woman!

9 Really not an excessive amount of alcohol, given there were six of us at dinner.

10 In these situations, Scott is usually bringing up the rear …

was going to do because I could see their eyes darting around looking for another rickshaw.

'I'll race you,' I yelled. 'Round the block. Winner gets twenty bucks!'

Carole and Clare were now clambering on a second rickshaw and screaming at Scott to hurry up. The drivers soon realized what was up, and that there was extra money involved in this for them, too.

'Go!'

Our driver took off like his rickshaw had wings. I've never seen anyone pedal so fast in my entire life. He could have generated electricity. Both bikes took the turn faster than was probably legal and suddenly we were in slow-moving traffic, trickling through the main streets of the Gaslight District. Think of it like duelling rickshaws along Old Compton Street in central London on a Saturday night. Our driver cut in front of two cabs and almost took out a group of Japanese tourists. My mum called back to them, 'Sorry, sorry,' as the rickshaw darted in and out of traffic like a pinball.

I hope, readers, you can appreciate how hard this was for the poor driver: hauling three adults, one of them me, at rubber-burning speed, while another rickshaw was chasing his tail – and gaining on him all the time.

At the second turn, before heading into the home stretch, the rickshaw carrying Carole, Scott and Clare got caught at a pedestrian crossing. They had to stop. I could hear the words 'no fair' echoing behind me when my rickshaw driver risked life and limb and jumped us onto the pavement, avoiding the next crowded intersection.

From the beginning, Carole, Scott and Clare's rickshaw driver was at a bit of a disadvantage because they'd been slower off the mark,[11] but I could see their driver had calf muscles that suggested he did more than pedal rickshaws during the tourist season. By the time we were all headed down the home stretch, weaving in and out of traffic, they'd almost caught up with us.

Something had to be done.

---

[11] Not my fault. Just because they didn't know the plan when we left the restaurant.

Up ahead and to my right, I could see a public parking lot. I told my driver to cut through the lot, missing the next block of traffic and, I hoped, bringing us back out in front of the restaurant where this Grand Prix had begun. Luckily for me, he was willing to take the risk. Once again, he shot the bike up on the pavement, and pedalled madly through the lot.

Carole's driver saw what had happened, but he figured he had strength on his side. He stayed on the street. My dad, meanwhile, was bobbing forward and back next to me in the rickshaw, as if his momentum would somehow help our pace.

Readers, my tactic paid off. Amid a cacophony of partying pedestrians, honking cars really annoyed with us, and blaring music from nearby clubs, I let out a cheer that rose above all of this when my rickshaw got to the restaurant inches before the other one.

I paid for the rides, tipped both drivers really well, and gave the prize money to the driver of my rickshaw. While we were all laughing and catching our breath, a group of Comic-Con fans came running up to us.

'I knew it! I knew that was Captain Jack I saw in a rickshaw.'

Needless to say, when Team Barrowman returned to the hotel, we all needed some refreshments. And then, after I'd made sure my parents were safely in their room, Carole, Clare, Scott and I ended up playing an unintentional game of 'Ding Dong Ditch'.

For those of you who may not know what this is, it's essentially the game that every child – no matter where he or she grew up – has played at some point in his or her childhood. You chase around your neighbourhood, ringing doorbells and running away.[12]

Gav, who had accompanied me on this trip, hadn't joined us for dinner that night because he had an early flight back to the UK the next morning. So, I decided to play the game on him. In my version of the prank, I didn't plan to 'ditch' after he answered; I planned to moon him when he opened his door.

---

12 In the interests of health and safety, I'm noting here that it's naughty.

By this time, Scott had given up on the three of us and he'd headed to our room. With Carole and Clare watching the hallway behind me for other guests or, God forbid, security, I loosened my belt and my jeans, ready to drop them when Gav came to his door.

I banged on room 316.[13] Nothing happened. I banged again. This time, in the spirit of the evening's events, I began singing Gav's name to the tune of 'A Bicycle Built for Two'.

'Gavin, Gavin, give me your answer do.'

Suddenly, Clare hissed,[14] 'Security!'

I started to run, forgetting that I'd loosened my belt. While I was at full sprint, my jeans locked around my knees and down I went, sliding face first across the carpet at maximum speed.

Clare and Carole leapt over me, laughing hysterically and calling out, 'Payback!' as they ran down the hallway towards their room.

I later learned from Gavin that he was in room 416.

---

[13] I made up this number to protect the innocent. Plus, I can't remember the real one.

[14] Actually, she yelled. Clare can't whisper to save herself.

In 2008, I researched the science of homosexuality in the documentary *The Making of Me*. Here I am in one of the laboratories.

With *I'd Do Anything* winner Jodie Prenger.

Tonight's the night: with my dancers on the set of my prime-time Saturday-night entertainment programme.

Does this jacket make my ass look big? Filming my CBBC show *Animals at Work*, which was broadcast in June 2009.

Clare, Gareth and me at Comic-Con. The rickshaw race was the same night.

This is the dinner that led to the rickshaw race in San Diego.

Scott and Clare feeling the pressure of Comic-Con.

At the 2008 Hub convention, I learned not to sit on coffee tables.

It's show time: my *Music Music Music* tour in 2009 was my best yet.

My mum and dad joined me on stage for 'Knock Three Times', which was an absolute riot.

My tour family. From l to r: James Gambold (back row); Gavin Barker, Matt Brind, Jamie Talbot, Daniel Ellis, Richard John, Jon Cooper, me, Mum, Dad, Jennie Griffin, James Pusey, Daniel Boys (middle row); Jamie Karitzis, James Robinson, Kate Kelly (front row).

In the Royal Albert Hall before one of the most exciting concerts of my life, with Mum, Dad and my best friend and mentor Beverly Holt.

On stage, doing what I love.

After receiving a standing ovation at the Albert Hall, I was overcome with emotion.

Just after the tour finished, I tore ligaments in my left ankle. Here I am recuperating at home in Sully.

On the famous Route 66, getting my kicks!

Taking a back seat with Myleene Klass for Children in Need.

About to perform the infamous 'banana trick' …

Dressed to the nines for my part in *La Cage aux Folles* in the West End.

Backstage with two of my 'Cagelles': Matt Krzan (left) and Nick Cunningham.

'Can we have a biscuit?' The amazing cast and crew of *La Cage aux Folles*.

With Carole and Eva Longoria Parker on Wisteria Lane.

On the set of *Desperate Housewives*.

Gabor and Rebecca make me a hippy for a flashback on *Desperate Housewives*.

In 2009, celebrating my twenty years in show business.

Accepting a highly prestigious award from Scott and Carole …

Whatever the future holds, 'I am what I am'.

CHAPTER TEN

'O CANADA'

'How do you solve a problem like a judge in jail?'

John Barrowman

Five things you should know about Toronto

1 You can take a ferry to an island and sunbathe nude
(Canadians will sunbathe in snow flurries).

2 It's not like America or the UK (it's Canadaland!).

3 Safeguards and trust are important (especially when
someone escapes via a hotel balcony).

4 When in Toronto, eat! (Food! Glorious food!)

5 I've looked at Falls from both sides now
(the Canadian side is better).

n June and July 2008, I travelled back and forth between Canada, the US and the UK to be a judge on the Canadian Broadcasting Company (CBC) version of *How Do You Solve a Problem Like Maria?* (I was working concurrently on a number of other commitments in Britain and the States.) Sometimes I flew weekly to Toronto and stayed – Thursday to Monday – in a condo in Yorkville.

On every trip across the Atlantic that summer, the plane hit some of the most violent thunderstorms I've ever experienced. I fly frequently. I know the signs. When the flight attendants buckle up, hold hands and begin to sing 'Kumbaya', the turbulence is going to be bad.

I loved everything about Toronto: the CN Tower, the great restaurants and, of course, the shopping.[1] However, I found that very little of my previous work on the BBC talent-search shows prepared me for the high drama and outrageous behaviour[2] that came with judging the Canadian *Maria* – especially when a Toronto jail ended up being alive with 'The Sound of Music'.

To begin with, the Maria who was the favourite of the other judges was not my favourite. I thought she was too vanilla; too bland for the role. The young woman who eventually won, Elicia MacKenzie, was one of my choices because she had energy and passion, and she sang from her heart.

As I did in the BBC version of the *Maria* show, I went to Maria School to work with and to meet the contestants. Many of the hopefuls knew me from my musical-theatre work, but more of them were familiar with me from *Torchwood* and *Doctor Who*.[3]

---

[1] Especially Canadian Tire.

[2] Not mine!

[3] Both shows are incredibly popular in Canada.

During one of my first days on set, I was working on a theatrical exercise with the contestants, and I said something silly about being gay.[4] Thanks to Clare, my niece, who was with me at the time,[5] an off-the-cuff expression from that day became the Barrowman phrase of the summer. Clare, I might add here, can spread family gossip or stir up drama faster than Perez Hilton and TMZ combined. There's some sentiment among my immediate family that she learned this trait from me. Never.

Anyway, I said something like: 'I'm just as much a gay man in Canadaland as I am in England.' And that was certainly true – I was on a CBC *How Do You Solve a Problem Like Maria?* float for the city's gay-pride parade one week (can't let a parade pass me by), and I discovered after only a few weekends in the city that Toronto is an open and very gay-friendly city.

Thanks to Clare, whenever anyone asked what John was doing that summer, the response was always, 'He's being gay in Canadaland.'

Unlike on the BBC talent shows, at the CBC, the panel of judges watched the Maria hopefuls on DVD in dress rehearsal before the live shows. This was not to pre-judge them, but to help the writers and the other judges – who had very little experience in this area – to craft a broad range of responses to each of the contestants' performances. It also meant the production team could time out the various sections of the script with more accuracy.

In these script meetings, each of us would suggest the kinds of things we might say if the performance that evening was a strong or a weak one. Given this was now my fourth time on a judging panel, I was never at a loss for something constructive and TV-friendly to say. There was one particular judge, though, who, when it was her turn to comment, would hem and haw and then finally say something like, 'Oh, I'll probably just tell her she's good,' or 'I'll probably say I liked what she did.'

Every time. When the show was down to its last six or so contestants, I couldn't help myself. On behalf of all talent-show judges everywhere, I gently lost it.

---

[4] Don't know what came over me. Never done that before.
[5] She'd come to Toronto from Milwaukee to spend the weekend.

'Stop being so nice. Stop being so Canadian. This is a contest. If she's rubbish, then tell her she's rubbish.'

One night during the live show, she made a comment suggesting a particular contestant, Donna Lajeunesse, had too much of an 'attitude'. I thought this was wrong of her. It's one thing to comment on a person's performance; yet another to comment on their personality.

First of all, if Donna did have some kind of 'attitude', if she was causing some discontent among the other contestants, then that conflict should have been worked out when she was at Maria School. The judge didn't need to humiliate her on live TV and perhaps bias the audience towards her. Donna looked perfect as an Austrian Fräulein, and she belted out her numbers with spirit and style. Anyway, the judge ragged on her attitude, calling her a 'diva', and commenting how she was badly behaved and how this kind of behaviour can't be tolerated in theatre ... blah, blah, blah.

Originally, the producers had decided they weren't going to come back to me for my comments after this judge had shared her opinion, but I planned to cut in quickly at a moment when she took a breath. During Barrowman family dinners, sometimes the only way you can get your say is to leap into the fray of the conversation when someone breathed. So I was ready when I heard this judge inhale.

'Sometimes when you're a diva,' I said, 'you're perceived as a bitch, but over the course of my career in theatre, every leading lady I've worked with has been a diva in some way and they've all been very successful, so ... well done, Donna.'

'Where's John this summer?'

'He's being gay and blunt in Canadaland.'

Despite some of the differences in our judging styles, the show's producers didn't have to do much work with me because I knew how to produce myself.[6] However, the same couldn't be said about Simon Lee, a fellow judge and Andrew Lloyd Webber's proxy during the early stages of the elimination process, when Simon had the final say on who should be saved in the sing-offs. Andrew only joined us later in the series as one of the judges.

[6] Thanks, Mel!

For years, Simon has been Andrew's musical supervisor for shows like *Jesus Christ Superstar* and *The Phantom of the Opera*, and he was also involved in the initial stages of the BBC's *How Do You Solve a Problem Like Maria?* However, I believed from the beginning that Simon was not a good choice as a judge, and in this venture he didn't represent Andrew's interests well at all. Early on, I mentioned to the series producer that she shouldn't put too much of the show on Simon's shoulders because I feared he might let the programme down.

For despite Simon's many talents, as a judge he was a stuttering, twitching mess most of the time. Unfortunately, his influence with the producers continued right up until his arrest. I don't claim to be prescient or perfect, but I knew many people who'd worked with Simon in the past, and, from the beginning of the production, I was worried about his professionalism. I was also aware of his personal struggles and how they might interfere with the show.

Sadly, it didn't take long for Simon's dramatics to go from petty to outrageous, and on the day after the show's semi-final, Toronto headlines read: 'Judge for CBC's *Maria* arrested after alleged assault, confinement at posh Yorkville hotel' and '*Maria* judge charged with assault'.

I didn't need anything nearly as histrionic for Simon to wear thin on me. The little things he did were quite enough. For example, I did most of the pre-air publicity for the show, and in return for my work, I was hoping I'd get to sing 'Every Little Thing She Does Is Magic' with the contestants, and have the opportunity to plug my album, *Another Side*, to the Canadian market.[7] This never happened. Instead, in rehearsals that week, the producers informed me that Simon was going to accompany the remaining Marias on the piano during the upcoming show. This didn't seem fair. Not only because I'd clearly been bumped, but also because Simon had to read his music during the accompaniment. As I said to the producers: if Simon had to read music while he played, how could he fairly judge the Marias' performances?

'Do you think the audience will notice that, John?' asked one of the producers.

---

[7] I'm a businessman too, you know.

Oh, yeah. Viewers are not stupid. They notice everything.

When I was a contestant on *Dancing on Ice*, I remember one week Phillip Schofield called out the final voting without a note card in front of him. Viewers wrote in and complained because they thought he was being told the answers in his ear. It didn't look kosher, even though it was, and the following week Phillip had the results on a card. This format has subsequently changed as viewers have become used to earpieces.

As we discussed Simon's planned performance, he piped up in the meeting – in a voice that sounded as if he was parodying a foppish Englishman – and explained he was a professional and would handle the situation appropriately. I let it go. Ultimately, the TV audience saw a few shots of Simon's hands that particular episode, and no shots of his music. Only the studio audience saw him for the entire number.

Normally, this kind of stuff wouldn't rile me, but on this occasion I thought that a great deal of the focus on Simon was at the expense of the Maria hopefuls. When I participate in shows like this, I always remind myself that as a judge I can be funny, sassy, maybe even a little in-your-face, but in the end the show is all about the contestants. I'll get another chance to perform, but these young men and women may not. Unfortunately, Simon's star turn was yet to come.

On the day of the penultimate show, Carole was visiting, and when we arrived at the studios for filming, the place was already buzzing madly.[8] No one on the team had seen Simon since the night before. Naturally, everyone was frantic. By the time Carole and I had made it to my dressing room, we had most of the story. Simon had been arrested and charged with assault, and would not be appearing on the programme anymore.

Earlier on that Sunday, Simon and his subsequent 'accuser' had had a very loud 'domestic dispute'. Both men were still in the throes of their Saturday-night partying in one of the more prestigious hotels in Yorkville – the Hazelton Hotel, just down the street from where I was living. The hotel had an outdoor patio restaurant at street level, and it was the kind of place where diners went to see and be seen; a place the likes of the Beckhams would frequent.

---

[8] And Clare didn't have anything to do with it.

According to one report, the 'domestic dispute' quickly became more outrageous and brunch diners were taken aback by the sight of a young man in his twenties climbing over the balcony of the hotel before shinning down the side and crashing down onto the restaurant patio.

'Oh, look, David, darling. A man's foot just landed in my sashimi.'

'How nice, Vicky, I have his elbow in my oysters.'

One published report then stated, 'The man stormed off, leaving the brunchers stunned, before returning without a shirt about ten minutes later and yelling at the restaurant patrons that he had forgotten something.'

Carole and I synthesized and filtered all the details we'd gathered since we'd arrived, and then I went off to a script reading with the two other judges and the show's producers. We were about twenty minutes into the meeting and still no one had asked the question that was looming like a big fat elephant in the room. I gave them a couple more minutes before I said, 'Um ... did you all hear that Simon's in jail?'

You'd have thought I'd just announced the Pope was gay or I was having Tom Cruise's baby. Jaws dropped. Coffee spilled. The producers were then forced to explain to the other judges that Simon had been arrested and he would not be available for either the semi-final or the finale of the show.[9]

I'm a good guy and my parents raised me well, but, honestly, can you blame me for not biting my tongue? I looked at the producers and at my fellow judges, I shrugged, and then I said (all together now), 'I told you so.'

The remaining Marias felt terribly let down. Simon had not only disappointed them, but he'd also let the programme down. In the end, his 'accuser' did not show up in court to press charges and the Canadian court exonerated Simon of all the charges against him.

'But where's John?'

'He's being gay, blunt, and gloating a teeny tiny bit in Canadaland.'

---

[9] Who knows when they were planning to tell us?

'Oh No, You Didn't!'

Oh yes, I did see my life flash before me during an evening performance of *Robin Hood* at the Birmingham Hippodrome in 2008, and all I kept repeating to myself was, 'Please don't let me die in tights.'

I've heard all the criticism about pantomimes before, and I hear it all over again from friends or colleagues when the announcement is made that, once more, I've agreed to perform in pantomime again at Christmas. I hear all about how panto is theatre at its lowest common denominator; about how panto is cheesy and outdated; and about how it's beneath a performer of my range; blah, blah, blah. This is usually my response: come see one of mine and I dare you not to have a good time. Can't be done.

Paul Elliot wrote my panto scripts for *Aladdin* and *Robin Hood*. He has a unique gift for appealing to the mums, dads, grans, uncles and aunties in the audience who are nostalgic for the pantos of their youth, but at the same time he's enough of a student of theatre and a whizz with a one-liner that his scripts also appeal to the wide range of children and young adults sitting next to those mums, dads, grans, uncles and aunties. Let's not forget that even Shakespeare was not above playing with cross-gender high jinks, mistaken identities and the theatrics of fools and fops.

Ever since I was a kid, I've loved to dress up and perform. As you know, that tradition continued when Clare and Turner were children and we would all dress up for our family performances at Christmas and the Barrowman New Year party. I've always adored working with children and for children. I enjoy seeing them laugh … and maybe even scaring them a little. On a whim, I did both to a whole crew of kids and their parents last year, when I stopped by the Doctor Who Up Close exhibition in the Red Dragon Centre at Cardiff Bay.

The exhibit is one of the best of its kind in the country. For a small fee, you can walk through the history of the Doctor and his companions – including yours truly as Captain Jack – checking out a lot of the costumes and props from across the series and from a number of recent episodes. You can also meet many of the Doctor's most famous enemies. On top of all of this, the exhibition has loads of details about how episodes were produced and images created. For any fan of the show, it's a treat.[1]

The Red Dragon Centre also houses my local cinema. One evening, when the movie Scott and I planned to see was sold out, we had about an hour to kill before the next showing. Since I didn't fancy heading home and coming back again, I suggested we take a peek at the *Doctor Who* attraction.[2] Poor Scott. In these situations, he usually rolls his eyes and wanders off to the nearest newspaper stand or bookstore.

As is often the case, a number of families were working their way round the displays when I entered, answering the trivia questions connected to each of the exhibits. No one paid much attention to the man in the baby-blue polo shirt who looked an awful lot like Captain Jack, as he snuck past the display of K9 …

I ducked round a dark corner to one of my favourite parts of the museum, where an evil Dalek was displayed in all its glory – with motion-sensored sound effects. On this day, the Dalek was presented in such a way that when visitors came round the curve from the first section of the exhibit, they're a bit taken aback, sometimes even freaked out by what confronts them. I figured, why not make this even scarier and more exciting for the unsuspecting families about to turn the corner?

I climbed up onto the display, and posed myself as if the Dalek was menacing Captain Jack. The first family who turned the corner didn't even bat an eyelid on seeing Captain Jack dressed in baby blue without

---

[1] Anyone reading this not a fan? What's wrong with you?
[2] Again. I never tire of it.

his coat, never mind that he was even in this particular exhibit. As the unsuspecting family leaned forward to take a closer look, I reached out and grabbed the mum's hand. She screamed so loud she scared the hell out of me and I screamed even louder. Her son, who was probably about ten, darted back round the corner, while his dad collapsed in hysterical laughter. I had barely enough time to assure them that, yes, indeed, I really was John Barrowman, before I had to hustle them onwards. I wanted to get back into position before the next victims – um, family – came bounding round the bend.

I could easily have stood next to the Dalek for another hour, but my popcorn and my partner were calling me.[3] Problem was, when I turned the corner to leave the exhibit, I had to walk through the gift shop that was, naturally, strategically placed on the way out. All the children and the parents whom I'd leapt out at and terrified had stuck around and bought up all the Captain Jack-related posters and action figures. Before I was able to make my escape, they cornered me for my signature – served me right (I loved it really).

When I'm performing panto, watching the enjoyment on kids' faces out in the auditorium is the best part of the experience. The biggest challenge is keeping my energy up between the matinee and evening shows. Any audience can tell when a performer is lagging, but in panto there's no room for even the smallest dip in enthusiasm. A crowd of younger people is very aware when you're not giving them all you've got – or, worse, when you're not taking seriously the role you're playing and the magic your character is a part of.

I watch a lot of movies in my dressing room during panto season and I try to pick films with exuberance that pops out through the screen and keeps my energy level peaked. This last panto season one of my favourite films was *Kung Fu Panda*. Man, I could do all his moves.

Panto is a blast to do, but it's also a serious business and it can have its own inherent dangers.[4] During my most recent foray to

---

[3] You don't want to know what Scott was calling me at this point. He was already in the cinema lobby.

[4] And I don't mean children and candyfloss.

Sherwood Forest as Robin Hood, we staged a diabolical move, where the Sheriff captured Robin and bound his hands and feet in cuffs, and then trapped him inside a deadly torture cage deep within his lair.

This cage was everything it appeared to be. Believe me. The cage had massive spikes, which were meant to make Robin Hood into mashed potatoes. Think that theatre sets are all created with smoke and mirrors? Think again. When the designers of the illusion constructed the cage, they knew they couldn't use fake spikes because, from the seats in the stalls, fake spikes looked like fake spikes. The result was that during every performance, I had to be spread out under countless very sharp and dangerous knife-like spears.

Obviously, safety was everyone's concern,[5] so the drop lever for the spikes had a number of protective features built into it. Nevertheless, whenever the lever was on notch #1, the spikes had only two notches left until … splat! As a final safety measure, the ensemble actors playing the Sheriff's evil minions were instructed to pay very careful attention to the man in the cage. If I was in trouble, they were meant to free me immediately.

One matinee performance, I was captured and bound, as usual, under the spikes. The Sheriff had not yet pulled the curtain around the table, which was the cue for me to be released and the effect to play out – as soon as I was freed, the spikes would come crashing down. As I was lying underneath those spears, I glanced up – and I noticed that the latches weren't connected all the way to their safest range. The lever was on the first safety, which meant that there were only two more left until I'd be a walking sieve.

I was clamped down with handcuffs, so there was no easy way to get me out of my predicament without ruining the effect for the audience. While the scene was playing itself out, I started to signal to the ensemble actors, my backup, that I wanted to get out. Pretty soon, I was really getting agitated … because no one was paying any attention to the cuffed man under the deadly spikes. Only when the Sheriff finally pulled

[5] Especially mine …

the curtain round the torture table, and I was hidden from the audience, was I released.

A bucketload of adrenalin and fear fuelled my anger. I leapt off the table so fast when the bindings were loosened that I scraped the skin off my wrists. Needless to say, everyone offstage knew at that point what had almost happened.

Clare, who was with me at the time, ran behind me as I charged to my dressing room, where I threw a chair across the room, shattering it against the door. I was so furious I could barely speak.[6]

Once I'd calmed down, and picked up the chair bits, the entertainer in me took over. I told Clare, 'Don't tell Grandma about the spikes. She'll panic and she'll never be able to enjoy the show.'

'What's John doing now?'

'Trying not to be Swiss cheese in pantoland.'

---

[6] I know – that's how mad and scared I was.

CHAPTER ELEVEN

'ON THE ROAD AGAIN'

'If it has tyres or testicles, it's going to give you trouble.'

Saying on a decorative tile above my back door

My seven all-time, to-die-for, definitive dream cars

1 Mercedes Gullwing (I'm drooling just writing this).

2 A 1964 Studebaker Super Hawk (a car for *Mad Men*).

3 A Tucker.

4 Aston Martin DBS (stands for 'damn brilliant sports car').

5 AMC Pacer (a seventies icon that reminds me of my childhood).

6 Range Rover.

7 Bentley Continental.

Given my love of driving, and my passion for cars – actually, my adoration of anything with a chassis, an engine, and more than one axle – I'm often asked why I've never appeared on BBC's *Top Gear*. The truth? I've never been asked. Because if I were to be asked, I'd be a guest faster than you could shift from first to third.

Top Gear is one of my favourite shows. I never miss watching the programme when I'm home and I record every episode when I'm not. I enjoy the entire team, their banter, and the show's overall format.

A few years ago, I got in a bit of trouble because, after an interview, when I thought my comments were being made 'off the record', I gave an impulsive answer to explain why I'd never been on *Top Gear*.

In my defence, a while before I made the remark, *Top Gear* had received a small number of complaints following Jeremy Clarkson's use of the term 'ginger beer'. However, a London free paper published my comment, which I'd thought was 'off the record', and as a result people at the BBC thought that Clarkson and I were having a public fight. I'm not sure that we ever really were, and I've consistently remained a fan of the show.

In the summer of 2009, my absence from prime-time car shows was remedied. I was asked to be a guest on *Fifth Gear* on Five. The programme had heard I was a petrol head beginning my own car collection, and their producers read in a *Motor Trend* magazine interview that one of my childhood dreams was to race a rally car, and that as an adult I'd like to buy my own some day and drive in off-road rally races. It seemed the perfect fit. And, I have to say, although I ended up destroying a £120,000 rally car in a death-defying crash on the show (and my mum yelled at me for days about my risk-taking[1]), it was a truly brilliant experience.

---

[1] Okay, that's my word. Hers were 'really stupid thing to do and don't ever do such a stupid, stupid thing again'.

My spectacular crash on *Fifth Gear* was, unfortunately, not my only crash of this summer – but my quick responses and fast thinking during a car accident in Bridgend proved to me that driving off-road might be a sport at which I'd excel. After all, it was in my genes. Driving off-road (and into snow banks and under snowploughs) were driving skills we practised as a family when we first moved to America.

In the early eighties, after our first few years in the US, our neighbours had a name for the Barrowmans.[2] We were labelled the family with the disposable cars because the drivers in the house at that time – my parents, Carole and Andrew – wrecked seven cars in a short period of time.

In their defence, not all of the accidents were the fault of their skills or lack thereof. During the first year that we lived in Prestbury, Illinois, my mum was driving her VW Rabbit on Hankes Road, the road that led into our neighbourhood, after a light snowfall, with my gran, Murn, sitting in her favourite seat in the car: the back seat. (Murn also liked travelling backwards in the extra seat at the very back of a Volvo station wagon we once owned. She and I would often ride back there when we took trips. Together we would wave,[3] pull silly faces and pick our noses at anyone who got less than two chevrons behind us.)

That wintry day, my mum's car skidded at a turn, the wheels caught on the lip of the road, the car flipped … and crashed down on its wheels in a nearby field. No one was hurt, but poor Murn was pinned in place, essentially caught in the space behind the seats, until my mum freed herself and then manoeuvred Murn out of her seatbelt.[4] When I came home in the school bus that day, I recognized my mum's car in the field, which sent me into a panic until I got home and saw my mum sitting safely on the couch – albeit sipping whisky rather than her usual sherry.

The family car at that time was a Caprice Classic with rear-wheel drive, and for many winters after that accident, the car had big bags of

---

[2] They probably had a few, but this was the one we heard about.

[3] And sometimes make other naughty gestures.

[4] No doubt in our minds that the belts saved them.

salt weighing down its rear to stop it fishtailing on the ice or snow. Driving in the Midwest, where winters sometimes brought 8–12 inches of snow in one storm a couple of times a month, meant that learning how to drive out of an icy skid and how to avoid sliding into ditches were must-have skills. I still pride myself on them to this day.

A few weeks after my mum's accident, Carole was waiting at the corner of Hankes Road for a city snowplough to pass – when the massive machine turned left and directly into her car. The plough's blade scraped up across the hood and kept coming. Carole was so stunned that this was actually happening, it took her a few beats to register that the blade was moving closer to the windshield – and to her head. She decided she'd better get the hell out of there.[5] She clambered out the passenger side of the car, screaming at the driver, who'd finally stopped, but not before he'd sheared a chunk off the front of the car.

Then it was Andrew and my dad's turn. Andrew's car had been sideswiped on the left while he crossed an Aurora intersection on his way home from school. A week or so later, when the car was repaired, my dad went to pick it up. As he pulled out of the body shop's parking lot, he was blindsided on the right side of the car. After swearing loudly (in Glaswegian) and freaking out the other driver, my dad reversed the car directly back into the repair bay. He climbed out to the stunned looks of the mechanics.

He said, 'You fixed the wrong side.'

The Barrowmans disposed of seven cars in those first years as American drivers. When my turn came to get my first car, I had learned from the entire family how to drive defensively. In America in the eighties, driver's education was sponsored by your local high school and so, as soon as I was eligible, I signed up for the driving classes and passed with chequered flags. On the day of my sixteenth birthday, the age when you're able to get a driver's licence in the US, I was first in line at the local Department of Motor Vehicles. I passed the road test at my first attempt.

[5] Duh!

Later that week, my dad took me to Bill Jacobs VW showroom in Joliet. (Despite the fact that the Barrowmans had wrecked a number of VWs in the past, we kept going back for another one.) My first car was a fire-red Scirocco. I adored it, and I think when I sat behind the wheel for the first time, at that moment I knew that, whenever I could afford it, I wanted to collect cars.

Around this time, I met Stacey Simmons, who became a close friend and confidante all through high school, and who also owned a red car, a Pontiac Firebird. I believe our first conversation, after I'd introduced myself to her, was about that car.

Stacey was a tall, leggy blonde. She liked clothes, especially Ralph Lauren. Even better, Stacey was a bit of a petrol head like me. She adored all the stuff a girl wasn't supposed to be into; and I loved all the things a boy wasn't supposed to like. We complemented each other perfectly.

Stacey was also a member of our high-school Pom Squad, the Tiger Paws. When I'd hang out at her house, I'd help her with the choreography for her dance routines. This, of course, fuelled the high-school rumour that we were dating, which was rubbish. We were BFFs.[6] When she and I went to parties, she was usually the designated driver because I'd be the one who'd like to have a drink.[7]

Stacey's mother, Lynn, and her father, Frank, were from a big real-estate family in Joliet, and it was Stacey's mother who first introduced me to 'Midwest Caviar'. It's still one of my favourite snacks. Take a block of Velveeta cheese, pour over a can of Hormel Chili with Beans,[8] add a carton of sour cream, and then heat in the microwave for a few minutes. Mix and dip. I'd devour the entire bowl. Loved the stuff!

Stacey's dad and I got along well, too. He was a really genuine guy, but one day – with absolutely no malice intended on his part – he said something that gutted me. I've kept this to myself all these years. But as I think about it now, in the context of these stories, I

---

[6] For readers, like, over, like, thirty, this means, like, 'best friends forever'.

[7] Always in moderation …

[8] For full impact later, you've gotta have the chili *and* beans.

believe it was another of those small, defining moments that's stuck in my psyche, and that may have had a bigger impact on me than I first thought.

Frank was typical of the generation of American men that emerged in the sixties, and which the US network AMC's terrific TV show, *Mad Men*, has epitomized. Frank came home from the office, tossed his jacket on a chair or table near the front door, loosened his tie, and accepted the cocktail Lynn would have waiting for him. One evening when he arrived home, I was sitting in the living room, waiting for Stacey. He and I chatted for a while.

'So, John,' he said, 'when are you going to stop all this funny stuff and think about getting a real job?'

I loved this family – still do – and I admired Frank very much. I thought he understood me. I laughed off his remark, and reminded him that acting *was* a real job, but I was hurt. At the time, his statement was one more added to all the others during middle and high school that made me even more determined to make my decision to be an entertainer pay off just as well as any 'real job'.[9]

Years later, when I was getting big jobs and well-paid work, my parents ran into Frank and Lynn, and Frank was impressed with my accomplishments. If he reads this, I'm sure he'll be surprised that his comment has stayed with me all these years afterwards – especially because he may not even remember the conversation. The incident has reminded me, though, that as adults we do have to be vigilant with our offhand comments and asides to the children in our lives because these kinds of remarks, in a child's head, can carry so much more weight than we intend.

The passion for cars that I shared with Stacey has remained as important in my adult life as it was in my youth and childhood, when I used to load cars into my Matchbox garage or race them on my Hot Wheels electric 'street speed challenge' track.[10] When I left for college,

---

[9] Check out *Anything Goes* for more details on my school experiences.
[10] 'Danger! Will Robinson' – maximum testosterone emissions for the next few paragraphs.

my dad traded in the VW Scirocco for an Isuzu Impulse with Lotus suspension,[11] and I've never looked back.

Many of the cars I've owned as an adult have associations with my youth. In my childhood head, a symbol of a person's success as a grown-up was to own a Mercedes. I've been lucky enough to afford two; I'm on first-name terms with my local Mercedes dealer, the Sinclair Group. In my garage, I have a slick black Volvo convertible, with champagne leather interior. With one touch, the car's hardtop frame rises majestically, as if the car was a Transformer – one of my favourite toys as a boy. I recently added a fire-red Cadillac to my stable; my first scarlet car since my youth, and a vehicle whose front makes it look like it should be a character in Disney's *Cars*.[12] My olive-green Renault Avantime, of which only a limited number were sold in the UK, reminds me of George Jetson's pod car, with its roof of glass and its sharp angles and futuristic shape, while my mint-green 1982 Mercedes SL is my Pam and Bobby Ewing car.

I used to own a DeLorean, the *Back to the Future* car, but because I have limited storage space for my car collection, I had to release this car back into the future. The first time I took the DeLorean out for a drive in Cardiff, I needed to fill up the tank. It took me forty minutes and a desperate phone call to its past owner in Ireland to find the location of the petrol cap.[13]

When my family returned to Scotland in 1972, after spending a year in the United States[14] at the behest of my dad's firm, Caterpillar Inc., one of the most prized possessions I brought back with me was my Big Wheel bike. Do you know the kind I mean? It was a low-to-the-ground riding tricycle, with a huge front wheel and big handles. The entire thing was made of heavy-duty plastic. My Big Wheel was yellow, with a red-and-black seat and thick black wheels. These particular bikes were popular in America in the sixties and seventies,

[11] Lotus suspension is not a yoga move.
[12] I've watched this movie a gazillion times.
[13] Tucked under the windshield.
[14] This year was also known as 'Barrowmans' Excellent Adventure', and marked our first escapades in the US prior to our emigration there in 1976.

and when I returned with mine to Mount Vernon in Scotland, I was the talk of the town.[15]

When I rode my Big Wheel, I could beat any kid on my street riding a bigger bike, plus I could generate the most amazing black skid marks on the pavement with it. I was known on Dornford Avenue as 'that wee demon driver'. All I needed to do to create these marks was to get myself going at high speed – preferably by beginning on the hill at the top of Dornford – then close to the corner I'd back-pedal really hard and pull the handbrake, and the Big Wheel would skid and spin wildly. Awesome!

One of my last rides as 'that wee demon driver' happened when I was racing my friend, Francis, from next door. I lost control of the Big Wheel, went flying over the handlebars, and hit the top edge of a low brick wall with my mouth. As you can imagine, when my mum reached me, I was bleeding badly. I had soaked through my shirt by then, and yet, because I was terrified of seeing blood, all the way to the hospital she kept telling me that it wasn't so bad and there really was no blood at all.

After that accident, I learned how to control my bike when I was speeding; and I applied the same rules to my driving when I got my licence. I'm a firm believer in the 'don't panic and drive' school of driver's education; the lesson taught me by my driver's ed teacher. His idea was that all drivers should know how – if it's possible – to get out of a dangerous driving situation without panicking and making the problem worse. When Clare and Turner were learning to drive, they practised manoeuvring out of dangerous situations in a neighbourhood cemetery. Why not? Everyone there was already dead.

Admittedly, I can be an impatient driver – a safe one, but most definitely impatient[16] – but I've never forgotten my driver's ed teacher's lesson about not panicking when facing a dangerous situation. It was a lesson that I recently had to put into practice – and it saved my family's life.

In June 2009, Scott, my parents and I were driving home after we'd

[15] At least among the five-year-olds on the street.
[16] I know. Hard to believe.

eaten out for lunch near my home in Sully. My parents were in the back seat, enjoying the view from the full roof of glass on my Avantime, and Scott was in the front seat, navigating.[17] It had been raining, but the downpour had stopped a short while ago.

Suddenly, up ahead, a car careened around a curve so fast that the driver had to swerve out into the other lane to avoid hitting the vehicle directly in front of him. The road was steamy wet and the speeding car lost its grip on the road's surface. Its abrupt swerve put it into the outside lane, and facing oncoming traffic. I was the oncoming traffic. I remember my mum screaming, 'Oh dear God, he's going to hit us,' and Scott recalled me saying, 'I've got to get off the road.'

Logic told me to slam on my brakes, but given the other car's complete loss of control, I knew that, if I stopped, the oncoming car would hit us head-on at full speed. More than one of us would die. Instead, I listened to my instincts. I accelerated. I swerved quickly round the oncoming car – missing it literally by inches – and crashed off the road into a gully, smashing first into a series of bushes and then a pole, which snapped under us on impact. The airbags deployed and, in a heartbeat,[18] the inside of the car filled with powdery smoke. My mum thought the car was on fire, but it turned out that the airbags had released a powdery substance upon impact.[19]

When I knew my family were fine, my adrenalin dissipated, my anger calmed,[20] and, while I waited for the emergency vehicles, I looked closely at the offending car's tyre marks. Then I examined mine, serpentining off the road to safety. I was so ready for *Fifth Gear* rally driving.

A month later, I joined the *Fifth Gear* crew at a rally track near Llangurig, Wales. Gavin and Rhys, my PA, came with me for company, and also because I wanted Rhys to film my circuit for me. I got suited up in a red fireproof jumpsuit, after which the show's host, Timothy

[17] Scott loves to help the satnav lady.
[18] All four, thankfully!
[19] I hope you never have to discover this for yourself.
[20] A little …

'Tiff' Needell, sat me in the Prodrive Impreza and gave me a quick lesson on rally driving.

I'm a regular viewer of *Fifth Gear*. Although I'd never met Tiff before, I knew of him by reputation and skill. For the first half-hour or so, Tiff tutored me on the car and the circuit while the cameras set up for my practice lap. I felt like that sixteen-year-old boy again, waiting to take his driving test. Inside the gloves, my hands were clammy and I could feel my adrenalin pumping.[21]

It was a familiar sensation. On *Torchwood*, especially during series two, I did most of the driving for shots that didn't require a stunt driver. This meant I was in control of the Torchwood SUV quite a lot. Burn didn't like to drive the SUV, as he thought it too difficult to handle; and Evie didn't like to drive fast, which was usually a prerequisite. Gareth didn't have any interest at all in getting behind the wheel, and neither did Naoko, so I – willingly, excitedly and possibly a touch too enthusiastically – always stepped up to the plate … wheel.

My favourite drive time in the Torchwood SUV was a scene in the 'Meat' episode. The entire crew was set up in a stretch of abandoned road that used to provide truck access for a company based near the docks in Cardiff. There was no traffic for the entire stretch of road. This meant that the opening truck accident, where the 'meat' is first discovered, could be set up across the full two lanes.

The four of us piled into the SUV. Burn was riding shotgun, holding the radio that cued me to drive into the scene, and Gareth and Eve climbed in the back.[22] I loved reversing quickly down the stretch of road to get into position and then – wait for it … 'Action!' – hitting the gas and racing from 0 to 50 mph in a short distance, before screeching to a stop on the director's mark. It was like drag racing with my dad's really expensive car.

The driving scenes ended up being the most fun I had that day because what no one had realized was that directly next to the

21 Love that feeling!
22 I think we may have left Coco at the Hub.

abandoned road was a field of pollinating ragweed. By early afternoon, most of the crew and a number of us in the cast were lined up under the make-up tents with red, itchy eyes and runny noses. The whole scene looked as if it was a set-up for an episode.

Whenever I drove for a scene, if a crew person could be spared, he or she would hide in the rear of the SUV and give me directions from inside the car. Late one night, when Clare and I were driving to Sully from Birmingham after a week of pantos, I *wished* we'd had someone giving directions from the back seat.

The M5 was completely shut down because of an accident. I did not want to spend the night stranded in traffic, so I pulled off the motorway and headed into the country. I told Clare to call Scott, who was already at home in Sully, and I asked him via Clare to guide us home. Scott loves globes and maps and anything with a legend, so he decided to navigate us home using Google Earth. I would have been faster having Clare use the stars to guide us.

Suddenly, in my Range Rover, I was careening through country lanes and winding roads originally designed for sheep.[23] I was tired, crabby and my Range Rover was getting its paint scratched. Needless to say, I started shouting at Scott via Clare while Scott returned the shouting back to me via Clare, who then started to shout at both of us for shouting at her. God, we needed a director in the back seat; if we'd been driving in the Torchwood SUV, alien technology might well have got us home with a lot less yelling involved.

I loved the Torchwood SUV, and, before it went to wherever discarded BBC cars go after they've disappeared from a series,[24] I was asked if I'd like to buy it. Given my passion for cars, I guess that wasn't too surprising. I did think about it for a few minutes, but decided, in the end, that a Dalek at my house was enough.

Here's another trivia fact for you for when you're playing 'I've Wasted My Life Watching TV, But I'm Happy': the Porsche that Jack

---

23 One sheep, and, if he was lucky, maybe a single, slim shepherd.
24 A crew member probably drives them into the TARDIS and then they're gone forever.

steals and drives during Day Three of 'Children of Earth' was my own car, used just for that episode.

While I turned down the purchase of the Torchwood SUV, I never forgot how to make many of the sudden stops and quick starts that filming in it had taught me. It was just as well – because I needed all my skills and wits about me the day I went rally driving.

During the filming of my practice rally run and my official timed ones on *Fifth Gear*, Tiff rode next to me in the car. After each run, I'm proud to share that he said I was a natural. When we drove to the open area near the course to practise stopping, skidding, turning and jumping, I actually forgot I was being filmed for a television show and I soaked up all of Tiff's insights and advice as if my life depended on it. As it turned out, it did.

On my first timed lap, I came in at 1:33. Tiff threw down the gauntlet and asked if I 'wanted to try to beat my own time'. Them are fighting words to me. Of course I did.

With Tiff reading aloud my pace notes from the initial timed run, I took the first two turns well, but I was coming into the third too fast. I skidded round the final curve too tightly and I lost control of the car. There was nothing I could do. As you can see on camera if you watch the show, I released the wheel and left the fate of Tiff and myself in the hands of the car god.[25]

We flipped three full rotations over the edge of the hill and slid down an embankment. For a fleeting moment, I did think I was in trouble, and that this jaunt in the countryside wasn't going to end well, but then I looked at Tiff and he was grinning, and when we landed, I started laughing, too.[26] We bounced hard on our wheels, and the car came to a really forceful stop. Tiff and I unbuckled quickly.

As I climbed from the wrecked car, I could see the crew rushing down the hill towards us, including Gav and Rhys, who was still filming. Gavin told me later that his heart stopped when he saw the car flip, and Rhys said his legs had felt like all the bones had been removed.

[25] Henry Ford.
[26] After swearing a few times into the camera.

When I got home that evening, that was pretty much what my mum threatened to do to me if I ever did something like this rally drive again. She gave me hell for about twenty minutes – after she'd checked me out herself and was reassured that I really was fine.[27]

After the crash, emergency personnel surrounded us almost immediately. As a precaution, I insisted a paramedic wash out my eyes. The camera inside the car had bounced loose a bit as we flipped, and the arm it was attached to had shattered the windscreen into tiny pieces, many of which ended up on Tiff and me.

After twenty-six years behind the wheel and twenty-three years in the entertainment business, I had finally made it onto a car show, but I went from first to *Fifth* and skipped *Top Gear*.

Oh, and don't tell my mum, but this Speed Racer may well do the whole rally race driving thing again.

[27] Even at forty-two, I'm still her baby.

`Two Men and Their Dogs´

There's an old gay saying[1] that not much comes between a gay man and his dog. This distinct bond has been written about a lot, and it's not difficult to see why. In a society that has not always condoned gay men having children, our dog, or in my case dogs, can be akin to having kids. And because many gay men, sadly, still find themselves ostracized from their families, a dog can be the one companion who loves unconditionally and wholeheartedly. I'm not saying that gay men love their dogs more deeply than other dog lovers, but dogs do play a role in our lives that is remarkable if not unique.

Scott and I pamper our dogs, we buy them toys[2] and, when we can, we travel with them. A few days before Harris joined our family, I was so excited I dashed into the Louis Vuitton store on Bond Street and bought an outrageously expensive doggy carrier. Oh my God, it was so fabulous I wanted to crawl inside and take a nap. When we brought Harris home, I set the carrier out on the floor and presented it to him. Ta da!

He stared at it. Sniffed at it. Tentatively, he stepped inside. I was already planning where I'd go with the LV on my arm and Harris snuggling inside. He sniffed around for a few minutes inside the carrier, and then he quickly backed himself out. He stared up at me with an expression that can only be described as saying, 'Well, that was a big waste of your money.' In the entire course of his puppyhood, I was able to get him inside the LV only one other time, and that was after pulling a Hansel-and-Gretel move and lining the interior with treats.

---

[1] Or maybe it's a gay old saying?
[2] I have enough to open a Pets R Us.

Our dogs not only have the run of our homes, but also of our lives, and when we lose them, we grieve deeply because we know in our hearts we've lost much more than just a pet. Between 14 March 2007 and 6 May 2008, Scott and I had to say goodbye to three dear family members: Penny, Tiger and Lewis.

Miss Moneypenny was the first dog I owned as a grown-up person living independently, without needing the permission of a parent to have, and when she died, her loss was devastating. Penny's health had been failing for quite a while before she died. She was nineteen and she was getting a bit leaky and pretty senile.[3] Her eyesight was severely diminished, and she moved only when necessary. But the vet always told me that as long as she was wagging her tail and she was eating well, then she was not in distress. And I clung on to that wisdom for as long as I could.

When Penny began to have difficulty getting outside on her own, I bought her doggy diapers and a little doggy stroller. Every night before bed, I'd wheel her out of my Cardiff flat and into the elevator, with Tiger and Lewis tagging along behind, and we'd all troop onto the Roald Dahl Way at Cardiff Bay, where we'd take a stroll. I'm sure we made quite a sight – a man, two dogs and a beautiful blonde spaniel stretched out in a padded stroller, leading the way.

One night, Scott and I came home after dinner and Penny was having seizures. We knew it was time to do the one thing I did not want to do: say goodbye to one of the first loves of my life. Before there was Scott, before there was fame, before there were any other dogs, there was Penny. She'd grown from a puppy to a mother[4] to the Grande Dame of my household. As I established myself in the theatre world and then in television, Penny shared in all my successes.

Scott drove to the vet's office while I sat in the back seat, with Penny wrapped in her favourite blanket on my lap. In the car, she had another seizure, and I did my best to hold her even tighter. She nestled into my lap for a few minutes, and then the weirdest thing happened. She

---

[3] Actually, she was a lot leaky, poor thing.
[4] Lewis was her son. She had a total of eight puppies in her lifetime.

suddenly let out a sad, mournful howl, as if she knew death was near. I'm not sure how Scott and I made it to the vet's office through our tears.

Penny's favourite treat was fresh chicken slices from M&S. The day before she died, Scott had wanted to make Penny feel better, and he'd given her more chicken slices than she usually ate. As we were driving to the vet's, Scott tried to tell me through his sobs that he may have inadvertently killed her with his sliced chicken.[5]

When the vet was ready to give Penny the injection, I cupped her little head in my hands, and I put my face right up close to her snout. I gently blew my breath into her face and I whispered over and over to her she was a good girl, my good girl. I knew Penny couldn't see me clearly anymore, but until she slipped away, I made sure she could smell me, and that she knew I was with her until her end.

All our dogs have had very distinctive personalities. Of the three in the family now, Harris is the baby brother of the crew. He's black and sleek, with boundless energy. He charges into everything – including regularly raiding the laundry baskets for socks and underwear that Scott and I later find spread across the lawn or dropped in the pool.

Charlie, our newest rescue dog, is the eldest, and is certainly the most neurotic of the three. He freaks at loud noises and is frightened of any confrontations with other dogs. When Harris is being too rambunctious, Charlie looks down his long regal nose at him, turns, and bounds away.[6]

Captain Jack, our Jack Russell, a rescue from Cardiff Dogs Home, had been abandoned in an apartment and was discovered only because his bark was so loud. Jack is the family thug, and a maniac for playing football. If you bring anything that looks even remotely like a ball into the house, you will have CJ at your feet the entire time, nudging you to play with him.

It most definitely doesn't have to be a real ball. Whenever Carole took a swim in the pool during a recent visit, she'd don a black Speedo swimming cap, which Jack would then chase up and down the length of the pool, barking as he went, because her head looked – to him –

5 I still kid him about this.
6 Charlie is very sensitive. He's our gay dog.

like a ball skimming across the water. When she turned, he'd try to bite at her noggin. It was hilarious to watch.[7]

Tiger, a rescue from Dogs Trust, joined the Barrowman–Gill household in 2006. He was a gorgeous, red-haired spaniel, and he was certainly the grumpiest dog we ever had. He was only with us for about a year and we did our best to love him madly. Whenever we'd lift Tiger a certain way – to put him in the rear of the car or to help him up on the couch – he'd nip at us. Scott and I always assumed his mild aggressiveness was because of his past experiences. He'd been abandoned at a dogs' home.

The night Tiger died, I'd been filming *Torchwood*. When I came home, I was having a lie-down in the bedroom. Tiger climbed onto the bottom of the bed and settled against my feet.

I've always believed that animals can be more sensitive and more connected to the natural world than we are. As many of you may know, I'm also very superstitious – and what happened next has always seemed like an omen to me. As I lay on my bed napping, a hawk swooped across the bay and flew against my window. I sat up, startled, and when I did, I noticed that Tiger was panting heavily. When I checked his gums, they were very pale. I knew he was in distress.

Scott and I took Tiger to the clinic immediately. One of the worst moments for me as a dog owner was when I had to leave Tiger overnight in that stark vet's cage. I didn't want him to think he was being abandoned all over again. As I reluctantly made my way out of the clinic, I kept calling back to him that we'd return, and that when he was well, we'd bring him home. I promised.

The next day, after exploratory surgery, the vet called and told us that Tiger was riddled with tumours. He'd likely been bleeding internally for a while. This explained why he'd always been so sensitive when we touched him. Poor Tiger had been ill for months. He died on the operating table that night, and never got to come home. I felt terrible about that for weeks afterwards.

---

[7] Though not quite so hilarious for Carole, who kept getting slightly mauled at every turn.

Scott was alone with Lewis when he died seven months later. I was filming *I'd Do Anything* and I was on a training mission with all the Nancy contestants in central London.

Lewis had been sick for about a year with various cancerous tumours. He'd been having regular blood transfusions and glucose injections and all sorts of other treatments, and, bless him, he kept fighting back. Some nights, when he seemed to be fading away, Scott would pour a couple of teaspoonfuls of thick sweet yoghurt onto his hand, and Lewis would lick up every drop and then almost immediately he'd rally for a few hours. For a long while, Scott had been the primary care-giver for Lewis in London because I was filming *Torchwood* in Cardiff and was travelling back and forth a lot.

The day before Lewis died, Scott had come home and found Lewis particularly lethargic. He packed him up and headed to the vet, hoping another transfusion might help, but the next morning, when Scott went in to collect Lewis, the vet told Scott that Lewis had had a seizure in the night, from a blood clot that had migrated to his brain.

While I was finishing up filming the segment with the Nancy contestants – on a boat on the Thames, out of phone reach – Scott was saying his final goodbyes to Lewis. Scott remembers that Lewis was lying on his side in the vet's cage, paddling his legs in the air like he was trying desperately to get up and escape out of there. Lewis looked so distressed that Scott knew he had to make this decision for Lewis as quickly as possible, even if it meant that I couldn't be there with them. Scott climbed into the cage next to Lewis and as the drugs dripped into Lewis's line, Scott recited in his ear all the silly gibberish phrases that had been their secret language for twelve years.

When Scott was finally able to reach me on the boat, we'd just docked. I told the contestants what was happening and Jodie said, 'Fuck this stuff and go to your family.' I knew then for sure she was something special.

The loss of Penny and Tiger devastated both Scott and me, but Scott was especially gutted by the swift deterioration in Lewis's health and his death. This is one of the reasons why one of our newest family members, Harris – a black spaniel like Lewis – is being completely spoiled by Scott.

Penny, Tiger and Lewis were cremated. We sprinkled most of their ashes in all the places they loved in Florida and in London, and the rest we spread under a tree in our garden in Wales. We miss them all, and feel blessed that they enriched our lives.

CHAPTER TWELVE

'A NIGHTINGALE SANG IN BERKELEY SQUARE'

★

'You're an impossible thing, Jack.'

The Doctor
'Last of the Time Lords', *Doctor Who*

Six and a half amazing things about playing Captain Jack

1 He has changed my life.

2 He has touched the lives of millions.

3 He got me a ticket to ride in the TARDIS (and to straddle it).

4 He brought me face-to-face with Davros (still get chills).

5 He introduced me to 'Sarah Jane'.

6 He introduced me to Catherine Tate.

6½ And did I mention I got to be in, on and near the TARDIS?

Prometheus, the Greek god, stole fire from Zeus, gave it to humans, and allowed them to use it to establish civilization. Because, you know, it's hard to invent the wheel, write poetry, make art, sing songs and dance when you can't cook your dinner and your toes are numb. Because of Prometheus's generosity – the whole bringing 'light' to humans thing – ordinary men and women back in the days of myths and stories considered him to be a pretty good god.

Unfortunately for Prometheus, Zeus was pissed at his disloyalty and his challenge to authority. Prometheus had to be punished. Poor Prometheus was chained to a big rock, where an eagle was sent to eat his liver.[1] As if this wasn't bad enough, because Prometheus was immortal, every day his liver regenerated and the eagle would swoop back and have another nosh.

As Captain Jack's character has developed over the years, I think he's becoming a twenty-first-century Prometheus, and in 'Children of Earth', the allusions and connections are even stronger. Both Prometheus and Jack are cunning, smart and immortal.

Before hard-core Woodies protest, yes, I know the debate. Technically, Jack is not immortal because he can die … he just doesn't stay dead. He rises, and he resurrects, and I realize that this may make him more Christ-like than Promethean, but I think that's quibbling. Plus, I think the darker, roguish qualities in Jack's nature make him more rebel than angel; however, I wouldn't rule out Russell T. Davies's connotations of either in Jack's make-up. After all, every culture from ancient times onwards has myths of men and women who sacrifice themselves for the good of others and then reappear, resurrect, or – like the Doctor – regenerate.

[1] I love liver. Especially sautéed with onions. Yum.

To continue: in one version of the myth, Prometheus is chained naked to a rock face. In 'Children of Earth', Jack is chained naked to a rock wall. This was a gruelling scene to film, mostly because, although I could struggle against the chains, I had to be held in one place.

I made sure I had some fun with these nude scenes too, though.[2] Before the filming of series three began, Euros Lyn, the director, asked me if I would be okay getting naked on camera.[3] If you've watched 'Children of Earth', you'll know that Jack is naked for most of the sequence that begins in the military jail cell and ends in the quarry where Jack, with Ianto's help, breaks out of his tomb.[4]

The scenes in the jail cell were filmed first, and a few days before we were due to begin, Ray Holman, *Torchwood*'s costume designer, asked me if I wanted a jock.[5] As you may know, I have no issues about baring my bum, but I did think about it for a beat or two in deference to my colleagues and the crew. However, in part of the sequence, viewers would see Jack in *all* his glory from behind. Ray, Euros and I therefore decided that if I were to wear a flesh-coloured jock, the strap of the jock would need to be digitally altered in post-production, so as not to affect the aesthetic of the scene.[6] So why bother? The three of us concluded it wasn't worth the hassle, and I declined Ray's offer.

(As it turned out, though, costume and I still had to do a little tucking on the day of the shoot, because when Jack rises from the ashes and faces Gwen, Ianto and Rhys, 'my boys' were clearly visible.)

The temperature on the day we were set to film was typical of the Cardiff climate: bloody cold. After the set designers did their initial prep work of the scene, they realized the problem I was going to have was with a different set of balls – the balls of my feet. The rocks were razor-sharp, and after Jack emerges from his tomb,[7] he must walk barefoot towards Gwen, Ianto and Rhys.

2 Unlike me, I know.
3 Bless. He had no idea.
4 Another biblical allusion, anyone?
5 To wear.
6 To say nothing of my arse.
7 Or womb?

While the cameras weren't rolling, a strategically placed towel covered my bare bits. As far as Gareth, Kai Owen (who plays Rhys) and Eve were concerned, underneath that towel was a jock – worn to protect their innocent eyes when Jack rises up[8] from the rubble and walks towards them.

Cameras roll. Sound runs. Action.

Jack climbs naked out of the rubble and walks towards his rescuers, who, if you watch the scene very carefully, are not just smiling broadly because they're thrilled that Jack is back and in one complete piece, but because I failed to tell them[9] that I had decided not to wear a jock. Their expressions are priceless, and they get even better when they try not to acknowledge that I have Always sanitary towels with trimmed wings stuck to the bottom of my feet.

The relationship between Jack and Ianto has grown over the series to become one of the strongest plot threads that you'll see in any dramatic TV show, and I'm so proud to be part of it given that it's between two men. In 'Children of Earth', the subplot and the banter surrounding Jack and Ianto's couple status brought humour and pathos to the episodes. I particularly loved the fact that in 'Children of Earth', the writers presented viewers with two distinct relationships at different points in their evolution – Rhys and Gwen contemplating buying a house and Gwen's pregnancy, and Jack and Ianto becoming a more public couple – and each was given the same emotional depth.

Fans have been devastated by Ianto's death and the tearing asunder of this iconic TV relationship. As a fan and as Captain Jack, I share their sadness, I really do – but I also like to think that Ianto and Jack's groundbreaking relationship will have set precedents for similar partnerships to be created in other TV shows. Plus, never underestimate the power of an imagination, especially Russell's. Who knows what (or who) is in Jack's future?

Nevertheless, the filming of the scene in which Gwen identifies Jack and Ianto's bodies was a heartbreaking one to film for the three of us.

[8] Cheeky!
[9] Oops.

The moment needed lots of tissues and a bit of humour to get Gareth, Eve and me through it.

Cameras roll. Sound runs. Action.

Gwen kneels next to Jack's draped body, which is spread out among all the dead from the 456's attack on Thames House.[10] She steels herself against what she's going to find. She gently lifts back the sheet. And I pop up in a fake beard and moustache, belting out 'Everything's Coming Up Roses' – with jazz hands.

Another poignant and brilliant experience I've had on a set as Captain Jack was the filming of 'Journey's End': the finale of *Doctor Who* series four. All the Doctor's companions – Catherine Tate's Donna, Billie Piper's Rose, Noel Clarke's Mickey, Freema Agyeman's Martha, Elisabeth Sladen's Sarah Jane, and Jack – came back to help the Doctor save the world … again.

I never feel complacent about filming on *Doctor Who* – because no matter how many times I'm invited back, for a big or small part, I'm thrilled. I love the fact that Captain Jack has become a mate of the Doctor. Every time I step on the *Doctor Who* set, time morphs for me to late on a Sunday night in front of a TV in a small suburb of Chicago, and I'm 'Wee John' curled up on the couch – with a cushion poised for maximum scare coverage – watching the Doctor battle Daleks, Autons and Davros.

For me, playing Captain Jack on this episode in particular, and in the series in general, has given me many memorable moments. One such was when all the companions were standing unified on the TARDIS, and we were all controlling it. Unless there's some kind of special anniversary episode in the future, when we all lumber onto the set with our zimmers leading a charge, such a gathering will never be seen on the TARDIS again.

Another was the moment when Sarah Jane and Jack came face-to-face with Davros. For my money, Davros was always more diabolical

---

[10] Did you notice that the wide tracking shot of the warehouse at the end of this scene mirrors the famous shot of the Atlanta railway station in *Gone with the Wind*? Loved that, Euros!

than the Master, darker than Darth Vader, and more evil than the Joker. Davros is the pinnacle of villainy, and Jack and the Doctor kicked his arse. How cool was that?

I realize that writing this next paragraph may plunge me even deeper into the valleys of geekdom,[11] but here goes anyway. I think the scene where Davros shoots Jack and he falls, and the Doctor, and everyone else watching, knows that Jack can't die, is an immeasurably important one when it comes to the Doctor's perception of Jack and their relationship. By using Jack in this way, the Doctor is finally admitting that Jack may not be a completely 'impossible thing' after all. The Doctor has finally accepted Jack for who he is – no longer only a 'fixed point in time and space', but a complex, deeply flawed, compassionate … human being. As a *Doctor Who* fan, filming this scene was like playing with live action figures – and I was one of them.[12]

Liz Sladen, who plays Sarah Jane, and I were standing together on set when Davros first came out from effects. Instinctively, I grabbed her hand and immediately she squeezed mine back. Davros freaked out both of us, and for a few seconds we stood and stared in terror as he moved in closer and began to speak.

The first time I met Liz was a couple of years earlier: I was in the lift going up to my flat in Cardiff Bay, which was also where she lived when she was filming *The Sarah Jane Adventures*. I apologized for my gushing even before I'd gushed.

'I'm really pleased to meet you. I'm a bit gobsmacked that I'm standing in front of Sarah Jane.'

'The feeling's mutual,' she replied. 'I love Captain Jack and John Barrowman.'

I offered that maybe Jack could do some work on *The Sarah Jane Adventures* some day, because I think they'd have good fun together, and I meant it. They would have an intriguing chemistry because Sarah Jane doesn't like or use violence and, well, Jack does.

Then there was the day I first met Catherine Tate, on the *Doctor*

---

[11] A place I adore.
[12] Just had a fan-gasm!

Who set. One of the ADs said, 'Catherine, this is John Barrowman.'

I couldn't help myself. I walked right up to her and said, 'Aw … rieeght,' mimicking the yob character she made famous from *The Catherine Tate Show*.

I regretted it immediately. I wished for a black hole to open up and swallow me right there – or, better yet, I thought about crawling inside the TARDIS, seeing the light and letting myself be disintegrated. Instead, I put my head in my hands, and moaned.

David Tennant stepped up next to me, and in a hushed voice he said, 'Don't worry. We've all done it.'

Catherine knew how iconic her comedy characters had become and she was fine with an occasional burst of dialogue or antics from her show seeping onto the set. She and I had a good laugh when we were working together.[13] She was naturally funny, plus she loved to sing. In fact, one day, after a particularly rousing rendition of '9 to 5' from Catherine,[14] I rang Trevor Jackson at Sir Cameron Mackintosh's office. I let him know that if there was ever another anniversary performance of *Les Mis*, Catherine would like to play Madame Thénardier. In fact, Catherine's a closet musical-theatre fan. Loves a bit of the sparkle, does our Catherine.[15]

Of course, changes are afoot on *Doctor Who*. I've no doubt when we look back on the new Doctor's first exploits, we'll all remember that we may have vented a bit about Matt Smith and how he's just not like David, but sometime after those initial little rants, we'll have adjusted and grown to love him, and we'll be travelling with our new Doctor wherever he may take us. It's the nature of the character that change is inevitable.

In my mind, Christopher Eccleston may have been the Doctor who launched Captain Jack, but David Tennant was my Doctor, the one I sailed with. Give me a moment or two, please.

The first time I met the new Doctor, Matt Smith, he'd come to the

---

13 You'd have to be dead not to.

14 She's a huge Dolly Parton fan.

15 Who, dear? Me, dear? Love a bit of sparkle, dear? Yes, dear. Thank you, dear!

BBC Television Centre in London to meet with the public-relations department. I was in the same office, reviewing my interview schedule for *Tonight's the Night*. I introduced myself and we chatted for about ten minutes. He said he'd love for his Doctor's and Jack's paths to cross in their futures. We laughed about a couple of our favourite *Doctor Who* moments, I wished him great success, and he left. As soon as he disappeared[16] down the hall, I turned to the others in the office and said, 'I feel as if I just cheated on David.'

The year between early 2007 and mid 2008 became 'the year of awful endings' for me. Russell T. Davies and Julie Gardner announced they were stepping away from the helm of *Doctor Who*; David Tennant revealed he was moving on to other galaxies; and, as I've mentioned, three of my beloved dogs passed away.

David's moving on made me melancholy for a while. I have to admit his leaving felt a bit like the other brother in the family leaving home. But then I realized that I love the show, I love David, and in the end every Doctor leaves us. David had lots of other things he wanted to do in the entertainment business, and I could understand and completely respect that.

When David came to see my 'An Evening with John Barrowman' concert in Cardiff, I made sure he was in a private box[17] because otherwise he'd have been mobbed. Playing the Doctor has changed his life, as much as playing Jack has changed mine, and David's genuineness and his compassion have never faltered.

For example, when it was announced this past year that mobile-phone numbers were going to be published, David texted all his friends who were actors, telling us which website to visit to have our numbers removed. I thought it was so sweet that he'd think about all of us in that way. That's the kind of dish we share on *Doctor Who*.

I was not surprised at Russell's announcement to turn the Doctor's universe over to Steven Moffat, a great writer who helped me to find Jack's voice. Russell and I are alike in many ways and one of our

---

[16] He didn't actually vanish. He took the elevator.
[17] Not the TARDIS.

similarities is that we not only embrace fresh challenges, but we actively seek them out. For Russell, like David, it was time to move on to something new. I must admit, however, that the part of his news that did come as a shock was learning that his new challenge might take him to work in the US.

I'd love to be sitting at an outdoor table at The Ivy in LA when Russell takes a meeting with a group of American producers and cuts right through their Hollywood bullshit. Russell doesn't conform to anyone's expectations but his own, and, like his writing, he sees a metaphor in most things, and most people's metaphors don't fit his expansive and creative way of thinking.

Russell's co-executive producer on *Doctor Who* and *Torchwood*, Julie Gardner, moved to the US to run BBC Worldwide, so I imagine Russell will be collaborating again with Julie.[18] If you want drama that pushes boundaries and is brilliantly written, you want Russell T. Davies on your script.

I'm never surprised when people move on. When I think back to some of my closing nights in the West End, I can still see two or three people who would sit, sobbing, on the couches in the corner, or stand gutting themselves at the bar, crying floods because the show had ended and things would never be the same again. I've never been like that. I get emotional, but I'll do it over a celebratory glass of champagne – not into a hanky. I'm always moving, and I'm always moving on to the next thing.

One of the newer areas I've moved into recently was to record a series of BBC Radio 4 *Torchwood* specials. The request came from BBC Radio through Gavin. Funnily enough, it arrived not long after I'd had an experience that related to the plot of the radio script.

I'd been invited to CERN in Geneva, Switzerland, by Royal Society Research Fellow, brilliant physicist, ex-D:Ream keyboard player, and really cool guy, Brian Cox, to visit the Large Hadron Collider[19] – where they hope to recreate and then study the conditions of the universe's creation. Scott and his parents, Sheelagh and Stirling, travelled with

[18] Only great things can come from that.
[19] Known as Alice – like Jack's daughter in 'Children of Earth'.

me, and each of us was able to step inside the collider tunnel itself, which is about seventeen miles long and runs deep underground along the French and Swiss borders.

On behalf of Captain Jack and myself, I planted my feet directly on the spot where the opposing particle beams will collide, recreating the Big Bang and obliterating that fixed point in space and time forever. I felt an incredible rush standing on that spot. In years past, what these scientists are now planning would have been the stuff of science fiction – only seen, perhaps, by Captain Jack in one of his futures – but yet here I was, standing on the site where a mind-blowing reality would take place.

Scott and his folks loved visiting the Hadron Collider at least as much as I did. In fact, for the Gills, I think it's safe to say that this visit to CERN to see the consequences of decades of scientific research, creativity and hard work ranked in their top-five all-time best experiences.

When I read the script for *Torchwood* 'Lost Souls', the first BBC Radio 4 special, I loved it and immediately agreed to sign up. Because of my visit to CERN, I was able to describe vividly to Gareth, Eve and Freema what I'd seen in the collider, helping them to visualize what we were performing.

The day I was in the studio for 'Lost Souls', relating my trip, I had one of those moments when you know it's you speaking, but it's as if you're listening rather than talking. I sounded as if I really knew what I was talking about! I could hear myself describe and explain in 'showbiz words'[20] what it was hoped the collider would achieve and what scientists might learn from it; sadly, three days later I couldn't tell you what I'd had for lunch that day. My brain works that way sometimes when it gets overloaded.[21]

Radio shows are very passive to perform. I had to stand in a room with a microphone, a music stand and my script. The space is dead space; its only ambience the layer of soundproof tiles.[22] I was in the

---

[20] Pithy, pointed, and with a little pizzazz.

[21] According to Carole, that's called being middle-aged. I've cut off her Malteser supply. See how you like that, Miss 'You're Older Than Me'.

[22] All the better for muffling your screams of boredom.

studio most of the time with Eve and Gareth, and, even with the three of us and our history together, we had a hard time getting anything beyond a little mild banter going among us between our takes.

It turned out that *Torchwood* 'Lost Souls' was the most downloaded radio programme on the BBC iPlayer and the most listened-to radio show in the history of BBC Radio 4 – which is why they came back to us and asked if we'd do three more. Of course! It's at times like this that I realize *Torchwood* has become this amazing, worldwide phenomenon. Because it's such an international hit, I don't think Russell and Julie will ever disconnect completely from their *Torchwood* family.

Russell and Julie are now based in Los Angeles, and so their move does, of course, raise the question of who will head up *Torchwood* on the production side. However, given that the show is as big a success in America as it is in the UK, I think that Russell and Julie will continue to be a part of *Torchwood*'s future on both sides of the Atlantic.

The more I get to know Jack's character, and the deeper Russell and his fellow writers for series three (John Fay and James Moran) delved into Jack's psyche and his personal history, the more Jack's relationship to humanity keeps evolving. For me, this depth makes Jack more and more interesting to play, and I think it's one of the reasons why Jack has become so iconic in popular culture. He's not afraid to challenge authority in all of its guises – alien and human – and he's demonstrated over and over again with Torchwood, and as a companion to the Doctor, that he will endure anything to protect and serve humanity. Like Prometheus, Jack is *with* the human race but not *of* the human race.

Do I think about this stuff when I'm playing Jack? Sometimes. Other times, I see these things in Jack's character when I'm watching the completed shows (which I do, the same as all of you), or when I'm reading emails from fans who have been affected in some way by a gesture, a comment, or a story arc involving Jack. For me, Jack has done much more than touch my life; he's changed it completely.

Playing Captain Jack has given me a freedom of choice and a level of clout and credibility in the entertainment business. Let me say it: playing Captain Jack has made me a celebrity. I'm noticed whether I'm running in for dog food to Costco in Cardiff or getting off the plane in South Africa, and I'm embracing and loving every minute of this fame. I have to say here that I have a difficult time listening to famous people,[23] many whose work I admire, whining about being a celebrity, or refusing to acknowledge that they are one, or even suggesting that being a celebrity is some kind of burden they have to bear so that they can continue to perform.

I once heard a famous actor[24] say that being a celebrity is the worst thing that can happen to an actor. First of all, I'm not sure what that means exactly. Was he suggesting that his ability to perform, to be the best he could be in a role, was hampered somehow by his celebrity status? Or was he suggesting that celebrities can't be serious actors? Either way, his statement says more to me about the actor himself than about the challenges of being a celebrity.

Years ago, when I first broke into television, there was a teeny, tiny part of me that said to the other voices in my head that, if I really made it, I might have to deal with the trappings of being famous. It's the nature of popular culture that celebrity status can come with entertainment success. For me, it's one of the possible by-products of being an entertainer, and, because of that, my attitude has been to embrace it, when necessary manage and control it, but above all else not to let it change who I am at my core.

Granted, there are certain things I can't do anymore. Riding public transportation can be difficult, so I have cars.[25] But as far as I'm concerned, being a celebrity has not only provided me with financial and creative freedom, but it's also given me the ability to open up opportunities for my family, friends, strangers and important causes, which might not have been possible before.

All thanks to my hero, Captain Jack Harkness.

[23] You know who I'm talking about.
[24] Not telling …
[25] Oh, the sacrifice.

`Zaza, Elphaba, Tottie and Me'

Most of my knowledge about multiple-personality disorder comes from movies like *Sybil*, *Primal Fear* and *The Incredible Hulk* (which is technically about a double-personality disorder, but you get my point). My pop-culture understanding of what I'm sure in reality is a terrible thing[1] is that the personalities are entirely separate from one another, and usually one is more dominant than the other.

Given that, I've decided my manager, my friend, my co-executive producer of *Tonight's the Night*, and the man who helped map my career with me, Gav Barker, has an alternate-personality disorder. Alternate not multiple because multiple suggests the whole 'look away from the camera, look back, and suddenly – yikes! – it's a different person' disorder. Not the case with Gav. His main personality shares space with all his alternate ones.

His first alternate is Olivia Obvious. She makes me laugh so she's one of my favourites. If I'm out somewhere with Gav – at a restaurant, say, or just walking along the streets of London or LA – and I say to him, 'Check out that hot guy over there,' Gav cannot check out that hot guy over there the way most of us could, should and would.[2] Gav can't give the time-honoured surreptitious glance, or the coy look over the shoulder, or even the peek from behind a magazine. Not if his life depended on it.

Instead, Gav Barker becomes Olivia Obvious. He might as well get up, walk across the room and eyeball the hottie at a three-inch distance from head to toe, including all the fun parts in between, for

---

[1] Or is it 'things', plural?

[2] Whether man or woman, the 'checking out a hottie' rules are the same.

all the subtlety he has in these situations. Olivia's tongue might as well hang out as she pants. When Olivia raises her head, I put mine in my hands.

Then there's the personality that appears most often with me on the phone or via email. Gav will say: 'You have got to give me an answer to this email right now!' or 'This question needs answering immediately because we need to move on this,' or 'You must correct this in that statement you made!' Let me introduce you to Patricia Pedantic. Patricia raises her head an awful lot when I have two or three significant projects running at the same time.

Patricia's close friend and confidante is Betty Bitchy, who tends to show her side most when Gav's driving. When someone cuts him up in traffic, Betty Bitchy appears. When someone is moving too slow, Betty takes over. Betty is a machine gun: her words fast and furious, her tongue a lethal weapon.

Alison Angry doesn't make an appearance very often, which is a good thing, but I can tell when Gav's about to lose it, and, in my own helpful way, I'll say, 'I see Alison's coming out?' Calms her down right away. Sometimes, when Gav gets too dogmatic about something and I see Alison in the wings, I'll say, 'Why don't you invite Patricia Pedantic to come out instead?'

This tendency of mine to give nicknames is one that was nurtured when I was growing up in the States, where everyone had one. There was BJ from *BJ and the Bear*, the Fonz in *Happy Days*, Bo in *The Dukes of Hazzard*, Mork[3] in *Mork and Mindy*, Gopher on *The Love Boat*, Ponch in *CHiPs* and, by far the father of them all, J. R. in *Dallas*.

In my family, none of us had a nickname. We weren't allowed. In fact, my parents were not afraid to chastise anyone who shortened any one of our names: 'That's not what we christened him,' they'd say, and then they'd demand a retraction. This whole purity-of-name notion changed when we stepped off the plane in Chicago. Suddenly, my brother Andrew was Andy to most of his friends and 'Wee John' stuck to me.

---

[3] You don't know – this may have been a nickname on Planet Ork.

For different reasons, my gran, Murn, who'd had at least one stroke by the time she first met Kevin, my brother-in-law, in 1980, always called him Gavin.[4] She couldn't get her tongue to say what I'm sure she knew in her head was Kevin. It always came out as 'Gavin'.

I thought this was hysterical. Remember, I was thirteen. I had a time-honoured duty to fulfil as a younger brother, plus a fascination with nicknames. I called him Gavin too. This, of course, has stuck, and every now and then, in memory of Murn,[5] I'll address Kevin as Gavin. I'm the only one who does, and he always answers.

I give nicknames to everyone I work with and those names often stick well beyond the duration of our working relationship. I labelled one of my J8 dancers from *Tonight's the Night* 'Jennie Fabulous', and that's what everyone called her on set. When she joined me on tour, I overheard someone introduce her to the tour crew as 'Jennie Fabulous'.

On *Torchwood*, we all had nicknames for each other; I was 'Jinny Baza'.[6] This past summer, I covered for Zoë Ball on her Saturday-morning show on BBC Radio 2 when she was on vacation, and I introduced myself as 'the Baza' a couple of times. 'Jinny' received a lot of listener texts too.

I have nicknames for my mum and dad now as well. My mum is known fondly around the house as 'Miriam'. This nickname came about after the first few months of our living in the States. My parents often had a hard time getting people to listen to exactly what they were saying, for their new neighbours were often distracted by their, at that time, very thick Scottish accents. For some reason, whenever my mum would introduce herself as 'Marion Barrowman', the person she was meeting always thought she was saying 'Miriam Barrowman'. The name stuck. She's 'Miriam', and my dad is 'Faither' (to be said with aforementioned Glasgow accent) or 'Big John', which my mum calls him frequently if both he and I are in the vicinity. This way, she

---

[4] No connection at all to the Olivia-Patricia-Alison Gav.

[5] I'm a grown man. I'd never call him 'Gavin' just for fun.

[6] For JB.

can distinguish who she's calling for and avoid saying, 'Wee John', which I hate.[7]

One of my favourite nicknames of all time is Carole's, mainly because it came to her inadvertently through my misbehaviour. The name has stuck to her not only with me, but also with every member of the extended Barrowman and Casey clans. I suppose it's not really a nickname since, by definition, it's longer than her given name, but – oh, who cares, here's the story.

The night before Carole's wedding in the August of 1982, her soon-to-be in-laws, Bud[8] and Lois Casey, held the groom's dinner[9] at Joliet Country Club, one of my infamous teenage haunts. I was a groomsman at the wedding, and I was also set to play my flute while guests were seated in the church. I had responsibilities.

Kevin, the groom, is from a large family, including two brothers (Kerry and Kelley) and three sisters (Kim, Kristi and Kolleen) and a busload, literally, of cousins, who all travelled down to the wedding from Minnesota. Many of them were invited to the groom's dinner. Needless to say, it was a terrific party, especially because Kelley, Kevin's youngest brother, and I turned out to be the same age – read underage back then – and the bar was an open one. Plus, I had the advantage of knowing the guys serving the drinks (from my occasional vodka-tonic charges on my dad's country-club tab,[10] when I hung out at the swimming pool on summer vacation), so the booze was flowing freely.

At some point, after dinner but before speeches started, Carole noticed that her youngest brother was nowhere in the dining room. When she found Kelley and me in the bar, let's just say, a little lubricated, she lost it. '*You* have responsibilities,' she hissed at me, oh so delicately.

My response – which is the one that everyone loves to remind her

[7] Well, wouldn't you rather be 'Big John' than 'Wee John'?

[8] His family nickname because his brother couldn't pronounce 'Donald'.

[9] This is an American tradition: the groom's parents host a meal for the wedding party the night before the nuptials.

[10] Children, I was severely punished every time I did this.

about – was yelled across the bar in pure brilliant Scottish, so practise rolling your 'r's before you say it. 'Carole, you're not my mother!'

My nicknames for Scott are Scottie – used mostly at home when I want him to fold the washing, empty the dishwasher or bring me some crisps – and Tottie, when I want ... never mind.

The family member with whom I share the most nicknames, though, is Clare.[11] She and I, in fact, have a kind of secret language with each other.[12] All our nicknames have something to do with what we're currently listening to, or are watching on television, or have seen at the theatre.

The most recent names that have lasted the longest with us are Elphaba, which we use to address each other, and which started minutes after seeing *Wicked* together in the West End; and, for me, Tracy Turnblad (from *Hairspray*, which Clare and I both love; we know the lyrics to *every* song).

One of the performance wishes that I granted on *Tonight's the Night* belonged to a young woman – a hairdresser whose mum had died of cancer when she was quite little – who wanted to sing 'Good Morning Baltimore' with the cast of *Hairspray*. On the Sunday night when we taped the performance, it was all I could do to keep myself from jumping onstage with them.

Finally, the newest additions to my personal nickname repertoire are 'Zaza' and 'Krystle'[13]. These relate to the persona of my latest role, Albin, and were created when I stepped into his stilettos in *La Cage aux Folles* in the West End in September 2009 (check out the picture section to see a photo of me in costume).

Zaza is a red-headed Ann-Margret lookalike with a set of gams that could stop traffic ... and they did. When Zaza was introduced to the public at a press photo shoot at the Menier Chocolate Factory in London in July 2009, she felt restricted by the photographer's forties-style calendar-girl poses. Zaza was not to be contained. She strutted the

[11] Clare and I also name all her handbags – gay uncle, remember? – but those would take up a whole section of their own.

[12] If I shared, well, it wouldn't be our secret anymore, would it?

[13] Of the Denver Carringtons.

whole entourage outside, took her 'bootay' onto the streets of London, and proceeded not so much to hail a couple of cabs as seduce them to stop.

Krystle, on the other hand, resembles her *Dynasty* namesake with her chic blonde looks and her restrained demeanour. Krystle is poised and pretty to Zaza's sassy and sexy: both represent two of the drag characters that make up Albin's repertoire at the nightclub La Cage aux Folles.

I know you all would have a fabulous time with either gal. If you're planning high tea at Harrods, Krystle will be entertaining company, but if you're looking for a high time at The Shadow Lounge in Soho, you'll need Zaza, dahling!

Jinny Baza, over and out.

CHAPTER THIRTEEN

'DESTINATION ANYWHERE'

'Here's to you … Mrs Barrowman.'

(With my apologies to Simon and Garfunkel.)

Six things I love to do on holiday

1 Not much of anything (even that's too much).

2 Avoid sitting too close to Scott on the plane.

3 Participate in local customs (unless they involve bloodletting or sautéed crocodile).

4 Shop for souvenirs (beads a requirement; bartering optional).

5 Send cheesy postcards (with added 'X's to show my location).

6 Play Marco Polo (mudslides included).

I love to go on trips with Scott, but he is not my favourite person to travel with. Once I get myself situated on a plane, I like to be left alone. On international flights, I take a black Louis Vuitton carry-on bag on board with me. My LV has everything in it I may need to occupy me during the journey: my computer, a couple of movies or a TV series on DVD that I want to catch up with,[1] a book,[2] a change of clothes, every charger for every portable electronic device I own, contact lenses and solution, my toothbrush ... and its charger, throat lozenges, Polysporin, a sleeping pill, chewable vitamin C, chewing gum, allergy nasal spray for Scott, my iPod, my BlackBerry, my Bose headphones, and my pillow.

When Scott travels, he carries a backpack. Inside, he tucks three or four clean hankies, two or three books, his iPhone, and the daily newspapers that he grabbed when we left the house, which, when we get settled, he spreads across his lap, the table, and usually well into my space.

Move over!

Scott is a travel fidget. He's the person you hate sitting behind, in front of or next to you, and when I write 'you', I really mean me. He stretches, adjusts, pokes, prods, stretches and adjusts, again and again. The annoyance of travelling with Scott is one of the reasons that, as soon as I could afford the extra expense, I paid for us to travel British Airways business class or Virgin upper class: that way, I get my own little pod, with walls and space to spread out, and Scott can't get too close.

Like many British families, Scott and I plan a trip together every year. Granted, it's not the only time we may travel together, but once a year we do organize a proper family vacation.

[1] On my last trip, I took *30 Rock* and *Entourage*.
[2] On my last trip, I took Joe Hill's *Heart-Shaped Box*.

In 2008 and 2009, I made a number of trips to America for work, including to Comic-Con in San Diego. If Scott is available, he'll join me on these sorts of jaunts. When we're together in LA, we stay at Le Montrose in West Hollywood. The hotel is in the neighbourhood where I used to live when I was filming Aaron Spelling's *Titans* in 2000. West Hollywood is on the edge of Beverly Hills and is home to a number of celebrities, but, more importantly, it has some of the best places for breakfast in the city. Scott and I love to eat a full American breakfast.

Another favourite hotel of ours is the Royalton in midtown Manhattan because that's where Scott and I began our tradition with the Easter Cat: a small, Beanie Baby-sized black cat with whiskers, white paws and a white face. The Easter Cat landed on Scott's pillow on Easter Sunday 1996. I was in New York filming *Central Park West*, and I wanted to create an Easter tradition that would be uniquely ours – so instead of an Easter Bunny, the Easter Cat brought Scott chocolate and a pair of Rollerblades.[3]

Scott was much more enamoured of the Easter Cat and the chocolate than the Rollerblades; Scott is decidedly non-athletic, but he's always a good sport. I'd been living in New York for the better part of a year, and was enjoying tearing round the Big Apple on blades. I'd been raving about them to Scott. So, while I was filming the following week, Scott decided to use his free time to learn how to Rollerblade.

In retrospect, I don't know what I was thinking, encouraging this behaviour. I think I somehow imagined that he and I could have these romantic rolls[4] around the park, weaving hand in hand along the paths, watching the other lovers stroll across the grass and cuddle on the benches. It'd be like our own version of *Barefoot in the Park*.[5] Instead, after three days of practice, Scott turned my Neil Simon romantic-comedy fantasy into a Dino De Laurentiis disaster film.

---

[3] So he's an odd Easter Cat.

[4] Well, we're not walking …

[5] Perhaps we'd call it *Wheeling in the Park*; *Rolling in the Park* sounds too much like a porn flick.

Scott spent two days going round and round and round the park and falling and falling and falling again. I'd come back to our room at the end of the day and Scott would be draped across the couch or the bed in complete agony, his body looking like he'd gone three rounds with a welterweight.[6] I've already shared with you how much he can moan when his body hurts. It was a painful experience all round.

On the third day ... well, that was the end of his Rollerblading career. Scott came shooting down a hill in the park, completely out of control. His options were limited. He couldn't figure out how to apply his brake without completely wiping out on the gravel path. There was no open grass to roll onto and drop to a stop, and he was heading at ever-increasing speed into a line of people – innocent women and children, no less.

Scott did the only thing he could. He swerved to his left and careened into a New York hot-dog vendor. The vendor's cart crashed over, hot dogs spilled out onto the ground, and Scott put both his hands on the hot plate to break his fall, resulting in a series of small burns across his palms. Despite all the stereotypes you may hold about people in NYC, the vendor was very nice about the entire incident. Scott dumped his Rollerblades – along with the forty-two hot dogs he'd spilled (and bought) – in a garbage can on the way out of the park.

Easter Cat, on the other hand, now travels with us everywhere. Scott remembers that there might once have been an Easter Dog, too, and that he always stayed at home, but he says he's lost track of him.[7] The Easter Cat was always more adventurous.

When Scott and I travel together, whoever remembers packs the Easter Cat; and when we travel individually, the Easter Cat is secretly hidden in the other person's suitcase. When we arrive at our destination, the cat is placed ceremoniously next to the bed.[8] The Easter Cat has been to Canada, Cambodia, Turkey, Lebanon, Mexico,

---

[6] And not in a good way.

[7] Don't tell Scott, but I think our real dogs may have chewed and destroyed the Easter Dog.

[8] Ah, isn't that, um, romantic?

Syria, Switzerland, Scotland, the US numerous times, and, most recently, to Barbados.

When I lived in Scotland, my family always took its vacation during the fortnight in July known as the Glasgow Fair, when Glasgow pretty much emptied out for those two weeks and families went south in search of sunshine and sand. For years, my mum and dad pulled a caravan, and for a couple of holidays that I remember during that time, we headed to the Isle of Wight.

I'm not sure what happened exactly to change this, but in the two years before we emigrated to the US, the caravan went by the wayside – literally – and our holiday shifted to an all-inclusive resort in Eastbourne. My guess? My mum finally figured out that caravanning essentially meant she was dragging her kitchen behind her. Plus, as Carole, Andrew and I got older, a holiday with five of us crushed in one room on wheels wore pretty thin.

Despite having lots of good fun on those early caravanning vacations, I would no sooner pitch a tent or hitch a caravan for my holiday now than I would hunt for my own food. My idea of roughing it on a trip is not having Grey Goose available in the minibar.

In my family, I'm not alone in this sentiment. Neither of my siblings has ended up being a very happy camper. And one year, when Scott and I took Clare and Turner on a trip out to California, Turner was so paranoid about staying in a motel that was 'close to the ground' that he made Scott and me shove the chest of drawers up against the door at night – so that no wild animals could break in.[9]

When I was young, I did love to sleep outside, as did Carole and Andrew. My dad, whom I've always thought secretly wanted to be Bob the Builder, came home one Saturday with enough plywood for an ark, and, in a single long weekend, proceeded to build a hut onto the back of our garage in Mount Vernon for the three of us to use as a playhouse. He didn't only make a sturdy wooden structure with a roof, windows and a door that would lock, but he also built two sets

[9] It was too late to stop the two uncles and the sister already inside.

of bunk beds inside the hut, for us to use when we wanted to have sleepovers with our pals. Since I shared a bedroom with Andrew, whenever he and his friends were using our room, I would transform the playhouse into my theatre, where I would practise my Jimmy Osmond and Lena Zavaroni impressions.[10]

In January 2009, when Scott and I were organizing our vacation for the year, I knew I wanted sunshine, soft sand, tropical drinks, scuba diving and a place that would force me to disconnect from the world of stage and television. Although Scott has travelled a lot and is more than capable of arranging all the planning involved in our holidays, I take a lot of pleasure in this part of the process.[11] We decided we'd take our proper vacation in Barbados, one of the coral islands that make up the string of islands in the West Indies. Given the emotional and physical demands of the months before this trip – with the whole 'Ballgate' debacle, a month-plus of panto in Birmingham, and all the preparations and planning for *Tonight's the Night* – I was ready for a break.

The plane banked and swooped over the tiny island airport, and my first vision of my holiday was stretched out in front of me in a long strip of white sand and sea the colour of cobalt. When we arrived at the Crystal Cove Hotel, I was so excited to be there I'm sure I skipped to the check-in desk.

'Good evening, sir, and welcome to Barbados. Your name?'

'Mr Barrowman and –'

'Ah, yes, sir,' he interrupted. 'The honeymoon suite for Mr Barrowman and Miss Gill.'

And then he looked up – and he slowly registered two men standing in front of him. He said nothing for a beat. Then lots of furtive glances passed back and forth between him and the staff, and then some throat clearing, and then came the clerk's profound apology.

Scott and I thought it was really funny and for most of the rest of

---

10 Which were not the same at all.

11 It's not because I'm controlling. Not me.

the vacation, I'd call him Miss Gill or even Mrs Barrowman every now and then, although the latter reminded me too much of my mum when I said it, so that didn't stick.

An embarrassed bellhop led Scott and I to our room: the honeymoon suite, where the bed was beautifully strewn with red rose petals, and towels had been decoratively shaped into two kissing swans and placed in the middle of the bed. The effect was very lovely, but not as lovely as the chilled bottle of champagne and the chocolates on the bedside table.

Later, I called down to the restaurant to make arrangements for dinner. I gave the maître d' my name, and he said, 'Oh dear, Mr Barrowman and, um, Mr Gill. Oh yes, we've all heard about what happened. We're so very sorry.' Word about Miss Gill had travelled fast.

We laughed when we saw the room, and, after taking a few pics of Miss Gill posing among the swans, we stepped outside and took in the beach views. I was glad we'd made the decision to head to the West Indies for this holiday. The tranquillity and the beauty of the setting was in stark contrast to our last holiday together in South Africa, where, at times, I'd felt like a prisoner inside the resort compound; we'd had to engage so many locks and alarms when we stepped outside that it had felt like *Prison Break*. And, during the night, those alarms kept going off because bands of youths would regularly try to break into the compound.

I loved a lot of things about South Africa – its intriguing geography, the fabulous wineries, and the local people I met at markets and out in the countryside – but I found the hypocrisy that came across from a number of white South Africans we had dinner with, and who talked about their society as if apartheid no longer existed, to be very disturbing. I know we were tourists and operating in a limited social milieu, but still.

In our entire two weeks there, neither Scott, Gav, Stu, or our friend, Ian 'Shirley' Temple, who joined us, ever saw a black South African in any service or retail position of power, and certainly not one that would put him or her in direct contact with a white customer or client. In every restaurant we ate in, the only black South Africans we saw were serving in the kitchen or cleaning up tables, and no one of any colour was eating with us or shopping with us as customers. Legal apartheid may be gone, but, in my opinion, financial and social apartheid has a chokehold on the country.

One morning, when the cleaning crew came into our condo and we were heading out, I told them that we had lots of extra fruit that I didn't want to go to waste and please to help themselves. The next day, their supervisor pulled me aside and chastised me quite severely, saying, 'If you give them extra food, they'll come to expect it.'

Once our trip took us out of Cape Town itself and into the hills and the countryside, the racial divide didn't seem as wide – or maybe the best that I can say is that the racial gulf wasn't so visible. I loved wandering in the markets and bartering for souvenirs. Scott might tell you I was lousy at bartering, but that would only be because he doesn't understand its nuances.

I swerved the car off the road one morning when we were heading to Table Mountain, a shiny beaded basket tempting me from a stall at the side of the road. The woman wanted $30 for it.[12] I paid her $20. Did I mention it was beaded? I could afford the $20 and she might otherwise have had to stand in the heat and the dust all day for another customer[13] like me to come along.

I also loved all the knick-knacks made from tin cans that the African children would sell. I bartered similarly for them. I bought a cool-looking Citroën car from a young boy made out of recycled Glade aerosol cans. It's one of my favourite souvenirs, and sits on a side table in the dining room in Sully.

Later that week, Gav, Stu, Scott and I decided to book a day trip to swim with the sharks.[14] The boat and its small group of passengers zipped out into the ocean, where anyone who wanted to could be lowered into a heavy, steel protective cage and then dropped underwater, where he or she came face-to-face with Jaws.

---

[12] Pretty much everyone wanted dollars.

[13] Okay … sucker.

[14] Swim out far enough, and you don't need reservations to let a shark gnaw on your flesh.

We all decided to sit up on the top deck of the boat and see how this whole thing played out, with a few other passengers going first, before we committed ourselves either way. I wanted to see how safe the 'cage keeps the sharks out' theory really was.

It didn't take long for us to realize that there was no way we were going down into the ocean in that cage. Not because the sharks came up really, really close, but because in order to get the sharks to come up really, really close, the tour operator and his buddy had to drop pounds of thick, raw chunks o' chum on top of the cage. Everyone who came up after the experience was covered in bloody bits of fish flesh and looked like rejects from Brian De Palma's *Carrie*. We all stayed put and we had much better views sitting on the boat deck, watching the sharks have a nibble at the other passengers. One poor woman freaked out so much when the chum hit her head and the sharks started to dive-bomb the cage that she had to be hauled out of the water, screaming hysterically. After an hour of this shark snacking, we were all hungry and bored. The movie was way more exciting.

We spent a much less messy day when we took the cable car up to the flat top of Table Mountain, which frames the city of Cape Town. The trip was fairly uneventful and the views stunning – until we had to be evacuated back down the mountain at top speed when the winds changed dramatically, the temperatures dropped from balmy to bloody freezing in a matter of minutes, and a huge band of heavy clouds cut right through the middle of the mountain.

The final leg of this holiday was our tour of the Stellenbosch wineries, where I fell in love with blended wines of every concoction: Cabernet Sauvignon and Merlot; and their Pinotage … to name two favourites. When we returned to London, Scott and I had wine packed in every nook and cranny of our luggage – but absolutely no more than our maximum customs allotment each.[15]

Before we left Cape Town for the wineries, I rented a helicopter to take all of us on an aerial tour of the Western Cape, including viewing the wildlife on the beaches and the marshes along the Atlantic coastline.

[15] Certainly not.

Those of you who know me well know I have a deep and enduring love/hate relationship with flying, but I have a passion for planes and anything that defies gravity. The helicopter, however, is not my favourite flying machine.[16] Nevertheless, the aerial tour came highly recommended and I thought it would be something we'd all enjoy.

Initially, the helicopter cruised at a very low height, and the panorama of the miles and miles of Cape coastline was stunning. For a quick detour, the pilot took us inland a little, over the townships that are, in fact, man-made slums and shanty towns. This part of the tour broke my heart to see, and I didn't feel right flying above people's homes and gawking into them. We asked the pilot to go back over the water, which he did, sometimes only by a matter of a few feet as he swooped in and out of the wake, sending flocks of birds into a frenzy ahead of us.

Before we had to head back to the airport, the pilot asked us if we'd like to experience a torque turn. Now, if you've ever flown in a helicopter, you'll know it's a very noisy machine and, even with headphones on, it can be difficult to hear clearly. I thought he'd asked if we'd like to see the 'stork run'; I thought it was another bird swoop, so I said with great enthusiasm, 'Absolutely!'

I discovered when I looked into it later that a 'torque turn' is actually one of the most dangerous tricks you can do in a helicopter. Although it was commonplace during the Vietnam War, most armed forces have since discouraged the manoeuvre because, well, it's an easy way to crash.[17]

The pilot pulled the helicopter into a steep, high climb with the nose right up in the air. Then he cut the tail rotor and, for a beat, we were hanging in mid-air, spinning on our axis. The pilot flipped the tail back up, and we dropped forward so fast it felt like we were free-falling on the world's wildest roller coaster, the ocean rushing towards us with full force and my stomach in my mouth. All of us inside the helicopter

---

[16] That would be the TARDIS.

[17] Plus, I think the whole hanging-in-the-air bit of the trick tends to make you an easy target.

did what I think it is fair to say most men would have done in a similar situation: we screamed like little girls.

Our most recent holiday in Barbados was much more tranquil and much less risky.[18] In the mornings, I'd get out of bed at around 7 a.m. and park myself in a deckchair at the lagoon pool, which looked out across the beach and the ocean. After that, I'd rouse myself for only the most necessary of physical functions. And as much as I love the active trips Scott and I take, where we explore new places and shop and visit historic sights and shop, I cherished the fact that when I roused myself from my deckchair one afternoon, I realized that I hadn't been on my phone or checked my email for three whole days.[19]

Every evening at 5 p.m., a number of families we'd met since we'd arrived at the resort joined Scott and me at the pool bar. The adults ordered mudslides,[20] but mine was kept on ice. Instead of drinking right away, I'd take all the kids into the pool and we'd play Marco Polo, or go to the beach and body surf, while all the mums and dads[21] got an hour to themselves to sip in the sun. A couple of the children were big *Doctor Who* fans, and young enough that they truly thought they were playing Marco Polo every night at 5 p.m. with Captain Jack, which, if you think about it, might well be exactly what Jack would want to play. He probably even knew Marco Polo.

Spending this time in Barbados and sharing some of our holiday with these other families made me understand another reason why my parents may have shifted our family vacation from the caravan to the resort at Eastbourne. A resort, especially one that you return to every year, allows families to connect with other families from walks of life that, in your home environment, you'd likely never have contact with. Plus, vacationing at a resort community usually means more friends for the children to play with and more eyes to watch them when they do.

---

[18] Really, Mum, it was.

[19] Who are you and what have you done with John?

[20] A delicious blend of vodka, Irish cream and Kahlúa.

[21] And Scott.

There is also another, very important bonus. I don't care if you're at Butlins in Minehead or at Crystal Cove in the West Indies, every resort has a karaoke night – and they're a hoot.

For the Crystal Cove karaoke evening, I played DJ. I insisted that all of the guests in the bar and main room, adults and children alike, get up and sing, and everyone did. The management told me the next day that my karaoke night was the best and most popular one they'd had since they opened.

I do like a good karaoke or a cabaret night. Always have. Years ago, when my friend from university, Marilyn, and my mum, dad and I were driving from Glasgow to London for my second audition for what was to be my debut in *Anything Goes*, we stayed at a hotel outside London the night before. The hotel had a piano bar and Marilyn, my mum and I commandeered it and entertained everyone for a couple of hours. We even made a few quid in tips. The next day, as my dad was checking out, the hotel manager asked if he could book the three of us for the following weekend.

The day after the Crystal Cove karaoke, Scott and I rented jet skis. In the mornings, the beach would swarm with entrepreneurial Rastafarians hawking such wares. For a tenner each, Scott and I got the run of our machines for the day. Barbados had very few rules, but the Rasta guy did suggest, for our own safety, that we didn't venture too far down the coastline … man. Scott and I headed out into open water, and thought, 'Hell – it's Barbados!' and we made a run for it. We drove the jet skis all the way down the coast, taking in the sights and sounds of the beaches and the other resorts as we cruised.

When we crossed back into the harbour, where a number of cruise ships had docked, we started waving to the tourists standing on the decks. Pretty soon, our waving turned to doing doughnuts and figure-of-eights and putting on a little show for the people waving back to us, and then pretty soon after that, a hulking, flashing coastguard boat headed towards us at quite a clip. The cruise-ship captains had notified the coastguard of a possible terrorist threat from two erratic jet-ski drivers in the harbour. Scott and I drove up next to the boat, apologized profusely, and got the hell out of there.

Before Scott and I left Barbados, we heard from our new friends that *the* place to dine was a restaurant called The Cliff. The problem was that in order to get a table, you usually had to book months in advance; to land the best table (called, naturally, Table #1), a table that appeared to float out over the water, was nigh-on impossible at short notice. This was the kind of restaurant where there are no prices on the menu and they happily accept a second mortgage or your first-born in order to secure a reservation.

However, while we were mudsliding one evening, one of the couples told me that they'd had to cancel their booking at The Cliff because they couldn't get a babysitter. Since my babysitting services were only available in the evenings at 5 p.m., and figuring that there was a chance other couples had had the same problem, I immediately rang the restaurant – and I got a slot for the following evening.

When Scott and I arrived, the manager greeted us at the door. He said he was so happy to see my name[22] on his list for the evening, and that he was a huge fan of *Doctor Who* and *Torchwood*. He escorted us to – drum roll – Table #1. We ate an amazing meal, sitting out over the ocean in the soft glow of black coral candelabra and my own contentment.

Have I mentioned how much I love being Captain Jack?

[22] And Miss Gill's ...

CHAPTER FOURTEEN

'I AM WHAT I AM'

'I believe in doing what I can, in crying when I must,
in laughing when I choose.'

Noël Coward, 'If Love Were All'

Eleven things you may not know about me

1 I shop at Costco (sometimes daily).

2 I have an obsession with flossing my teeth
(sometimes ten times daily).

3 I love kitchen gadgets (size doesn't matter).

4 I love 'Swedish Fish' (a delicious gummy candy my
family brings me by the ton).

5 I'm allergic to shellfish (everything swells).

6 I'd love to own my own hotel and spa some day.

7 I have a room full of shoes (organized in plastic
containers from ... Costco).

8 I put on a massive fireworks display for my friends in July.

9 I get bored quickly.

10 I love a scary read and a frightening film.

11 I'll watch anything about a crash, cyclone, tornado
or hurricane (can't help myself).

'Mornin', dear!'
'Lovely day.'
'Hmm, yes.'
'What'll you have for your brekkie?'
'Toast, strawberry jam and black coffee, please, love. Oh, and today, I think I'll be gay!'

My family tree is a long and ancient one, with branches stretching from the north-eastern coast of Northern Ireland to the midlands of Scotland. The Barrowman name, as with many of all our names, is a derivation of a medieval profession – just like Carpenter, Cooper, Miller, Potter, Reeve, or my personal favourite, Rimmer.[1] The Barrowmans were highly skilled and very spiritual workers. I kid you not. Barrow men were paid to guard ancient burial mounds, called barrows, and their duty was to make sure the grave mound wasn't robbed or desecrated before, I'm guessing, the soul had a chance to ascend to the afterlife. Of course, it's possible that my ancestors just spent a lot of time in the fields shovelling shit and pushing a wheelbarrow, but I prefer my first version.

When I was asked to participate in the BBC documentary series *The Making of Me*, one of the things that attracted me to the project was that the documentary would trace my roots in a different way from a traditional family history. Instead of genealogy and lineage, the show explored biology and genetics to help me understand one of my most defining characteristics – being gay.

Since my career began, I've always been open about my sexuality, but that doesn't mean I don't have questions about it. I was lucky

---

[1] Guess what his ancestors did …

enough to be raised in a family where sex was not a four-letter word. I'm a very curious person. I love the kind of television show where things or events or even people are taken apart to see what makes them tick. Whether it's a brand-new car or a plane crash,[2] I'm intrigued about how and why things work the way they do, myself included.

The producers of the series explained to me that this documentary was going to explore current medical facts, scientific knowledge and psychological tests, many of which they'd apply to me, all with a mind to answer the question: what shapes a person's sexuality? Or, in my mind, what makes me gay?

Although I think the numbers are shrinking, there are still people who believe that being gay is a lifestyle choice, and that one morning I woke up and decided to be gay. I knew that participating in *The Making of Me* was a risk because, from the beginning, I agreed that I would go wherever the science, the tests and their conclusions took me. This meant that I had to be open to discovering things about myself that I didn't already know. The big question the show was exploring through my journey was one of the most interesting questions human beings ask: is our sexuality a product of our nature, or the result of how we've been nurtured?

My answer before the show? I was born gay. Homosexuality is part of my nature; it's as much a part of who I am as the colour of my eyes, the size of my feet and the fact that I can roll my tongue. But my agreement with the producers was that, no matter what happened, I would take the risk of learning something I might not want or like to know.

The journey to answer the key question was an incredible one, and it started with a series of phone calls to my immediate family, who would have to be involved in the process, and who the producers needed to interview extensively. With Carole and my parents, they wanted to explore through stories and photographs the possibilities of relatives, distant and immediate, who might also have been gay; and as part of the investigation, they needed DNA samples from my mum

---

[2] Can't help it. Love watching disaster docs and aircraft-crash investigations.

and Andrew. Carole and my parents spent hours with the producers, narrowing down images and telling tales that would become part of a filmed family dinner at my parents' house in Brookfield, Wisconsin.

In typical Barrowman fashion, the major drama of this dinner was not whether we wanted to reveal that one of my mum's great-uncles, a particularly dapper bachelor who always had lots of young, good-looking male friends surrounding him, was gay, or – and I love this one – that my dad's great-uncle, also another lifelong bachelor, had frequent 'hunting' weekends 'up north' but, according to my parents, never seemed to come home with any game.[3] Oh, so gay. No. None of that was the least bit controversial. The family drama involved food – as it so often does with us. How much and what should we have? What about dessert? Do we eat before we film? Should we use the good china? Who's sitting where? We're not using paper plates. We're using my good dishes.[4] Can we have a drink when this is going on?[5]

I'd arrived in Chicago from London the day before, and I'd driven up that morning to Brookfield, a suburb of Milwaukee, to film the family gathering. Because a number of the tests I'd be participating in were to be conducted at Northwestern Memorial Hospital in Chicago, I was staying at a hotel in Chicago. The crew and producers for the documentary had already been in the States for a couple of days and they'd met with and interviewed my family beforehand.

Like many of our family dinners, this one started out relatively subdued – until I asked my mum a question that related to an avenue of enquiry the documentary was exploring: the role of a mother in shaping the sexual orientation of her children.[6] I asked my mum if she thought she'd been a domineering mother, and, if so, might she have influenced my being gay?

The look on my mum's face was a fierce combination of 'how dare you' and 'he so came out that way'. It was also hilarious. Clare's drink

---

[3] I'm sure he bagged plenty.
[4] Mostly from my mum.
[5] Mostly from all of us.
[6] This sentence could have come out all wrong.

shot out her nose, Kevin choked a bit on his beer, Carole had to leave the table, and my dad and I completely cracked up – and I mean side-splitting, wee-your-pants cracking up. After that, all professionalism, poise, and most of the script went right out the condo window.

Turner arrived late at the family dinner because of his work schedule. I greeted him at the door with the cameraman in tow. Like a typical Barrowman, Turner paid the camera no mind, sat down at the table, and, with very little prompting, gave his opinion on what he thought made his uncle gay.

'I don't care.'

Which, hurrah, is probably the answer you'd get from many in Turner and Clare's generation.

Along with the Barrowman anecdotes from our family tree, this journey of discovery also involved a number of very intriguing scientific tests, including, at one point, a severe anxiety-causing one. The first assessment I was put through took place on the day following the family dinner, and was carried out at a lab at Northwestern University Hospital. These initial tests were designed to monitor my arousal response to a variety of erotic images.[7]

The room was like thousands of doctors' offices around the world. I stripped to my skin, sat on the chair, and electrodes were placed around the tip, base and head of my penis, which was then draped with a towel. First, via a computer screen, the researchers showed me images of monkeys[8] and lots of pretty landscapes. Then they transitioned to male nudes, female nudes, male-on-male sex, male-on-female sex, and female-on-female sex.

So there I was: completely naked in this sterile office, with a towel over my crotch, my willy completely covered in wires, watching all variety of porn known to man … and woman, while researchers outside were watching me watching all this stuff inside. I knew exactly what would happen. Nothing. No erection happening here. As it turned out, it didn't matter. The test was all about blood flow.

---

[7] Aka porn.
[8] Really, they did. Kinda creepy ones, too. Like *Wizard of Oz* monkeys.

The researchers told me that this was a test the US Army had used in the fifties – on men who refused to go into the military because they claimed they were gay. When I thought about it later, those test results must have been a bit of a double-edged sword for the person being examined. On the one hand, you'd get out of the army, but on the other, you'd be out of the closet … at a recruiting station in Alabama in the fifties.[9]

The researchers explained that they could see when blood started pumping into my penis before anything under the towel noticeably changed. I sat there concentrating on all those images and didn't get an erection, but, according to the researchers, I reacted exactly the way a normal gay man should have reacted. The blood flow increased to my penis when I was shown the male-on-female erotica. Well, it would, wouldn't it? There was a boy involved. Absolutely nothing stirred for the female-on-female images, but when I'd viewed the male-on-male porn, I was off the scale. Overall, I got an A+ in that exam.

Guess what? I'm Supergay![10]

The test that caused me some distress was one that had to be done in an enclosed MRI machine. I'm claustrophobic when I'm in confined spaces – which is probably why I had to get out of the closet as soon as possible. This time, the electrodes were connected to my brain and my reaction was scanned while I watched similar pornographic images as before, only this time on a screen above my face. Same subject, different positions; plus this time they showed me pictures of male athletes and female athletes in their standard running, jumping and kicking poses. After I'd viewed each image, I had to press a button from one to four, with one being a turn-on and four being not so much.

I was fine inside the machine for the first couple of minutes, until I suddenly felt a panic attack coming on: dry mouth, pulse racing, stomach rolling, tingling in my arms. Most of the time when an attack like this happens, I use what I call 'distraction therapy', which means I force my brain to disconnect from the panic by reciting a song, or

[9] Not going to be your best day.
[10] I'm having T-shirts made.

imagining my happy place,[11] or telling myself a very linear story in my head. If that doesn't work, I do my best to let the attack run its course, reminding myself, as it does, that panic attacks are not fatal.

Panic attacks are not fatal. Panic attacks are not fatal.

Over the years, I've been onstage in the middle of a number and suffered a panic attack, been in the TARDIS with the Doctor and kept one at bay, and, most recently, during my show in Oxford on my concert tour, I let one charge through my system while I sang on.

I've been told that panic attacks are often triggered for no reason, but agoraphobia or, in my case, mild claustrophobia can be a catalyst. My mum suffers from panic attacks on occasion, as do Carole and Clare. Because Carole and I were aware of them when Clare had her first one as a child, we taught Clare our 'distraction method'. Clare mastered this so well that she got to a point where she didn't need to wake her parents every time she felt an attack coming in the middle of the night; instead, she'd read aloud to herself from Arnold Lobel's *Frog and Toad are Friends*. Most of the time, this technique works for me too,[12] but, ironically, watching porn wasn't distracting enough.

At one point during the test, as I started to feel the anxiety growing, I realized I was hitting the buttons more slowly after each image. I pushed through the attack and eventually got myself back in control.

The next day, the researchers met with me to explain my test results. They projected the scan of my brain onto a large flat screen and amazingly, as I watched, I could see the panic attack occurring. For the first time I saw my brain in anxiety mode, which was riveting.

During the panic attack, the part of my brain tied to arousal continued to fire, despite my stress. In fact, on the screen it looked as if fireworks were going off in my head; yet my reactions and my hands had slowed down. Even during the panic attack, my brain continued to act homosexually.[13]

During *The Making of Me*, I also interviewed people, gay and not

[11] An aisle in Costco or a Ralph Lauren store.
[12] Distracting myself – not reading *Frog and Toad*.
[13] Definitely need to have those T-shirts made.

gay, who had something to contribute to my investigation. One of the more fascinating, but ultimately more disturbing and sad, interviews was with a man who claimed he'd been cured of being gay.

This man, let's call him Mike, was in his fifties, and he felt his life before he was cured of his homosexuality was dreadful. He explained to me that he was always getting laid, always hanging out in bars, and always doing the things his parents and his church had taught him were wrong. Eventually, he participated in a 'cure' sponsored by his church and now claimed he had everything he had ever wanted. He was married, had children, a nice house and a good job. And yet, to me, he seemed so unhappy, so very angry and so very gay.

Mike believed that, as a gay man, he could never settle down, never have children, and never live on his farm with his white picket fence. While we were talking, he was not really interested in listening. He didn't want to hear that I had all the things he had, too – a loving family, a beautiful house, a successful and fulfilling career – and that I had achieved them without denying who I was.

I was really interested in Mike's perspective, but his story profoundly bothered me. He admitted he was making a choice to live as a heterosexual because he felt his true self was 'wrong'. He claimed he didn't like himself when he was gay. His solution was to repress his true feelings. That's all despairing enough, but what was especially perturbing was that he wanted to berate me for living my life openly and honestly as a gay man. I have no problems with others living in denial and being unhappy, but don't spread your anguish around. I think Mike had scared himself straight by sacrificing his true feelings, and he was angry with me because I represented something he did not think was possible – that a person can be gay and happy.

Mike and I said our goodbyes and I wished him well. I thought a lot about him on the trip back to the hotel. Mike had grown up during the sexual revolution of the sixties, seventies and eighties, as many of us did, and I think he equated his extreme promiscuity with being gay, when, in fact, his promiscuity was a product of all sorts of other things. Gay men do not have a monopoly on sleeping around. Have you ever been in a straight club in London's West End on a Saturday night?

One of the things I've learned over the years, and that I'll stand up for much more now than ever before, is that I will not tolerate people telling me – either directly or indirectly – that the way I live as a gay man is wrong or, worse, immoral. And while I'm on the topic, I'm taking back the phrase 'family values' from fundamentalists and Christian conservatives. I have strong family values. I live according to those values and I share them with millions of other men and women who are living, loving, and creating families in non-traditional ways. End of rant.[14]

Admittedly, I agreed to *The Making of Me* with an agenda – to try to better understand my own sexuality, while at the same time presenting some understanding to others of what it means to be gay. The documentary succeeded in both of these areas as far as I'm concerned.

What was my answer at the end of the journey? I discovered that we are all complex and unique beings and that our DNA can't be fully explained … yet. I also learned that our sexuality is decided long before we're born, and whether or not we are gay is the result of the interaction of many related biological and hormonal factors. One day, scientists might find a 'gay gene', but that gene may hold such a myriad of branches that to pinpoint only one as a true 'gay gene' may be something for Captain Jack's future, but I'm not sure it's in mine.

As it turned out, Andrew and I share a similar genetic code; yet I'm gay and he's not. What I learned from this was that even if they do discover that 'gay gene', it may still be only one of many elements that make a man gay. What made Scott gay may not be the same combination of factors that made me gay.

One of the most fascinating revelations presented to me during the filming was this: the more boys a woman carries in her womb, the more likely she is to have a son who is gay. I was the third boy to occupy my mother's womb.[15] A number of my gay friends are the third or fourth in a family of boys. This is not to say that men who are

14 For now …
15 I made that sound like I was squatting for a few months. Sorry, Mum.

the eldest and are gay can't be explained. Their determining factors may just be a different mix.

I received lots of letters after *The Making of Me* aired in the UK and on BBC America, particularly from young men struggling with their sexuality and from parents of gay children, who were moved and pleased with the programme.

Simon from Leeds wrote a letter that was typical of the many I received from gay men. 'I came out in 2003, and was basically snubbed by my family, who were unable to accept my sexuality. I was punished by parents who thought I was "making a choice" and intentionally trying to hurt them ... I forced my mum to sit down with me and watch [*The Making of Me*]. Through tears and pain, we watched it, and slowly my mum has begun to accept that it is not embarrassing to have a gay son ... Thank you for helping bring my family back together.'

And then a letter from April, who lives in Texas, and who sent this to me on Mother's Day in 2009. April wrote that when her daughter was four, she had asked her, 'What can I be when I grow up?'

April had replied, 'Baby, you can be anything you want to be!'

'Mommy, I want to be a boy.'

April told me that although she had accepted that she had a transgender daughter, she was having a difficult time understanding her daughter's decision to begin the process of becoming a male. Then she came across *The Making of Me* on YouTube.[16] April told me in her letter: 'I was so moved and captivated that I asked my daughter to watch it with me. We would stop the video and laugh, then argue, then cry and hug.'

April closed her letter with this: 'Some day, I will probably have to say goodbye to my baby girl. And when that happens, I will cry, be sad, and then put her pictures away. Then I will greet the son that will be coming into my life with open arms and a loving heart.'

I regard *The Making of Me* as one of my most important accomplishments. Letters like Simon's and April's reaffirmed why the documentary was important to do, and why, instead of going on another talk show

---

16 Yeah, again, YouTube!

and being silly and camping it up a little, I chose to explore this issue seriously and with respect. With programmes like this, I'm not helping anyone to be gay or trying to make them come out. Men like Simon are already gay, and the choice to come out is theirs and theirs alone. But, in my own way, I hope I'm helping them to be comfortable, confident, and accepting of themselves. Bottom line: I want to spread the word that being gay is normal.

In spring 2009, during an interview for a newspaper, the journalist asked me how old I was when I *decided* to be gay. Clearly, there's still work to be done, and I'm honoured to do my part to educate and affirm whenever I can. I love being a gay icon[17] and I love representing the gay community, and I hope I'm doing them proud. Nothing makes me smile more than when I speak to a young gay man or woman and he or she tells me that I really helped them to come to terms with their life. That's absolutely brilliant.

Unfortunately, some latent prejudices still persist. Too often I'm described in the press or on TV as a 'gay actor', or a 'homosexual entertainer',[18] and more recently I've noticed the word 'flamboyant' sneaking into introductions of me. This is a code word for 'gay'. Unless I'm belting out 'I Am What I Am' in sequins and stilettos, or I'm dressed in a sparkling suit – with a belt with bling – for a Busby Berkeley number on *Tonight's the Night*, I'm not flamboyant. Is Andy Roddick described as a straight tennis player? Angelina Jolie, a heterosexual actor? Bruce Willis, a straight leading man? I don't think so; and unless Bruce Willis steps into a pair of Jimmy Choos and wraps himself in a feather boa, he's not flamboyant, either.

Describing people in this way may be subtle,[19] but it's prejudice, and I'm not embarrassed to call people on their ignorance or to challenge them on their inaccurate perceptions. Now, a caveat here: if you find yourself in a situation where you may get hurt if you call

---

[17] Love the flag, the outfits, the secret handshake, the motto …

[18] Seriously, what the hell does that mean? And don't you want to see that performance?

[19] As a sledgehammer (and not Scott's).

attention to prejudiced behaviour, then absolutely do not. Be a man (or a woman) and walk away. But if you are in a situation where people are being derogatory, stand up for yourself. Call them on it. Sometimes when you do, they will apologize and admit to having not really thought about their language in that way before. When I called the journalist's attention to the question about when I 'decided' to be gay, she apologized immediately.

I've always tried to apply this attitude in all spheres of my personal and professional life; I believe it's important to do so. An experience I once had with the producers of a TV show is a good example of this. I was in my dressing room, watching movies and passing time with Clare, when one of the producers joined us with some notes for me about my performance.

'John,' he said, after he'd checked off a couple of other points, 'we wondered if you really wanted to reveal that you're gay?'

Whoa. Clare's eyes widened and, when she saw my expression, she shifted away a little to give me a wider berth. I stared at the producer for a very long, dark minute. Did he think that maybe I should have saved this detail for dinner conversation, in case, after the pudding, I was suddenly caught humping the waiter?

'I really hope I didn't hear that coming out of your mouth,' I stated, 'because I'm not going back into the closet for anyone.'

The incident was even more offensive because they sent a gay producer to discuss this with me, as if somehow this would ease the blow. I could tell he was terribly embarrassed. He should have been.

'We think it might change how people feel about you,' he continued.

'For Christ's sake!' I yelled. 'You've hired me to be a professional, not to have sex! Being a gay man has nothing to do with my abilities on this show.' I was even more furious because, as I've stated, one of my explicit missions as an entertainer is to work to create a world where no one will ever make a statement like that to anyone who's gay.

'Who told you to say this?'

He tried to back down, to soften the statement somehow, especially when he realized I was getting angrier. I also think he could see that

Clare, all 5'3" of her, was rising up on her flip-flops preparing for an attack. She was hissing and spitting in the corner.[20]

'I'm not changing who I am for you or anyone else,' I seethed, livid now. 'I find it highly offensive that you as a gay man have said this to me. I don't care who told you to say it. You should have stood up to whoever put you up to this. Grow some balls, man.'

Later, after I'd calmed down and Clare had been contained, the producers apologized profusely[21] and we all moved on from this incident. I hope that, in standing up for myself in this way – on this particular occasion, and all the many other times I've done so – I've also stood up for those who don't quite have the voice, or the confidence, that I do. As my parents taught me, speak up for yourself (especially if you have something to say) and speak up for others (especially if they can't).

When my parents and I sat at their kitchen table in Illinois many years ago, and I told them I was gay, they embraced me immediately – but that does not mean it was easy for them, or that it's easy for other parents, either. Families need time to adjust and come to terms with what they are being told. For my parents – and, keep in mind, this was almost twenty years ago now – their readjustment had a lot to do with their fears about AIDS and HIV.

That said, nothing angers me more than when I hear about parents who have abandoned or disowned their children because they're gay. No matter how hard a parent may try, he or she is not going to change that child's fundamental biological make-up. Instead of making a son or a daughter's life more miserable, step up to the parenting plate, help them understand who they are, and support them in living happy, productive lives – because, in the words of Jerry Herman, 'life's not worth a damn, till you can say … I am what I am'.

---

20 That's my girl!
21 They really did – most sincerely.

`NOCD – Not Our Class, Dear!'

Even before there was any sound in the movies, people were talking about Palm Springs, about catching a glimpse of Clark Gable or Greta Garbo at the famous El Mirador Hotel. In the 1950s, when Palm Springs really became the 'playground to the stars', you might have spotted Frank Sinatra on the golf course or Dean Martin at the nineteenth hole waiting for him.

Today, a stargazer can see an entire galaxy of them when the movie world and its celebrities come for the Palm Springs Film Festival. But if it's me you're looking for there, you'll need to book a table at Trio or peek over the patio wall at my close friends Brett and Javier's house, where you'll find me lounging by the pool while basking in the healthy glow of a 'Three Olives' bubble-gum-flavoured vodka martini.

Palm Springs is a desert town, nestled in the Coachella Valley under the shoulders of the San Jacinto mountains, and it's become one of my favourite destinations, especially because the area has everything I want in a weekend getaway: good food, great friends, hot weather – and a Costco. When I was in LA filming *Desperate Housewives* in spring 2010, I'd travel with Brett and Javier to their house in Palm Springs on most weekends.

Now, because of the combination of Hollywood history, old-school Californian aristocracy and gay-friendly fabulousness that make up the character of Palm Springs, the film version of Dominick Dunne's *The Two Mrs Grenvilles* became our movie of choice on one or two of those weekends. The film was Claudette Colbert's last movie[1] and stars Ann-Margret as a chorus girl: the daughter-in-law

---

[1] Worth watching for that reason alone.

Colbert's matriarch considers 'not of her class'. The movie is wonderful fun and the three of us were quoting from it liberally one afternoon when I decided to look seriously at buying my own house in Palm Springs.

We were checking out our final open house with our realtor and I was loving what I saw. We had welcomed the realtor into our imaginary version of *The Two Mrs Grenvilles*, so the silliness had multiplied. It should go without saying, given the nature of these table talks, that we were all a bit loopy and it was going to cause some trouble.

The house I was interested in was spacious with good-sized bedrooms. Like our home in Cardiff, it had a pool and a beautiful view from the patio. I decided we all needed to go back to the realtor's office so I could crunch some numbers.

The realtor told us his office wasn't far, but it was difficult to find if you didn't know the area. We agreed to follow close behind. His car was a fairly nondescript silver sedan, but the traffic was light so we figured, no worries. Brett and I climbed into Javier's SUV. The realtor pulled into some traffic, and we pulled out close behind. As Javier is wont to do when in a car, even when he's driving, he began to sing. Since he is of Mexican descent, he sings in Spanish – which then elicits from me an attempt to sing along, also in Spanish.

'Jav, the realtor's getting too far ahead,' Brett pointed out from the back seat.

The realtor's car was indeed a few cars ahead, so Javier sped up a little[2] and cut in front of the cars separating us as they slowed for the next stop light. This, with a squeal of brakes, brought us dangerously close to the realtor's bumper because he didn't move as quickly off the green light as we expected. Meanwhile, Javier was really getting into the groove, singing and gesturing towards the realtor's car, and Brett and I had moved into full *Mrs Grenville* action, pointing at the realtor in an admonishing way.

The realtor pulled away from the light and sped up. We did too. He made an illegal turn, and we followed right behind. Abruptly, he pulled

---

[2] Well, more than a little, but within the speed limit.

a quick left and swerved into a strip-mall parking lot that had a few storefronts and a bank drive-through.

'Jeez. We'd never have found the office tucked in here,' commented Brett.

Javier pulled his SUV into an empty spot and we pushed open our doors. Suddenly, the realtor slammed his car into reverse. As he burned rubber past us, we could see clearly that he was a she and the terrified middle-aged woman, mobile phone in hand, that we'd been following was *not* our realtor.

I love the American desert: the heat, the stunning mountain vistas, the long open roads and the clouds of dust kicked up by fast wheels. Other than helping children, of course, the desert was one of the reasons I agreed to participate in the BBC's Children in Need (CIN) 'Around the World in 80 Days' relay in the late summer of 2009. The other reason was that Myleene Klass would be my partner.[3]

For the first part of our leg of the race, Myleene and I drove an electric car, a Tesla Roadster, through the Arizona desert, across the famous Route 66. The trip was amazing in many ways, but in retrospect I spent most of my time teaching Myleene how to enjoy American junk food. I began the trip with long sticks of strawberry liquorice called Twizzlers, then advanced to the tropical-flavoured liquorice known as Pull-n-Peel, and then somewhere in Texas we ended with a traditional bonfire and the making of S'Mores.[4]

One of many notable stops on our trip was at an old mining town: Oatman, Arizona, which could have been a movie set dropped from the Universal lot. Donkeys wandered aimlessly along the streets and up on the sidewalks.[5]

With my encouragement, Myleene pulled the car closer to a pack

---

[3] Myleene was my TV wife during filming. Don't lie: you have a work spouse too. A person you spend as much time with on your job as you spend with your partner at home.

[4] A delicious sandwich of sweet gooeyness: toasted marshmallow and melted chocolate between two graham crackers.

[5] You think you have some asses in your neighbourhood …

of the donkeys so that we might say hello and, I have to admit, taunt them with our treats. We discovered – not so much to our surprise as to our horror – that donkeys love Twizzlers too. Who knew? We couldn't get their heads out of the car. Believe me, we tried. I feared for my face. Myleene feared for her snacks.

Then, in a bit of a panic, I yelled at Myleene to floor the gas pedal; I mean the electric accelerator. When we pulled away from the pack, we heard a dull thump and we really thought we'd hit the rear of one of the donkeys. We hadn't. But can you imagine that headline?

Barrowman's Twizzler Results in Injury to Donkey's Ass.

CHAPTER FIFTEEN

'THE BEST OF TIMES'

'Rachel: I tried, but I don't have a gag reflex.
Emma: When you're older, that will turn out to be a gift.'

Glee, episode two

Notes from twenty years
in show business

1 Always sign your own cheques.

2 Wear your costumes home just once per show.

3 Pantyhose are one of the worst fashion accessories ever.

4 Treat your dresser and make-up artist with the same respect as your co-stars.

5 Performing Jerry Herman is not the same as performing David Mamet.

6 Vamping[1] is a time-honoured theatrical skill.

7 Always celebrate with champagne. The second bottle can be cava.

---

[1] Don't get all *Twilight* on me. This is a theatre term and means 'improvising'.

One evening, after a matinee performance of *La Cage aux Folles*, an elderly lady – carefully coiffed, tastefully dressed, and waiting patiently at the kerb for her driver – spotted one of the Cagelles darting out of the stage door to grab a bite to eat between shows.

'You know,' she said to him as he walked past, 'you queers sure do know how to have a good time.'

To have spent my twentieth anniversary in show business in 'highest drag', playing Albin in *La Cage aux Folles* – one of the most iconic roles in musical theatre – was without a doubt a career high. To follow that blockbuster run a few months later with a six-show arc as the murderous eco-terrorist, Patrick, on one of my favourite American TV shows, *Desperate Housewives*, was like being given an amazing present, opening it, and finding another cool gift inside.

Desperate Housewives was especially exciting because, as you know, since getting hooked on *Dallas* in the late seventies I've loved night-time soap operas that have a bite in their tone and high glamour in their production values. Plus, I've spent a lot of my professional life surrounded by one or two divas and a smattering of desperate housewives.[2]

I have to say, though, that if it hadn't been for Bernie Cribbins, the anniversary of my twenty years in entertainment would have come and gone without the scrumptious cake, the expensive champagne, the cheers and toasts, and – what would have been really sad – I would've missed being awarded the historic and acclaimed golden penis.[3] Seriously, none of this would have happened if not for Bernie doing the math.

[2] I'm not naming names … and no, not my mum.
[3] Relax. I'll get there.

His reminder came in the form of a sweet card to my dressing room at the Playhouse Theatre a couple of days before the actual date marking the anniversary. In the card, Bernie wrote that on the following Saturday, 3 October 2009, it would be twenty years since I made my stage debut in *Anything Goes* at the Prince Edward Theatre. In that production, Bernie played Moonface Martin to my Billy Crocker and we rocked. Playing Billy was the first of many career- and life-changing roles that I've had so there was something exactly right about Bernie being the one to remind me of the significance of the dates.

In a marriage, the twentieth anniversary is traditionally marked with gifts of china, but no one seemed to know if there was a similar tradition in the theatre world. I think that's why Carole and Scott decided to start one just for me, and they used Bernie's idea from twenty years ago as their inspiration. While working on *Anything Goes* in 1989, Bernie would, at the end of every week, present someone in the cast – someone who'd gone above and beyond in their mistakes, slip-ups, flubbed lines or general idiocy – with what he dubbed the 'Dick of the Week' award. This award was handmade and quite amazing in its anatomical accuracy and, oh my, it disappeared after the show's run ended.[4]

While Scott and Carole were thinking up traditions, I reserved the upstairs bar at the Playhouse Theatre, and sent word round to the cast, crew and friends to celebrate my anniversary with me after Saturday's evening performance. But that was as far as I got. Immediately, everyone insisted I step away from the planning and let others take care of this particular event. You can't organize your own party, they exclaimed. Since the anniversary was coming within two days of my official opening night in *La Cage* on 5 October, I took their advice and got on with my work as Albin, leaving Carole, Scott and Gavin to the party details.

The 'Albins' I know in real life may sometimes be sad, but even when they're alone, they're never shabby. Aging drag queens are immaculate, particular and proud. Glamour defines them even as they age and it becomes more difficult for them to show it; while they may be riddled with self-doubt and wrinkles, they reveal those vulnerabilities

---

[4] Still to this day have no idea who might've taken it.

in quiet moments – not in tacky slippers and manky robes. Consequently – and especially given *La Cage aux Folles* is a big bold burlesque musical, and not Chekhov or David Mamet – I wanted my Albin to be immaculately groomed and a tender man … and I wanted my Zaza to be fucking fabulous.

If you saw the show, you'll know that I played Albin with less angst than the actors before me and my Zaza was more 'ravishing, sensual and fabulous'[5] than she'd been before too. Audiences loved them both because bums filled the seats and fans blocked the road every night outside the stage door. The box office soared – and there's nothing shabby about that.

My last role in a musical before *La Cage* had been stepping in as Billy Flynn in *Chicago* in 2004 at the Adelphi Theatre, so it had been a few years and lots of television work since I'd been on an eight-shows-a-week regimen. Thankfully, it didn't take long for old habits and rituals to return.

Every evening, as the cast gathered for the show, I'd wander round the dressing rooms, especially to the Cagelles',[6] and say hello. I'd banter a little with my terrific co-star, Simon Burke, who played Georges (our production was the first time two gay men had played Albin and Georges), I'd flirt with Matt Krzan, my show boyfriend,[7] and I'd dispense any wisdom, wit and wackiness necessary to get us pumped for a great show. I have to say, though, that this cast was not one that needed much pumping from an outside source. Their energy and passion were always palpable and I'd work with them again in a heartbeat. Jonathan Stott, our wonderful company manager, must have felt like a circus ringmaster most of the time.

At 6.30 p.m., my make-up artist, Laura Richardson, and my dresser, Meghan Fletcher, would begin my transformation to Albin for 'A Little More Mascara'; a song I didn't really like when I started rehearsals, but which became one of my favourites as the run

---

[5] Herman's description of Zaza from 'A Little More Mascara'.
[6] Had to be sure the boys were in fine form.
[7] Matt was my work spouse for *La Cage*.

continued. Sometimes the process began with shaving, and not only my face.[8] Even now, when I read about the things actors do to prepare for parts – how they gained or lost weight, played with their left foot – I have to laugh. My preparation for *La Cage* was learning how to put on false eyelashes while singing tricky lyrics and dancing in a tight corset.

And don't get me started on the pantyhose. Who the hell invented these … these … torturous things? Putting on pantyhose with speed and precision takes practice, patience and manicured nails. You have to be able to pull on the hose without snagging the nylon, which, despite Meghan buying the kind of orthopaedic hose a 100-year-old nurse with screaming varicose veins would wear, I still managed to do, sometimes two pairs a night.

And then, just when I'd think all was well, I'd have to spend precious but necessary time adjusting and lining up … my boys. For those of you who don't know, pantyhose have a seam that intersects the panty, and if my boys were not lined up properly against said seam, I'd be sobbing by the end of Act One.

After the 'five minutes till curtain' call, the cast gathered onstage behind the safety curtain for a mic check and an opening chant. I don't think it matters if you're in a football strip or sequins and frilly knickers,[9] every team has a starting ritual. The cast would huddle together in our 'sparkle dust' and 'bugle beads' with our toes pointed into a circle and we'd chant: '*Un*! *Deux*! *Trois*! Woo! Get Rrready! Can you just not? Can't even get a biscuit in this place! Or a drink!' Followed by wild applause from all.[10]

In the Playhouse Theatre, most of the time you could get a biscuit or two, but you could also just as easily catch a cold or an infection as well. The dressing rooms in this theatre are in the basement of the building. Walking down the two flights of stairs from the stage door at

---

[8] Some days this could add twenty minutes to the dressing routine.

[9] Under the football strip?

[10] Sounds way better when you hear it. Ask me to chant if you ever run into me.

street level was like stepping into, if not the bowels of hell, then maybe the waiting room set up right before the inferno.

The dressing rooms had no natural light, bad airflow, the ceilings were low, and the floors cracked and uneven. The entire underworld space was about as big as a two-car garage. To make matters even worse, the wardrobe laundry room, with its constantly running washing machine, contained an ancient dryer that vented – get this – directly into the main hallway. As a result, if someone coughed on Monday, we all had the plague by Tuesday.[11]

After settling into my dismal and dilapidated dressing room, I bought a humidifier, an air conditioner, a couple of gallons of purple paint and three packages of floor tile, and spruced up the room to meet basic human-rights standards.[12] You're welcome, next actor who gets the room.

The Playhouse Theatre in its infancy was known for its burlesque shows and its performances of comic operas, so it was fitting that *La Cage* was running there. One of the brilliant elements of Herman's show is the theatre-within-the-theatre pretext. The audience of *La Cage* at the theatre in London is transported to the French Riviera and becomes the imagined audience for La Cage – the cabaret bar – on the Riviera. This illusion creates moments during the cabaret numbers set in La Cage when the performers have room to improvise – sometimes deliberately, sometimes not so much. When a performer improvises, the band is vamping too, repeating the same bars until the performer moves on. One night, a lady[13] sitting at a cabaret table looked up Zaza's dress about two bars before she was invited to do so, creating the opportunity for my vamp that lasted for 298 bars: a theatre record.

Despite the elderly matron's statement to one of the Cagelles at the start of this chapter, this entire cast had fun on and off the stage, whether gay or not, and I know my performance was more spirited because of their boundless energy. Some of my favourite moments

---

[11] Almost all of us fell victim to a chest crud or bad cold during this run.

[12] As defined by Zaza.

[13] I use the term loosely.

came at the close of Act One, when, after singing 'I Am What I Am', Albin pulls off Zaza's wig and, with hair and damaged dignity in hand, dashes out through the fire exit. Someone from stage management was always waiting to escort me quickly back to my dressing room, but, still, do you really think I could let such opportunities for mischief pass me by?

Sometimes, during the matinees, I'd come charging out through the exit doors and the construction workers on the building site across the street would whistle at me … until one day I mooned them and then the whistles became grunts as they figured out what was under the frillies. Once, I burst out the door, spotted my handler from stage management, and, instead of running to the stage door to my right, I hiked up my gown and ran the other way, towards the Thames, chasing a bus that had just pulled away from its stop. Folks at the rear of the bus were laughing and waving for me to hurry up, while stage management was sprinting behind me, screaming, 'John, stop! John, right now! Stop!'

Occasionally, the frantic costume changes and the nature of the theatre's layout behind the scenes contributed even more to this manic madness. The backstage areas of the theatre are about as spacious as the dressing rooms; swinging a hamster would've been dangerous, never mind the proverbial cat. Plus backstage was home to the giant birdcage. We'd have to dash up one flight of stairs to get to stage left and a different flight to stage right, both marked with big black arrows on all the hallways. For the first few performances, finding the Holy Grail would have been easier than navigating the corridors to get onstage.

For a few scene changes, I was able to dart behind the safety curtain for my next cue on the other side of the stage, saving some seconds and lots of energy. For other entrances, I'd have to dash back down the narrow stairs (sometimes meeting two performers and someone from wardrobe with her arms full of ostrich feathers rushing up the same stairs), sprint across the front of the house using the tunnel underneath the stage, and hike back up the stairs on the other side – all in time for my cue. And may I just remind you that I was often doing this dashing in *very* high heels. This sprinting behind the scenes got to be such a defining characteristic of the show that I decided to attempt to set a record for the fastest backstage costume change from a blue-suited Albin to a pink chiffon high drag Zaza.

Night one: we needed to set our baseline. Go!

I came running offstage so fast, with so much momentum, that I almost took out two of the crew, a couple of Cagelles, and the full-length mirror standing in the sliver of an alcove where three dressers, supervised by Meghan, waited to assist. First, dresser one helped me off with my jacket and shirt, while dresser two loosened my belt and pants. At the same time, I'd lift my feet out of Albin's loafers and dresser three slipped off my socks and lined up Zaza's heels. Dressers one and two then set Zaza's pink chiffon dress on the floor, and I'd take off my trousers and step into the dress.[14] Dresser two pulled up the chiffon while dresser one zipped. Dresser three shoehorned me into the heels. Dresser one handed me Zaza's earrings. I clipped them on while diamonds were fastened around my neck, and then – the pièce de résistance – Zaza's big blonde wig[15] was lowered onto my head and fitted at lightning speed with a million kirby grips. Finally, all dressers put the last few touches to the ensemble, including hooking the train of the dress over my wrist.

Voila! Zaza is here – in 44 seconds.

Next night. Go! Running. Dressers. Jacket and shirt. Belt and pants. Loafers. Heels. Pink chiffon. Boobs. Zip. Wig. Kirbies. Hook. Zaza!

A new *La Cage* record – 34 seconds.

Give this frantic backstage pace, it's not surprising there were wardrobe or prop malfunctions. A couple of times during the cabaret scene, my nipple tassels didn't spin properly due to a faulty connection,[16] and one night my garter broke during the same number and dangled visibly between my legs. Another time, when my false eyelashes slipped off during 'Mascara', I worked 'ooh, she's getting a little askew' smoothly into the lyrics while repositioning the lash like a pro.

Yet the best vamp of all was during my final performance. At the

---

[14] For this change, the boobs were sown into the dress so no bra and falsies were needed.

[15] I called this wig the Krystle Carrington (from *Dynasty*).

[16] On the tassels! Not my nipples.

end of the cabaret scene, I choreographed my own dance number.[17] Instead of standing in the middle of the Cagelles spinning my martini as I was supposed to do, I danced, ending with full splits right on the mark. It took two Cagelles to hoist me off the floor and offstage, but it was worth it.

In 1978, aged eleven, I travelled across the United States with my parents, my gran and my brother for a road trip to California. Like many tourists, we visited the Universal theme park and took a tour of the Universal lot. Thirty-two years later, on my first day on that same lot to film *Desperate Housewives*, I felt as if I was that kid again. And because I was stepping onto a set with a number of strong professional women, I figured that – no matter what anyone had told me about their demeanours or their working style – there had to be some competition among them. And so, when I first arrived on Wisteria Lane, I was cautious and stepped lightly until I figured out the set's dynamics.

Luckily, the two women with whom I had the most contact during my filming – Drea de Matteo and Eva Longoria Parker – were wonderful, and the rest of the cast and crew were so welcoming that they made me feel like one of their own from the start.

During that first afternoon on the set, my weird sort of déjà-vu nervousness was heightened because my initial introduction to the full *DH* cast came within a couple of hours of my transatlantic trip from London to LA – but even if I hadn't been a bit jet-lagged, the surroundings at Universal would have knocked me for six; that location would easily overwhelm even the most jaded among us.

The *Desperate Housewives* set is on the 420-acre Universal lot, which is really a small city with its own fire station and sheriff's department. The lot's been home to so many classic films and TV shows that when I'd get shuttled from my trailer to the lower set (where many of the interiors for *DH* are shot), I'd be a bit gaga, as we passed the still-standing set of the original *Phantom of the Opera*, the burned-out set from Tom Cruise's *War of the Worlds*, or the Bates Motel from *Psycho*.

---

[17] Ask Scott. I practised at home.

On days when we were filming on Wisteria Lane, the trailers for the actors were located on what was called the Upper Lot. There, I'd simply step outside my trailer … and the huge concrete pool and the tall blue wall from *The Truman Show*[18] would be ten feet from my door. In the distance, I could see the adobe rooftop of Steven Spielberg's DreamWorks.

Wisteria Lane is a real street with real houses, and not simply chipboard facades. Inside each one of these real houses, the main rooms are fully furnished as lived-in sitting rooms. I know this to be true because one day on set between scenes, Carole and I went on a secret mission to explore the inside of the houses (especially Gaby's house, because Clare is a huge fan of Eva Longoria Parker). As we dashed upstairs in Gaby's house, we discovered – just in the nick of time – that the houses on Wisteria Lane have no upstairs!

The other big difference between these houses and yours and mine is that, when necessary, a wall or a column can easily be removed to accommodate any camera angle. Outside on the lane itself, all the bursting blooms, beautiful flowers and lush full trees are plastic – gorgeous, but plastic nonetheless.

During the read-through of the script for my first episode on the show, Marc Cherry, the show's creator and writer, sat at the head of the big table with the full cast surrounding him like family; just as Russell did on *Torchwood* and *Doctor Who*. Felicity Huffman sat across from me on that first read-through and, although I didn't have any scenes with her, our paths crossed a number of times in the make-up trailer; a trailer that has to be one of the biggest and best-equipped make-up trailers in the entertainment industry.

When I first stepped into this trailer to get my hair darkened to play the role of the dastardly Patrick, I couldn't believe how spectacular the set-up was. Each of the ten-plus make-up and hair stations had flat-screen TVs above the mirrors and each one was kitted out equally so the main women on the show (Eva Longoria Parker, Felicity Huffman, Marcia Cross and Teri Hatcher) had the same amenities and comforts.

---

[18] One of Scott's favourite films.

The show even has its own *Desperate Housewives* bottled water. Lest you think that only the theatre world is a small one, the make-up artist assigned to me for my time on *DH* was the same person I'd worked with on *Titans* in 2000. Neither Gina nor I had changed a bit.

Most of my filming time was spent with Drea de Matteo, who played Angie, Patrick's ex-wife and ex-partner in eco-terrorism. Drea was brilliant to work with. When we first met, we hit it off immediately. She said something smart-ass tinged with a few expletives, I replied with something equally fucking funny and we were off.

In fact, Drea decided early on in our relationship that I was her long-lost brother from another mother but the same father. She and I had similar personalities and tendencies: a quick mind,[19] a highly developed sense of humour and the urge to play on set. Drea and I had so much fun that Brett, Javier and I created a drink for her that we'd sip when we'd go to Brett and Javier's place in Palm Springs on the weekends. We called it our Desert Matteo. Rim of brown sugar on the glass. Shot or two or three of tequila (Drea's favourite drink). Splash with pink grapefruit juice. Squirt of lemon or lime (can go either way). Cheers, Drea!

As it turned out, my biggest challenge during *Desperate Housewives* was that, since mine was a guest role, I had lots of down time. For those of you who know me well, boredom is not a good state for me to be in. When I was not on the lot waiting to be called to the set, and I'd shopped as much as I could,[20] I'd visit friends, like Julie Gardner (and her soon-to-be-born son), her partner, and Russell and his awesome surfboard.[21] I also spent time in Florida with my parents.

When I was on set and had down time between takes, my options were limited, so I'd entertain the crew with my Cher impressions … and my infamous – but pretty amazing – banana trick.

I'm not sure how this particular trick first came about,[22] but over

---

[19] Read 'naughty'.

[20] Can't believe I just said that …

[21] Oh, I'm so kidding about the board. He's actually into Rollerblading on the beach.

[22] That's my story and I'm sticking to it.

the years I've become quite adept at demonstrating – how shall I put it? – a particular oral skill with a banana as my prop. I do not take this talent lightly, nor do I flaunt it; however, when the situation is right, and the audience of an appropriate age, give me a bunch.

One afternoon, amidst a raucous amount of hoots and hollers, I performed for the *DH* crew, and let's just say that when I finished, all the men on the set, most of whom were not gay, applauded vigorously. But the best part of sharing this particular talent that afternoon was the good it later went on to achieve for a small segment of mankind.

The next evening, as I was leaving the set, I stopped at the *Desperate Housewives* production offices to pick up a few things. The receptionist asked if I'd wait a few minutes because someone wanted to meet me. I agreed, thinking a *Torchwood* or *Doctor Who* fan was in the building.[23]

The receptionist returned with a poised and professional young woman. She was clearly a bit shy, even a bit embarrassed, certainly a little uncomfortable, but with some prompting from the receptionist, she admitted that she'd heard about my banana trick and asked if I'd please give her a lesson.

She even had her own bananas ready.

The other delight of my time on *Desperate Housewives* was filming scenes with Eva Longoria Parker. Like Drea, Eva is smart, sexy and a pistol of energy. Not a lot of people know that while she's filming *Desperate Housewives*, she's also working on her Masters degree in Chicano Studies. She'd often tuck herself off in a corner between takes with a book and her ever-present highlighter.

That's not to say she was anti-social, though. One weekend, when Scott, Stu, Gavin and I went to Las Vegas, she arranged a table for us at her restaurant, Beso. For Carole's birthday, Eva also arranged for our table at Beso in LA, where we all drank far too much white sangria, a specialty of the house.[24] Meanwhile, on set, there were times when she'd join me in a show-stopping tap-dance routine on the stairs at

[23] They're everywhere.
[24] Because of all the fruit, it's actually *muy* healthy.

Angie's house (which is where most of my scenes were filmed). Now *that's* entertainment.

On the night in October 2009 when I marked my twentieth anniversary in show business, the flowers and cards, the champagne and calls from friends, family and casts and crews from days gone by touched me deeply.

As we gathered to celebrate, I'd all but forgotten about Bernie Cribbins's 'Dick of the Week' award until, with a great flourish, Carole and Scott presented me with their updated, homemade version. To memorialize my entertainment journey from a 'glimpse of stocking' to high drag, they honoured me with the 'Dick of the Decades' award: a stunning golden penis under glass.

I learned later in our car ride home from the party that Scott and Carole had as much fun creating this award as I had receiving it. They had scoured the adult sex stores in Soho to find the perfect penis,[25] one that was an admirable size and as golden as an Oscar. In every sex store, they asked the person behind the counter if he or she had any golden penises and, if they did not, did they have one that could be spray-painted and would absorb gold paint.

Thank God for Britain's relentless health and safety standards that have reached into all aspects of our lives, because at least one store assistant insisted that, if they spray-painted the penis – and at this juncture he paused and looked forcefully at Scott and Carole – they'd better not insert it anywhere.

When Carole and Scott finally found the perfect specimen,[26] they were forking out the money when the cashier asked why they needed a golden penis anyway.

'It's for a special award,' said Carole.

Without missing a beat, the cashier replied, 'What would I have to do to win one?'

---

[25] Tough job.
[26] See the pic at the end of the photo section.

TABLE TALK #11

'Goodnight and Thank You'

Help with the dishes? Don't be silly. You were my guests. Where's Scottie? He loves to do dishes.

Before you brave your journey home, I'd like to thank you for joining me, for allowing me to share my stories with you, and for supporting all that I've done these last few years.

A couple of months ago, I was explaining to my nephew, Turner – who is now nineteen and in his second year at university – about these table talks, these family vignettes, and how I wanted them to capture the tone and the content of the kinds of conversations the Barrowmans often have when we gather for family dinners or parties.

'So you've basically talked about farting, shite and sex.'[1]

And, Turner, your point is?

For the most part, I hope I've covered more than those three significant subjects.[2] Before I call you a taxi,[3] are there any questions remaining that I haven't covered in my table talks? There are? Okay. Fire away.

'Is there some part of your body you do not like, and if so, would you consider plastic surgery?'

I'm comfortable with all my bits and bobs. Oh, maybe I'd like my love handles[4] to be smaller, but it doesn't take much to sort them out. When my days are more flexible, I'm confident that I'll have time to get to the gym in the mornings. I'll take care of them that way. But

[1] Oh, he knows me so well.
[2] In fact, I don't think I've told one single farting story.
[3] You're a taxi! (Sorry … couldn't resist.)
[4] Or, as Clare calls them, 'muffin tops'.

I have nothing against plastic surgery, especially if it makes a person feel more confident about his or her body, and boosts their self-esteem.

'To whom would you give your last Rolo?'

First of all, my regular sweetie of choice isn't usually a Rolo, but if it were, I'd have to give it to my Jack Russell terrier, Captain Jack. Jack has to take a pill every night, and I discovered from his vet that a Rolo is the one chocolate treat you can give to most dogs. So I bought a carton of Rolos at Costco, and each evening I stick his pill deep inside the caramel.

'If time travel really did exist, where would you go and why?'

Hmm. I'd like to be very noble and say I'd travel back to some terrible epidemic or disaster,[5] taking a vaccination or medical supplies with me, but that would have to be my second trip. On my first trip, I'd love to travel back to the Hollywood of the thirties and forties and star in the classic MGM musicals of the time. Perhaps have the chance to perform with Gene Kelly, and have the opportunity to be part of a big, extravagant Busby Berkeley number for the man himself. I'd call him 'Buz' for short.

The film *For Me and My Gal* would suit my time-travel dream just fine. Plus, it would have the added bonus of allowing me to co-star with Judy Garland. Judy's daughter, Lorna Luft, has been my friend for over twenty years. We first met at a charity luncheon in London, at which we were seated together. Most recently, I was a guest on Lorna's BBC Radio 2 tribute concert to her mother. If I'm imagining a little time travel, it would be amazing to sing with Judy Garland as part of the journey.

'If you could do a remake of a movie musical, which one would you choose?'

You'd probably expect me to say *For Me and My Gal*, but I picked that film in answer to your last question because of the conflagration of its actors and director.[6] Funnily enough, though, my choice for a remake would be of another classic Judy Garland film.

[5] Love those disaster docs!
[6] Doesn't have anything to do with sex, Turner.

If I could change a few things about it, then I'd love to do a new version of *A Star Is Born*. In my staging, I'd include additional songs – maybe add 'I Know Him So Well', which would fit perfectly because I'd also adapt the film's original 1937 Dorothy Parker script so that the romantic relationship is between two males; one on the rise to stardom, the other on the downturn. I'm too old now to play Billy Crocker, or many of the leading male roles that are part of the classic Hollywood movie musicals, but in *A Star Is Born*, Norman Maine could and should be a man in his forties.[7]

'Is there any item or gizmo you carry everywhere you go?'

I would be completely lost without my BlackBerry, my black MacBook and my dental floss. Oh, and a packet of baby wipes.

'If you could be a superhero, who would you be? If you could have a superpower, what would it be?'

I don't have to think about this one for very long. I'd want to be able to fly; and I'm happy to say that I'm already a superhero, but if being Captain Jack doesn't count, then I'd love to pull on the iconic blue tights and red Speedos and be Superman.

'Is there a person, living or dead, real or fictitious, with whom you'd like to have dinner, and why?'

As long as you're picking up the tab, I'm inviting two people to dinner. The first person I'd choose would be my gran, Murn, who loved a good laugh, appreciated a good meal, and relished a good blether. She died when I was a teenager; given how close she and I were when I was growing up, I know she'd be bursting with pride for all that I've accomplished. I'd love to take Murn out to a fabulous restaurant and let her have the run of the entire menu – especially the desserts. I'd also let her wrap in her napkin as many rolls as she could fit in her handbag for later.

My second person would have to be one of my musical muses, Cole Porter. I imagine he'd be great company and I'd enjoy flirting a little with him. One of the areas of musical theatre that I'd like to learn more about, and perhaps even attempt to tackle some day if the right project

7 Early forties. Very early forties.

should arise, is the art of writing lyrics. Cole Porter was the master at packing irony, double entendres, colourful details and pointed generalities into a song's lyrics without them losing their heart. Cole and I would order champagne and caviar, and I'd make sure we got a table near the piano. How delightful!

'What would you eat for your last supper?'

Honestly, if I knew I was facing the end and I had enough energy to eat a last meal, I probably wouldn't. I'd find another organ to exercise and go out a different kind of satiated.[8]

Oh, if you insist. I'd gorge myself on shellfish, from prawns to shrimp to scallops to lobster. I'd dip them in butter, in olive oil, or in a sweet Thai sauce – and I'd hope that death would come swiftly before my allergy to all of them killed me slowly.

'Do you and Scott have the same taste in fashion? And do you share your clothes with him?'

Don't get me started. This subject is a bit of a touchy one in the Barrowman–Gill household. Scott and I have quite different tastes in fashion. He tends towards plain Ralph Lauren T-shirts and his favourite pair of tan Lucky jeans that I bought for him years ago in New York, and that he plans to wear until there's no thread count left. He's coming close.

Yet this man, who's colour-blind and hates to shop, has no problem borrowing[9] my flashy clothes, particularly my pink polo shirts and my trainers. This likely wouldn't bother me if I'd already worn the shirt or the shoes, but sometimes I've not even taken the price tags off. I like to be the first person to wear an item I've purchased. I have a similar issue[10] with books and magazines. Please don't crack the spine or flick the folios before I get the chance to be the first one into the pages.

'If you were invisible for a day, what would you do?'

I'd hide out in the locker room of the Welsh rugby team, or any

[8] Sorry – that's my last sexual reference … maybe.
[9] Stealing.
[10] It's not a hang-up or a neurosis, thank you very much.

professional male sports team for that matter. I love a man in a uniform.

'Why do you wear your watch on your right wrist?'

I know now that most people who are right-handed wear a watch on their left wrist, but when I got my first watch – a birthday present from my mum and dad when I was in primary school – I put the timepiece on my right wrist without knowing that detail. My reason was a logical one. When I was writing papers or taking notes in school, I could easily flip my wrist, sneak a peek at the time, and know exactly how long before the bell. Wearing a watch on my left wrist feels clumsy to me now.

'Do you still enjoy going to see shows in the West End?'

Whenever I can, I go to the opening nights of my friends' productions. The thrill of going to see a show has never faded for me. I love to be in the audience, and although I usually try to be a bit inconspicuous, it doesn't always work out. I went to see *Priscilla, Queen of the Desert*, with Jason Donovan,[11] and towards the end of the second act, the safety curtain dropped. Having been in this situation before myself in a number of productions, I knew something had gone awry with the set mechanics.

Once, when I was playing Joe Gillis in Andrew Lloyd Webber's *Sunset Boulevard*, the stage mechanics shut down and wouldn't rise up, leaving the floors of the set stuck at unsafe levels for the actors. When the safety curtain had been down for over fifteen minutes, a couple of us from the cast crawled underneath and led the audience in a singalong until the glitch was repaired.

After about ten minutes, the *Priscilla* audience was growing restless. I was hoping I hadn't been spotted.

'John, give us a song!' called someone from the other side of the balcony.

I laughed and called back, 'It's against theatre rules for another professional to perform in the audience.'

It didn't matter. The woman who'd called to me began to sing 'Any

[11] Loved the show!

Dream Will Do' – and pretty soon the entire balcony was crooning a cappella.

'Do you like to entertain at your home, and if so, what was the last occasion when you played host?'

In the spring of 2009, I wanted to greet my Sully neighbours, and say thank you to the cast and crew of *Torchwood* now that the filming of 'Children of Earth' was completed. (Plus, I really wanted to show off my new house to family and friends.)

I ordered lots of everything, including enough fireworks to start my own Mardi Gras. The party was such a success that the next day I had to repaint all the interior walls, replace a few lamps, and accommodate a sprinkling of stay-over guests recovering from the festivities, who were stretched out across our couches.

In the morning, everyone who slept over helped Scott and me clean the house. As we did, Scott and I revelled in how much we enjoyed being hosts, and how proud we were finally to have enough space to throw such a bash.

We repeated the tradition again this summer, and marked the American Fourth of July celebration with a BBQ and fireworks. This time, the walls survived.

On your way out, make sure you touch the Dalek for good luck. Till next time, goodnight and – from the bottom of my heart – I thank you.

Index

(In subentries, the initials JB, JB Sr, MB and SG denote John Barrowman, John Barrowman Sr, Marion Barrowman and Scott Gill; italic *n* signifies a footnote.)